25
of the
GREATEST
SERMONS
ever preached

25
of the
GREATEST SERMONS
ever preached

Jerry Falwell
Compiler and Editor

BAKER BOOK HOUSE
Grand Rapids, Michigan 49506

Permission to use the following material is gratefully acknowledged:

"The Pilgrim's Staff," by Robert Murray McCheyne, from *A Basket of Fragments,* copyright © 1975 by Christian Focus Publications, used by permission; "Ten Reasons Why I Believe the Bible Is the Word of God," by R.A. Torrey, from *R.A. Torrey,* copyright © 1950 by Fleming H. Revell, used by permission of Baker Book House; "God Is Near," by F.B. Meyer, from *F.B. Meyer,* copyright © 1950 by Fleming H. Revell, used by permission of Baker Book House; "Get on the Water-wagon," by Billy Sunday, from *The Best of Billy Sunday,* copyright © 1965 by Sword of the Lord Publishers, used by permission; "The Good Fight of Faith," by J. Gresham Machen, from *God Transcendent and Other Selected Sermons,* Ned B. Stonehouse, ed., copyright © 1949 by William B. Eerdmans Publishing Co., used by permission; "The Conquest of Fear," by George W. Truett, from *Follow Thou Me,* copyright © 1932 by Harper Brothers, used by permission of Harper and Rowe Publishers; "Heaven," by G. Beauchamp Vick, *Sword of the Lord,* January 2, 1981, copyright © 1981 by Sword of the Lord Publishers, used by permission; "Pay Day—Some Day," by R.G. Lee, *Sword of the Lord,* June 3, 1960, copyright © 1957 by R.G. Lee, used by permission of Miss Hildred Phillips, 508 Stonewall, Memphis, Tennessee; "What Must I Do To Be Saved?" by John R. Rice, from *The Rice Reference Bible,* copyright © 1981 by Sword of the Lord Publishers, used by permission.

Special thanks to Allen McClellan who compiled and edited the sermons contained in this volume and wrote the biographical sketch of each preacher.

To Evangelist B.R. Lakin, that great soldier of the cross and prince of preachers. A blessing to untold millions, he has faithfully preached the gospel for more than sixty years.

Introduction

Preaching is the declaration of the message of God. It has always been the God-appointed means of propagating the gospel of Jesus Christ. The apostle Paul stated: "It pleased God by the foolishness of preaching to save them that believe" (I Cor. 1:21). Soon after I was converted in 1952, I began reading the sermons of great preachers. While a sermon is generally better heard than read, something struck me while reading the sermons of great preachers. I recognized that they clearly pointed to the reality of Christ and the urgency of salvation.

If you are a preacher, reading the sermons of great preachers will not in itself make you a great preacher, but it will make you a better preacher. In fact, it will make you a better person. Every Christian would do well to have his or her faith challenged and motivated by the reading of great preaching. However, words alone will not change your life. You must respond in obedience to the principles of God's Word and let His Spirit apply its truths to your life.

This volume contains twenty-five of the finest and most blessed sermons from some of God's choicest servants from the past. Though these preachers represent a wide range of denominational backgrounds, each was greatly used of God to influence his own generation. These sermons were chosen for several reasons: their historical value, their depth and beauty of expression, their clear presentation of the gospel, and the fact that each one was used of God in a unique and special way. Each message exalts Christ above all else. The messages by Edwards, Moody, Lee and Rice were used of God to bring millions to Christ. They represent some of the greatest evangelistic sermons ever preached in the English language.

Some of the sermons were preached out of deep personal conviction in times of crisis; for example, Machen's "Fight the Good Fight of Faith'" was his last chapel address at Princeton Theological Seminary before he separated from them over the issue of liberalism. William Carey's impassioned appeal for a mission to the heathen shocked the complacent English Christians of his day. In time Carey went to India and became one of the greatest missionaries of all time. Billy Sunday's "Get on the Water Wagon" was preached constantly throughout the Prohibition controversy of the early twentieth century.

These sermons are great for several reasons:

1. *Classic.* They are the true classics which have stood the test of time. Even Edwards' "Sinners in the Hands of an Angry God" still can be read with great profit and conviction more than two hundred years later. Whitefield and Wesley were contemporaries who both became experts at open-air preaching to the masses. Though they differed

theologically they were both greatly used of God during a period of unprecedented revival both in England and America. McCheyne's "The Pilgrim's Staff" is a message of encouragement and compassion unsurpassed in any generation.

2. *Convicting.* Another striking feature of these sermons is the convicting nature of each one. These were not mere intellectual addresses. Each was a sermon straight from the soul of the preacher. The reader can sense the presence of God in Meyer's "God is Near." One can easily detect the love of God and the compassion of Christ in Smith's "As Jesus Passed By" and Wesley's "God's Love to Fallen Man." They are sermons that convict the soul and move the reader to do something about what he has read.

3. *Clear.* The sermons in this volume are not complicated intellectual treatises that leave the reader uncertain of the point being made by the speaker. Each is strikingly clear in its content and purpose. Talmage makes it clear that Christ is everything. Spurgeon draws us to the cross as our only hope and glory. Parker offers hope to the weary. Whitefield declares with certainty that salvation is by grace. Torrey makes it plain that the Bible is indeed the Word of God.

4. *Courageous.* These sermons were preached by real men to real people with real needs. They were courageous declarations of truth to men who often did not want to hear the truth. Edwards suffered great personal persecution because of his insistence upon personal conversion. Finney was criticized for merely trying to raise money with his message on stewardship. Carey was scorned by the religious establishment of his day for his appeal to use "means" to reach the heathen. These are courageous sermons by men of courage. They are life-changing messages because they were preached by men whose lives had been changed by the grace of God.

Reading and applying these twenty-five sermons could be one of the greatest blessings of your life. If you are a layman, let God speak to your heart as though these men were preaching to you. If you are a preacher, you will not find better models of great messages anywhere than right here. However, even memorizing the words of these sermons will not bring anybody to Christ nor change anyone's life. These messages must grip your soul before they can be translated properly to your life or your audience. May God bless you through these sermons as He has Me.

Jerry Falwell
Lynchburg, Virginia

Contents

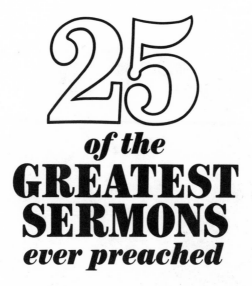

25
of the
GREATEST
SERMONS
ever preached

Jonathan Edwards
(1703—1758)

Jonathan Edwards is considered by many to be the first of the great American-born preachers. He was born the son of a minister in 1703 in East Windsor, Connecticut, and started on the road to distinction early. With ten older sisters to help teach him, Jonathan was only twelve when he attained a working knowledge of Latin, Greek, and Hebrew. He graduated from Yale University when he was seventeen. At nineteen he began preaching and was ordained as a Congregationalist minister five years later.

In 1727 Edwards became a pastor in Northampton, Massachusetts, where he remained for twenty-two years. During this time his preaching was a principal factor in the first Great Awakening. In 1750 he went to Stockbridge, Massachusetts, to serve as pastor and missionary to the Indians.

Edwards's voice and manner were not ideal for pulpit oratory. Poor eyesight forced him to hold sermons close to his eyes as he read them word for word. But his intellect and imagination enabled him to present truth in a powerful way. He was endued with Holy Spirit power and emotional fervor that distinguished him from the other Puritan leaders of his day. Edwards profoundly influenced George Whitefield, Thomas Chalmers, and David Brainerd (who was engaged to Edwards's daughter before his untimely death). A notable philosopher and deep thinker, Edwards ranks as one of the greatest preachers of colonial America.

The following sermon, "Sinners in the Hands of an Angry God," is his most celebrated, and one of the most famous ever preached by anyone. It was a powerful impetus to the great revival in New England. He preached the sermon in Enfield, Connecticut, on July 8, 1741.

Edwards accepted the presidency of Princeton College in 1758. He died from a smallpox vaccination shortly thereafter.

1

Sinners in the Hands
of an Angry God
By Jonathan Edwards

Their foot shall slide in due time (Deut. 32:35).

There is nothing that keeps wicked men at any one moment out of hell, but the mere pleasure of God.

By the mere pleasure of God, I mean His sovereign pleasure, His arbitrary will, restrained by no obligation, hindered by no manner of difficulty any more than if nothing else but God's mere will had, in the last degree, or in any respect whatsoever, any hand in the preservation of wicked men one moment.

The truth of this observation may appear by the following considerations:

1. There is no want of power in God to cast wicked men into hell at any moment. Men's hands cannot be strong, when God rises up. The strongest have no power to resist Him, nor can any deliver out of His hands.

He is not only able to cast wicked men into hell, but He can most easily do it. There is no fortress that is any defense from the power of God. Though hand join in hand, and a vast multitude of God's enemies combine and associate themselves, they are easily broken in pieces. They are as great heaps of light chaff before the whirlwind or large quantities of dry stubble before devouring flames. We find it easy to tread on and crush a worm that we see crawling on the earth. It is easy for us to cut or singe a slender thread that anything hangs by. Thus easy is it for God when He pleases, to cast His enemies down to hell. What are we, that we should think to stand before Him, at whose rebuke the earth trembles, and before whom the rocks are thrown down?

2. They deserve to be cast into hell. So that divine justice never stands in the way, it makes no objection against God's using His power at any moment to destroy them. Yea, on the contrary, justice calls aloud for an infinite punishment of their sins. Divine justice says of the tree that brings forth such grapes of Sodom, "Cut it down; why cumbereth it the ground?" (Luke 13:7). The sword of divine justice is every moment brandished over their heads, and it is nothing but the hand of arbitrary mercy and God's mere will that holds it back.

3. They are already under a sentence of condemnation to hell. They do not only justly deserve to be cast down thither, but the sentence of the law of God, that eternal and immutable rule of righteousness that God has fixed between Him and mankind, is gone out against them, and stands against them, so that they are bound over already to hell. "He that believeth not is condemned already" (John 3:18). Every unconverted man properly belongs to hell; that is his place; from thence he is. "Ye are from beneath" (John 8:23); and thither he is bound; it is the place that justice, and God's Word, and sentence of His unchangeable law assign to him.

4. They are now the objects of that very same anger and wrath of God that is expressed in the torments of hell; and the reason why they do not go down to hell at each moment is not because God, in whose power they are, is not at present very angry with them—as He is with many miserable creatures now tormented in hell, who there feel and bear the fierceness of His wrath. Yea, God is a great deal more angry with great numbers that are now on earth, yea doubtless with some who may read this book, and may be at ease, than He is with many of those who are now in the flames of hell.

So it is not because God is unmindful of their wickedness, and does not resent it, that He does not let loose His hand and cut them off. God is not altogether such a one as themselves, though they may imagine Him to be so. The wrath of God burns against them; their damnation does not slumber. The pit is prepared; the fire is made ready. The furnace is now hot, ready to receive them; the flames do now rage and glow. The glittering sword is whetted and held over them, and the pit hath opened its mouth under them.

5. The devil stands ready to fall upon them and seize them as his own, at what moment God shall permit him. They belong to him; he has their souls in his possession and under his dominion. The devils watch them; they are ever by them, at their right hand. They stand waiting for them like greedy, hungry lions that see their prey and expect to have it but are for the present kept back. If God should withdraw His hand, by which they are restrained, they would in one moment fly upon their poor souls. The old serpent is gaping for them; hell opens its mouth wide to

receive them; and if God should permit it, they would be hastily swallowed up and lost.

6. There are in the souls of wicked men those hellish principles reigning that would presently kindle and flame out into hell fire, if it were not for God's restraints. There is laid in the very nature of carnal men, a foundation for the torments of hell. There are those corrupt principles, in reigning power in them and in full possession of them, that are seeds of hell fire. The principles are active and powerful, exceedingly violent in their nature; and if it were not for the restraining hand of God upon them, they would soon break out. They would flame out after the same manner as the same corruption, the same enmity, does in the hearts of damned souls and would beget the same torments as they do in them. Sin is the ruin and misery of the soul; it is destructive in its very nature; and if God should leave it without restraint, there would need nothing else to make the soul perfectly miserable. The corruption of the heart of the man is immoderate and boundless in its fury. While wicked men live here, it is like fire pent up by the course of nature; and as the heart is now a sink of sin, so, if sin was not restrained, it would immediately turn the soul into a fiery oven or furnace of fire and brimstone.

7. It is no security to wicked men for one moment that there are no visible means of death at hand! It is no security to a natural man that he is now in health, and that he does not see which way he should now immediately go out of the world by any accident, and that there is no visible danger, in any respect, in his circumstances. The manifold and continual experience of the world, in all ages, shows this is no evidence that a man is not on the very brink of eternity and that the next step will not be into another world. The unseen, unthought-of ways and means of persons going suddenly out of the world are innumerable and inconceivable. Unconverted men walk over the pit of hell on a rotten covering, and there are innumberable places in this covering so weak that they will not bear their weight, and these places are not seen. The arrows of death fly unseen at noonday; the sharpest sight cannot discern them. God has so many different unsearchable ways of taking wicked men out of the world and sending them to hell that there is nothing to make it appear that God had need to be at the expense of a miracle, or to go out of the ordinary course of His providence to destroy any wicked man, at any moment. All the means that there are of sinners going out of the world are so in God's hands, and so universally and absolutely subject to His power and determination, that it does not depend at all the less on the mere will of God, whether sinners shall at any moment go to hell, than if means were never made use of, or at all concerned in the case.

8. Natural men's prudence and care to preserve their own lives, or the care of others to preserve them, do not secure them a moment. To

this, divine providence and universal experience do bear testimony. There is this clear evidence that men's own wisdom is no security to them from death: that, if it were otherwise, we should see some difference between the wise and politic men of the world and others, with regard to their liableness to early and unexpected death. But how is it in fact? "How dieth the wise man? as the fool" (Eccl. 2:16).

9. All wicked men's pains and contrivances which they use to escape hell, while they continue to reject Christ, and so remain wicked men, do not secure them from hell one moment. Almost every natural man who hears of hell, flatters himself that he shall escape it. He depends upon himself for his own security. He flatters himself in what he has done, in what he is now doing, or what he intends to do. Every one lays out matters in his own mind as to how he shall avoid damnation and flatters himself that he contrives well for himself and that his schemes will not fail. They hear indeed that there are but few saved and that the greater part of men that have died heretofore are gone to hell; but each one imagines that he forms plans to effect his escape better than others have done. He does not intend to go to that place of torment; he says within himself that he intends to take effectual care and to order matters for himself so as not to fail.

But the foolish children of men miserably delude themselves in their own schemes and in confidence in their own strength and wisdom; they trust to nothing but a shadow. The great part of those who heretofore have lived under the same means of grace, and are now dead, are undoubtedly gone to hell, and it was not because they were not as wise as those who are now alive. It was not because they did not lay out matters as well for themselves to secure their own escape. If we could come to speak with them and inquire of them, one by one, whether they expected, when alive, and when they used to hear about hell, ever to be subjects of that misery, we doubtless should hear one and another reply, "No, I never intended to come here. I had arranged matters otherwise in my mind. I thought I should contrive well for myself; I thought my scheme good. I intended to take effectual care, but it came upon me unexpectedly. I did not look for it at that time, and in that manner; it came as a thief. Death outwitted me. God's wrath was too quick for me. O my cursed foolishness! I was flattering myself and pleasing myself with vain dreams of what I would do hereafter; and when I was saying peace and safety, then sudden destruction came upon me."

10. God has laid Himself under no obligation, by any promise, to keep any natural man out of hell one moment. God certainly has made no promises either of eternal life, or of any deliverance or preservation from eternal death, but what are contained in the covenant of grace, the promises that are given in Christ, in whom all the promises are yea and

amen. But surely they have no interest in the promise of the covenant of grace who are not the children of the covenant, who do not believe in any of the promises and have no interest in the Mediator of the covenant.

So that, whatever some have imagined and pretended about promises made to natural men's earnest seeking and knocking, it is plain and manifest that whatever pains a natural man takes in religion, whatever prayer he makes, till he believes in Christ, God is under no manner of obligation to keep him a moment from eternal destruction.

So it is that natural men are held in the hand of God over the pit of hell; they have deserved the fiery pit and are already sentenced to it, and God is dreadfully provoked. His anger is as great toward them as toward those that are actually suffering the execution of the fierceness of His wrath in hell; and they have done nothing in the least to appease or abate that anger. Neither is God in the least bound by any promise to hold them up for one moment. The devil is waiting for them. Hell is gaping for them. The flames gather and flash about them and would fain lay hold on them and swallow them up. The fire pent up in their own hearts is struggling to break out, and they have no interest in any Mediator. There are no means within reach that can be any security to them. In short they have no refuge, nothing to take hold of; all that preserves them every moment is the mere arbitrary will and uncovenanted, unobliged forbearance of an incensed God.

Application

The use of this awful subject may be for awakening unconverted persons to a conviction of their danger. This that you have heard is the case of every one out of Christ. That world of misery, that lake of burning brimstone, is extended abroad under you. There is the dreadful pit of the glowing flames of the wrath of God. There is hell's wide gaping mouth open; and you have nothing to stand upon, nor anything to take hold of. There is nothing between you and hell but the air; it is only the power and mere pleasure of God that holds you up.

Your wickedness makes you, as it were, heavy as lead, to rend downwards with great weight and pressure towards hell. If God should let you go, you would immediately sink and swiftly descend and plunge into the bottomless gulf. Your healthy constitution, your own care and prudence, and best contrivance, and all your righteousness would have no more influence to uphold you and keep you out of hell than a spider's web would have to stop a falling rock. Were it not for the sovereign pleasure of God, the earth would not bear you one moment, for you are a burden to it. The creation groans with you. The creature is made subject to the bondage of your corruption, not willingly. The sun does not willingly shine upon you, to give you light to serve sin and Satan. The earth does not willingly yield her increase, to satisfy your lusts; nor is it willingly a stage for your wickedness to be acted upon. The air does not willingly serve you for breath to maintain the flame of life in your vitals, while you spend your life in the service of God's enemies.

The wrath of God is like great waters that are restrained for the present. They increase more and more, and rise higher and higher, till an outlet is given, and the longer the stream is stopped the more rapid and mighty is its course when once it is let loose. It is true that judgment against your evil works has not been executed hitherto; the floods of God's vengeance have been withheld. But your guilt in the meantime is constantly increasing, and you are every day treasuring up more wrath. The waters are constantly rising and waxing more and more mighty; and there is nothing but the mere pleasure of God that holds the waters back, that are unwilling to be stopped and press hard to go forward. If God should only withdraw His hand from the floodgate, it would immediately fly open, and the fiery floods of the fierceness and wrath of God would rush forth with inconceivable fury and would come upon you with omnipotent power. If your strength were ten thousand times greater than it is, yea, ten thousand times greater than the strength of the stoutest, sturdiest devil in hell, it would be nothing to withstand or endure it.

The bow of God's wrath is bent and the arrow made ready on the string. Justice directs the bow to your heart and strains at the bow. It is nothing but the mere pleasure of God, and that of an angry God without any promise or obligation at all, that keeps the arrow one moment from being made drunk with your blood.

Thus all you that never passed under a great change of heart, by the mighty power of the Spirit of God upon your souls; all you that were never born again, and made new creatures, and raised from being dead in sin to a state of new, and before altogether unexperienced light and life, are in the hands of an angry God. However you may have reformed your life in many things, and many have had religious affections and may keep up a form of religion in your families and closets and in the house of God, it is nothing but His mere pleasure that keeps you from being this moment swallowed up in everlasting destruction.

The God that holds you over the pit of hell, much in the same way as one holds a spider, or some loathsome insect, over the fire, abhors you and is dreadfully provoked. His wrath towards you burns like fire; He looks upon you as worthy of nothing else but to be cast into the fire. He is of purer eyes than to bear to have you in His sight. You are ten thousand times more abominable in His eyes than the most hateful venomous serpent is in ours. You have offended Him infinitely more than ever a stubborn rebel did his prince; and yet, it is nothing but His hand that holds you from falling into fire every moment. It is ascribed to nothing else, that you did not go to hell the last night; that you were suffered to awake again in this world, after you closed your eyes to sleep; and there is no other reason to be given, why you have not dropped into hell since you arose in the morning, but that God's hand has held you up. There is no other reason to be given, while you have been reading this address, but His mercy; yea, no other reason can be given why you do not this very moment drop down into hell.

O sinner, consider the fearful danger you are in! It is a great furnace of wrath, a wide and bottomless pit full of the fire of wrath, that you are held over in the hand of a God whose wrath is provoked and incensed as much against you as against many of the damned in hell. You hang by a slender thread, with the flames of divine wrath flashing about it and ready every moment to singe it and burn it asunder; and you have no interest in any Mediator, and nothing to lay hold of to save yourself, nothing to keep off the flames of wrath, nothing of your own, nothing that you have done, nothing that you can do, to induce God to spare you one moment.

And Consider Here More Particularly:

1. Whose wrath it is. It is the wrath of the infinite God. If it were only the wrath of man, though it were of the most potent prince, it would be comparatively little to be regarded. The wrath of kings is very much dreaded, especially of absolute monarchs, who have the possessions and lives of their subjects wholly in their power—to be disposed of at their mere will. "The fear of a king is as the roaring of a lion: whoso provoketh him to anger sinneth against his own soul" (Prov. 20:2). The subject who very much enrages an arbitrary prince is liable to suffer the most extreme torments that human art can invent or human power can inflict. But the greatest earthly potentates, in their greatest majesty and strength, and when clothed in their greatest terrors, are but feeble, despicable worms of the dust in comparison with the great and almighty Creator and King of heaven and earth. It is but little that they can do, when most enraged, and when they have exerted the utmost of their fury. All the kings of the earth, before God, are as grasshoppers; they are nothing and less than nothing. Both their love and their hatred are to be despised. The wrath of the great King of kings is as much more terrible than theirs as His majesty is greater. "And I say unto you my friends, Be not afraid of them that kill the body, and after that have no more that they can do. But I will forewarn you whom ye shall fear: Fear him, which after he hath killed hath power to cast into hell; yea, I say unto you, Fear him" (Luke 12:4,5).

2. It is the fierceness of His wrath that you are exposed to. We often

read of the fury of God, as in Isaiah 59:18: "According to their deeds, accordingly he will repay, fury to his adversaries." So Isaiah 66:15: "For, behold, the Lord will come with fire, and with his chariots like a whirlwind, to render his anger with fury, and his rebuke with flames of fire." And so also in many other places. Thus we read of "the winepress of the fierceness and wrath of Almighty God" (Rev. 19:15). The words are exceedingly terrible.

Consider this, you that yet remain in an unregenerate state. That God will execute the fierceness of His anger implies that He will inflict wrath without any pity. When God beholds the ineffable extremity of your case, and sees your torment to be so vastly disproportioned to your strength, and sees how your poor soul is crushed, and sinks down, as it were, into an infinite gloom, He will have no compassion upon you. He will not forbear the execution of His wrath, or in the least lighten His hand. There shall be no moderation or mercy, nor will God then at all stay His rough wind. He will have no regard to your welfare, nor be at all careful lest you should suffer too much in any other sense than only that you shall not suffer beyond what strict justice requires. Nothing shall be withheld because it is so hard for you to bear. "Therefore will I also deal in fury: mine eye shall not spare, neither will I have pity: and though they cry in mine ears with a loud voice, yet will I not hear them" (Ezek. 8:18). Now, God stands ready to pity you; this is the day of mercy; you may cry now with some encouragement of obtaining mercy. But when once the day of mercy is passed, your most lamentable and dolorous cries and shrieks will be in vain; you will be wholly lost and thrown away of God, as to any regard to your welfare. God will have no other use to put you to but to suffer misery; you may be continued in being to no other end—for you will be a vessel of wrath fitted to destruction; and there will be no other use of this vessel but only to be filled full of wrath. God will be so far from pitying you when you cry to Him that it is said He will only "laugh and mock." "Because I have called, and ye refused; I have stretched out my hand, and no man regarded; but ye have set at nought all my counsel, and would none of my reproof: I also will laugh at your calamity; I will mock when your fear cometh; when your fear cometh as desolation, and your destruction cometh as a whirlwind; when distress and anguish cometh upon you. Then shall they call upon me, but I will not answer; they shall seek me early, but they shall not find me: for that they hated knowledge, and did not choose the fear of the Lord: they would none of my counsel: they despised all my reproof. Therefore shall they eat of the fruit of their own way, and be filled with their own devices. For the turning away of the simple shall slay them, and the prosperity of fools shall destroy them" (Prov. 1:24-32).

If you cry to God to pity you, He will be so far from pitying you in your doleful case, or showing you the least reward or favor, that instead of that He will only tread you under foot. And though He will know that you cannot bear the weight of Omnipotence treading upon you, yet He will not regard that, but He will crush you under His feet without mercy. He will crush out your blood, and make it fly, and it shall be sprinkled on His garments, so as to stain all His raiment. He will not only hate you, but He will have you in the utmost contempt; no place shall be thought fit for you but under His feet, to be trodden down as the mire of the streets.

3. The misery you are exposed to is that which God will inflict, to the end that He might show what the wrath of Jehovah is. God hath had it on His heart to show to angels and men, both how excellent His love is and also how terrible His wrath is. Sometimes earthly kings have a mind to show how terrible their wrath is by the extreme punishments they would execute on those that provoked them. But the great God is also willing to show His wrath and magnify His awful majesty and mighty power in the extreme sufferings of His enemies. "What if God, willing to show his wrath, and to make his power known, endured with much long-suffering the vessels of wrath fitted to destruction?" (Rom. 9:22). And seeing this is His design, and what He has determined, even to show how terrible the unmixed, unrestrained wrath, the fury and fierceness of Jehovah is, He will do it to effect. There will be something accomplished and brought to pass that will be dreadful with a witness. When the great and angry God hath risen up and executed His awful vengeance on the poor sinner, and the wretch is actually suffering the infinite weight and power of His indignation, then will God call upon the whole universe to behold the awful majesty and mighty power that is to be seen in it.

Thus it will be with you that are in an unconverted state, if you continue in it; the infinite might, and majesty, and terribleness of the omnipotent God shall be magnified upon you in the ineffable strength of your torments. You shall be tormented in the presence of the holy angels, and in the presence of the Lamb. When you shall be in this state of suffering, the glorious inhabitants of heaven shall go forth and look on the awful spectacle, that they may see what the wrath and fierceness of the Almighty is; and when they have seen it, they will fall down and adore that great power and majesty.

4. It is everlasting wrath. It would be dreadful to suffer this fierceness and wrath of Almighty God one moment, but you must suffer it to all eternity. There will be no end to this exquisite, horrible misery. When you look forward you shall see a long forever, a boundless duration before you, which will swallow up your thoughts and amaze your souls; and you will absolutely despair of ever having any deliverances, and end, any mitigation, any rest at all. You will know certainly that you

must wear out long ages, millions of millions of ages, in wrestling and conflicting with this almighty merciless vengeance. Then when you have so done, when many ages have actually been spent by you in this manner, you will know that all is but a point to what remains, that your punishment will indeed be infinite. O, what can express what the state of a soul in such circumstances is? All that we can possibly say about it gives but a very feeble, faint representation of it; it is inexpressible and inconceivable, for "Who knoweth the power of God's anger?"

How dreadful is the state of those who are daily and hourly in danger of this great wrath and infinite misery! But this is the dismal case of every soul that has not been born again, however moral and strict, sober and religious they may otherwise be. Oh that you would consider it, whether you be young or old! There is reason to fear that there are many who will read this book, or who have heard the gospel, who will actually be the subjects of this very misery to all eternity. We know not who they are or what thoughts they now have. It may be they are now at ease, and hear all these things without much disturbance, and are now flattering themselves that they are not the persons, promising themselves that they shall escape. If we knew that there was one person, and but one, of those that we know, that was to be subject of this misery, what an awful thing would it be to think of! If we knew who it was, what an awful sight would it be to see such a person! How might every Christian lift up a lamentable and bitter cry over him! But alas! Instead of one, how many is it likely will remember these solemn reflections in hell!

And now you have an extraordinary opportunity, a day wherein Christ has thrown the door of mercy wide open and stands calling and crying with a loud voice to poor sinners, a day wherein many are flocking to Him and pressing into the kingdom of God. Many are daily coming from the east, west, north, and south: many that were very lately in the same miserable condition that you are in, are now in a happy state with their hearts filled with love to Him who has loved them, and washed them from their sins in His own blood, and rejoicing in hope of the glory of God. How awful is it to be left behind at such a day, to see so many others feasting while you are pining and perishing, to see so many rejoicing and singing for joy of heart while you have cause to mourn for sorrow of heart, and to howl for vexation of spirit! How can you rest one moment in such a condition? Are not your souls as precious as the souls of those who are flocking from day to day to Christ?

And let every one that is yet out of Christ, and hanging over the pit of hell, whether they be old men and women, or middle-aged, or young people, or little children, now hearken to the loud calls of God's Word and providence. This acceptable year of the Lord, a day of great mercy to some, will doubtless be a day of as remarkable vengeance to others.

Men's hearts harden, and their guilt increases apace at such a day as this, if they neglect their souls. Never was there a period when so many means were employed for the salvation of souls, and if you entirely neglect them, you will eternally curse the day of your birth. Now, undoubtedly, it is as it was in the days of John the Baptist; the axe is laid at the root of the trees, and every tree which brings not forth good fruit, may be hewn down and cast into the fire. Therefore, let every one that is out of Christ, now awake and flee from the wrath to come. The wrath of Almighty God is now undoubtedly hanging over every unregenerate sinner. Let every one flee out of Sodom: "Escape for your lives, look not behind you, escape to the mountain, lest you be consumed."

George Whitefield
(1714—1770)

George Whitefield had the unlikely beginning of being born the son of tavern keepers in Gloucester, England, in 1714. In this environment he had little Christian influence as a child but displayed unusual ability in school. Whitefield chose to go to college at Oxford, where he met John and Charles Wesley and joined their "Holy Club." He graduated in 1736 and began to preach in jails as an ordained deacon.

When many ministers refused to have Whitefield in their churches due to his pulpit excess, he resorted to preaching in the open fields, for which he became renowned. Whitefield traveled to America in 1738 and began a home for orphans; he consequently traveled throughout the colonies and Great Britain preaching and raising financial support for his work. In fact, he made thirteen trips across the Atlantic in his lifetime and visited Spain and Holland, as well as other countries in western Europe. Whitefield's preaching played a significant role, as did that of Jonathan Edwards, in the Great Awakening. He had a marked influence on contemporaries such as John Wesley and Benjamin Franklin, with whom he remained close friends until his death in 1770.

Whitefield was known for the tremendous power he held over large congregations. His open-air meetings quite frequently involved crowds in excess of 25,000, and sometimes larger. He once preached near Glasgow, Scotland, to more than 100,000 people in one gathering. This remarkable feat could be accomplished without the aid of modern amplifiers due to the tremendous quality of his voice. It was estimated that 10,000 people were converted in that meeting. Whitefield worked largely alone in his ministry, and his sermons bear out the fact that he continually wrestled with souls. Wherever he preached, he left an unforgettable impression.

The Method of Grace
By George Whitefield

They have healed also the hurt of the daughter of my people slightly, saying, Peace, peace; when there is no peace (Jer. 6:14).

As God can send a nation or people no greater blessing than to give them faithful, sincere, and upright ministers, so the greatest curse that God can possibly send upon a people in this world is to give them over to blind, unregenerate, carnal, lukewarm, and unskillful guides. And yet, in all ages, we find that there have been many wolves in sheep's clothing, many that daubed with untempered mortar, that prophesied smoother things than God did allow. As it was formerly, so it is now; there are many that corrupt the Word of God and deal deceitfully with it. It was so in a special manner in the prophet Jeremiah's time; and he, faithful to his Lord, faithful to that God who employed him, did not fail from time to time to open his mouth against them, and to bear a noble testimony to the honor of that God in whose name he from time to time spake. If you will read his prophecy, you will find that none spake more against such ministers than Jeremiah, and here especially in the chapter out of which the text is taken he speaks very severely against them. He charges them with several crimes; particularly he charges them with covetousness: "For," says he, in the thirteenth verse, "from the least of them even unto the greatest of them every one is given to covetousness; and from the prophet even unto the priest, every one dealeth falsely."

And then, in the words of the text, in a more special manner he exemplifies how they had dealt falsely, how they had behaved treacherously to poor souls: says he, "They have healed also the hurt of the daughter of my people slightly, saying, Peace, peace; when there is no peace." The prophet, in the name of God, had been denouncing war against the people; he had been telling them that their houses should be left desolate,

18

and that the Lord would certainly visit the land with war. "Therefore," says he, in the eleventh verse, "I am full of the fury of the Lord; I am weary with holding in: I will pour it out upon the children abroad, and upon the assembly of young men together: for even the husband with the wife shall be taken, the aged with him that is full of days. And their houses shall be turned unto others, with their fields and wives together: for I will stretch out my hand upon the inhabitants of the land, saith the Lord."

The prophet gives a thundering message, that they might be terrified and have some convictions and inclinations to repent. But it seems that the false prophets, the false priests, went about stifling people's convictions, and when they were hurt or a little terrified, they were for daubing over the wound, telling them that Jeremiah was but an enthusiastic preacher, that there could be no such thing as war among them, and saying to people, Peace, peace, be still, when the prophet told them there was no peace.

The words, then, refer primarily unto outward things, but I verily believe have also a further reference to the soul, and are to be referred to those false teachers who, when people were under conviction of sin, when people were beginning to look toward heaven, were for stifling their convictions and telling them they were good enough before. And indeed, people generally love to have it so; our hearts are exceedingly deceitful and desperately wicked; none but the eternal God knows how treacherous they are.

How many of us cry, Peace, peace, to our souls, when there is no peace! How many are there who are now settled upon their lees, that now think they are Christians, that now flatter themselves that they have an interest in Jesus Christ; whereas if we come to examine their experiences we shall find that their peace is but a peace of the Devil's making—it is not a peace of God's giving—it is not a peace that passeth human understanding.

It is a matter, therefore, of great importance, my dear hearers, to know whether we may speak peace to our hearts. We are all desirous of peace; peace is an unspeakable blessing; how can we live without peace? And, therefore, people from time to time must be taught how far they must go and what must be wrought in them before they can speak peace to their hearts. This is what I design at present, that I may deliver my soul, that I may be free from the blood of all those to whom I preach—that I may not fail to declare the whole counsel of God. I shall, from the words of the text, endeavor to show you what you must undergo and what must be wrought in you before you can speak peace to your hearts.

First, then, before you can speak peace to your hearts, you must be made to see, made to feel, made to weep over, made to bewail, your actual transgressions against the law of God. According to the covenant of works, "the soul that sinneth it shall die"; cursed is that man, be he what he may, be he who he may, that continueth not in all things that are written in the book of the law to do them.

We are not only to do some things, but we are to do all things, and we are to continue to do so, so that the least deviation from the moral law, according to the covenant of works, whether in thought, word, or deed, deserves eternal death at the hand of God. And if one evil thought, if one evil word, if one evil action deserves eternal damnation, how many hells, my friends, do every one of us deserve whose whole lives have been one continued rebellion against God! Before ever, therefore, you can speak peace to your hearts, you must be brought to see, brought to believe, what a dreadful thing it is to depart from the living God.

And now, my dear friends, examine your hearts, for I hope you came hither with a design to have your souls made better. Give me leave to ask you, in the presence of God, whether you know the time, and if you do not know exactly the time, do you know there was a time when God wrote bitter things against you, when the arrows of the Almighty were within you? Was ever the remembrance of your sins grievous to you? Was the burden of your sins intolerable to your thoughts? Did you ever see that God's wrath might justly fall upon you, on account of your actual transgressions against God? Were you ever in all your life sorry for your sins? Could you ever say, My sins are gone over my head as a burden too heavy for me to bear? Did you ever experience any such thing as this? Did ever any such thing as this pass between God and your soul? If not, for Jesus Christ's sake, do not call yourselves Christians; you may speak peace to your hearts, but there is no peace. May the Lord awaken you, may the Lord convert you, may the Lord give you peace, if it be His will, before you go home!

But, further, you may be convinced of your actual sins, so as to be made to tremble, and yet you may be strangers to Jesus Christ, you may have no true work of grace upon your hearts. Before ever, therefore, you can speak peace to your hearts, conviction must go deeper; you must not only be convinced of your actual transgressions against the law of God, but likewise of the foundation of all your transgressions. And what is that? I mean original sin, that original corruption each of us brings into the world with us which renders us liable to God's wrath and damnation. There are many poor souls that think themselves fine reasoners, yet they pretend to say there is no such thing as original sin. They will charge God with injustice in imputing Adam's sin to us, yet they tell us we are not born in sin. Let them look abroad and see the disorders in it, and think, if they can, if this is the paradise in which God did put man. No!

everything in the world is out of order.

However, therefore, some people may deny this, yet when conviction comes, all carnal reasonings are battered down immediately, and the poor soul begins to feel and see the fountain from which all the polluted streams do flow. When the sinner is first awakened, he begins to wonder, How came I to be so wicked? The Spirit of God then strikes in, and shows that he has no good thing in him by nature; then he sees that he is altogether gone out of the way, that he is altogether become abominable, and the poor creature is made to lie down at the foot of the throne of God and to acknowledge that God would be just to damn him, just to cut him off, tho he never had committed one actual sin in his life.

Did you ever feel and experience this, any of you—to justify God in your damnation—to own that you are by nature children of wrath, and that God may justly cut you off, tho you never actually had offended Him in all your life? If you were ever truly convicted, if your hearts were ever truly cut, if self were truly taken out of you, you would be made to see and feel this. And if you have never felt the weight of original sin, do not call yourselves Christians. I am verily persuaded original sin is the greatest burden of a true convert; this ever grieves the regenerate soul, the sanctified soul. The indwelling of sin in the heart is the burden of a converted person; it is the burden of a true Christian. He continually cries out: "Oh! who will deliver me from this body of death, this indwelling corruption in my heart?" This is that which disturbs a poor soul most. And, therefore, if you never felt this inward corruption, if you never saw that God might justly curse you for it, indeed, my dear friends, you may speak peace to your hearts, but I fear, nay I know, there is no true peace.

Further, before you can speak peace to your hearts you must not only be troubled for the sins of your life, the sins of your nature, but likewise for the sins of your best duties and performances.

My dear friends, what is there in our performance to recommend us unto God? Our persons are in an unjustified state by nature; we deserve to be damned ten thousand times over; and what must our performance be? We can do no good thing by nature: "They that are in the flesh cannot please God."

You may do things materially good, but you cannot do a thing formally and rightly good; because nature cannot act above itself. It is impossible that a man who is unconverted can act for the glory of God; he cannot do anything in faith, and "whatsoever is not of faith is sin."

After we are renewed, yet we are renewed but in part, indwelling sin continues in us, there is a mixture of corruption in every one of our duties, so that after we are converted, were Jesus Christ only to accept us according to our works, our works would damn us, for we cannot put

up a prayer but it is far from the perfection which the moral law re-
quireth. I do not know what you may think, but I can say that I cannot
pray but I sin—I cannot preach to you or any others but I sin—I can do
nothing without sin; and, as one expresses it, my repentance wants to be
repented of, and my tears to be washed in the precious blood of my dear
Redeemer.

Our best duties are so many splendid sins. Before you can speak
peace to your heart you must not only be sick of your original and actual
sin, but you must be made sick of your righteousness, of all your duties
and performances. There must be a deep conviction before you can be
brought out of your self-righteousness; it is the last idol taken out of our
heart. The pride of our heart will not let us submit to the righteousness of
Jesus Christ. But if you never felt that you had no righteousness of your
own, if you never felt the deficiency of your own righteousness, you cannot come to Jesus Christ.

There are a great many now who may say, Well, we believe all this;
but there is a great difference between talking and feeling. Did you ever
feel the want of a dear Redeemer? Did you ever feel the want of Jesus
Christ upon the account of the deficiency of your own righteousness?
And can you now say from your heart Lord, Thou mayest justly damn
me for the best duties that ever I did perform? If you are not thus
brought out of self, you may speak peace to yourselves, but yet there is
no peace.

But then, before you can speak peace to your souls, there is one particular sin you must be greatly troubled for, and yet I fear there are few
of you think what it is; it is the reigning, the damning sin of the Christian
world, and yet the Christian world seldom or never thinks of it. And
pray what is that?

It is what most of you think you are not guilty of—and that is, the sin
of unbelief. Before you can speak peace to your heart, you must be
troubled for the unbelief of your heart. But can it be supposed that any of
you are unbelievers here in this churchyard, that are born in Scotland, in
a reformed country, that go to church every Sabbath? Can any of you
that receive the sacrament once a year—oh, that it were administered
oftener!—can it be supposed that you who had tokens for the sacrament,
that you who keep up family prayer, that any of you do not believe in the
Lord Jesus Christ?

I appeal to your own hearts, if you would not think me uncharitable,
if I doubted whether any of you believed in Christ: and yet, I fear upon
examination, we should find that most of you have not so much faith in
the Lord Jesus Christ as the Devil himself. I am persuaded that the Devil
believes more of the Bible than most of us do. He believes the divinity of
Jesus Christ; that is more than many who call themselves Christians do;

nay, he believes and trembles, and that is more than thousands amongst us do.

My friends, we mistake a historical faith for a true faith, wrought in the heart by the Spirit of God. You fancy you believe because you believe there is such a Book as we call the Bible—because you go to church; all this you may do and have no true faith in Christ. Merely to believe there was such a person as Christ, merely to believe there is a Book called the Bible, will do you no good, more than to believe there was such a man as Caesar or Alexander the Great. The Bible is a sacred depository. What thanks have we to give to God for these lively oracles! But yet we may have these and not believe in the Lord Jesus Christ.

My dear friends, there must be a principle wrought in the heart by the Spirit of the living God. If I ask you how long it is since you believed in Jesus Christ, I suppose most of you would tell me you believed in Jesus Christ as long as ever you remember—you never did misbelieve. Then, you could not give me a better proof that you never yet believed in Jesus Christ, unless you were sanctified early, as from the womb; for they that otherwise believe in Christ know there was a time when they did not believe in Jesus Christ.

You say you love God with all your heart, soul, and strength. If I were to ask you how long it is since you loved God, you would say, As long as you can remember; you never hated God, you know no time when there was enmity in your heart against God. Then, unless you were sanctified very early, you never loved God in your life.

My dear friends, I am more particular in this, because it is a most deceitful delusion, whereby so many people are carried away, that they believe already. Therefore it is remarked of Mr. Marshall, giving account of his experiences, that he had been working for life, and he had ranged all his sins under the Ten Commandments, and then, coming to a minister, asked him the reason why he could not get peace. The minister looked to his catalog. "Away," says he, "I do not find one word of the sin of unbelief in all your catalog." It is the peculiar work of the Spirit of God to convince us of our unbelief—that we have got no faith. Says Jesus Christ, "I will send him [the Comforter] unto you. And when he is come, he will reprove the world" of the sin of unbelief; "of sin," says Christ, "because they believe not on me."

Now, my dear friends, did God ever show you that you had no faith? Were you ever made to bewail a hard heart of unbelief? Was it ever the language of your heart, Lord, give me faith; Lord, enable me to lay hold on Thee; Lord, enable me to call Thee my Lord and my God? Did Jesus Christ ever convince you in this manner? Did He ever convince you of your inability to close with Christ, and make you to cry out to God to give you faith? If not, do not speak peace to your heart. May the Lord awaken you and give you true, solid peace before you go hence and be no more!

Once more, then: before you can speak peace to your heart, you must not only be convinced of your actual and original sin, the sins of your own righteousness, the sin of unbelief, but you must be enabled to lay hold upon the perfect righteousness, of the Lord Jesus Christ; you must lay hold by faith on the righteousness of Jesus Christ, and then you shall have peace. "Come," says Jesus, "unto me, all ye that labor and are heavy laden, and I will give you rest."

This speaks encouragement to all that are weary and heavy laden; but the promise of rest is made to them only upon their coming and believing, and taking Him to be their God and their all. Before we can ever have peace with God we must be justified by faith through our Lord Jesus Christ, we must be enabled to apply Christ to our hearts, we must have Christ brought home to our souls, so as His righteousness may be made our righteousness, so as His merits may be imputed to our souls. My dear friends, were you ever married to Christ? Did Jesus Christ ever give Himself to you? Did you ever close with Christ by a lively faith, so as to feel Christ in your hearts, so as to hear Him speaking peace to your souls? Did peace ever flow in upon your hearts like a river? Did you ever feel that peace that Christ spoke to His disciples? I pray God He may come and speak peace to you. These things you must experience.

I am now talking of the invisible realities of another world, of inward religion, of the work of God upon a poor sinner's heart. I am now talking of a matter of great importance, my dear hearers; you are all concerned in it, your souls are concerned in it, your eternal salvation is concerned in it. You may be all at peace, but perhaps the Devil has lulled you asleep into a carnal lethargy and security, and will endeavor to keep you there till he gets you to hell, and there you will be awakened; but it will be dreadful to be awakened and find yourselves so fearfully mistaken when the great gulf is fixed, when you will be calling to all eternity for a drop of water to cool your tongue and shall not obtain it.

If you do not, then show yourselves men, and this morning go away with full resolution, in the strength of God, to cleave to Christ. And may you have no rest in your souls till you rest in Jesus Christ! I could still go on, for it is sweet to talk of Christ. Do you not long for the time when you shall have new bodies—when they shall be immortal, and made like Christ's glorious body? And then they will talk of Jesus Christ forevermore. But it is time, perhaps, for you to go and prepare for your respective worship, and I would not hinder any of you. My design is, to bring poor sinners to Jesus Christ. O that God may bring some of you to Himself! May the Lord Jesus now dismiss you with His blessing, and may the dear Redeemer convince you that you are unawakened, and turn the wicked from the evil of their way! And may the love of God, that passeth all understanding, fill your hearts. Grant this, O Father, for Christ's sake; to whom, with Thee and the blessed Spirit, be all honour and glory, now and forevermore. Amen.

John Wesley
(1703—1791)

Born in Epworth, Lincolnshire, England, in 1703, John Wesley was one of nineteen children. The "father of Methodism," he was the son of an Anglican minister. His mother, Susanna Wesley, was a godly woman with an exceptional teaching ability which helped create scholars of her children. John attended Charterhouse School at the age of ten and then went to Oxford University, where he graduated in 1724. After being ordained as a priest of the Church of England in 1728, Wesley returned to lecture at Oxford. It was here that he and his brother Charles headed a group of extremely devoted students who were called "methodists" due to their methodical approach to religious life.

Wesley was converted after making a missionary trip to America in 1735; he realized that he did not have a personal relationship with Jesus Christ, although he had been in the ministry for several years. Shortly thereafter he was introduced to open-air preaching by George Whitefield and became an itinerant evangelist. As he preached about holy living and personal religious experience, crowds as large as 20,000 came to hear him. He organized his converts into societies and officially established Methodism in 1784 when he separated from the Church of England. The entire course of a nation was altered as God used Wesley to bring about a revival of Christianity in Great Britain. Many historians agree that his efforts saved England from the horrors of the French Revolution.

Wesley was systematic in his work and was a man of great discipline. He rose at four o'clock each morning, traveled on horseback, and preached several times a day for over fifty years. He rode 250,000 miles in his lifetime and preached over 40,000 sermons. A classical scholar who composed hymns on horseback, Wesley published a thirty-two volume work at seventy years of age. At the age of eighty, he regretted that he could preach only twice a day. He died after a short illness in 1791, never having "retired" from preaching.

God's Love to Fallen Man
By John Wesley

Not as the offence, so also is the free gift (Rom. 5:15).

How exceedingly common, and how bitter, is the outcry against our first parent for the mischief which he not only brought upon himself, but entailed upon his latest posterity! It was by his willful rebellion against God, "that sin entered into the world." "By one man's disobedience," as the apostle observes, the many, as many as were then in the loins of their forefathers, were made, or constituted sinners. Not only were they deprived of the favor of God, but also of His image, of all virtue, righteousness, and true holiness, and sunk partly into the image of the Devil: in pride, malice and all other diabolical tempers, partly into the image of the brute, being fallen under the dominion of brutal passions and groveling appetites. Hence also death entered into the world, with all his forerunners and attendants: pain, sickness, and a whole train of uneasy as well as unholy passions and tempers.

"For all this we may thank Adam," has been echoed down from generation to generation. The selfsame charge has been repeated in every age and every nation where the oracles of God are known, in which alone this grand and important event has been discovered to the children of men. Has not *your* heart, and probably *your* lips too, joined in the general charge? How few are there of those who believe the scriptural relation of the fall of man who have not entertained the same thought concerning our first parent? Severely condemning him, that, through willful disobedience to the sole command of his Creator, "Brought death into the world and all our woe."

Nay, it were well if the charge rested here, but it is certain it does not. It cannot be denied that it frequently glances from Adam to his Creator.

Have not thousands, even of those who are called Christians, taken the liberty to call His mercy, if not His justice also, into question on this account? Some indeed have done this a little more modestly, in an oblique and indirect manner; but others have thrown aside the mask and asked, "Did not God foresee that Adam would abuse his liberty? Did He not know the baneful consequences which this must naturally have on all His posterity? Why then did He permit that disobedience? Was it not easy for the Almighty to have prevented it?" He certainly did foresee the whole. This cannot be denied. "For known unto God are all his works from the beginning of the world." (Rather from all eternity, as the words *ap aionos* properly signify.) It was undoubtedly in His power to prevent it, for He hath all power both in heaven and earth. But it was known to Him at the same time that it was best upon the whole not to prevent it. He knew that, "not as the offence, so is the free gift": that the evil resulting from the former was not as the good resulting from the latter, not worthy to be compared with it. He saw that to permit the fall of the first man was far best for mankind in general, that abundantly more good than evil would accrue to the posterity of Adam by his fall, that if "sin abounded" thereby over all the earth yet grace "would much more abound," yea, and that to every individual of the human race, unless it was his own choice.

May the Lover of men open the eyes of our understanding to perceive clearly that by the fall of Adam mankind in general have gained a capacity, first, of being more holy and happy on earth, and secondly, of being more happy in heaven than otherwise they could have been.

First, mankind in general has gained by the fall of Adam a capacity of attaining more holiness and happiness on earth than it would have been possible to attain if Adam had not fallen. If Adam had not fallen, Christ had not died. Nothing can be more clear than this, nothing more undeniable; the more thoroughly we consider the point, the more deeply shall we be convinced of it. Unless all the partakers of human nature had received that deadly wound in Adam, it would not have been needful for the Son of God to take our nature upon Him. Do you not see that this was the ground of His coming into the world? "By one man sin entered into the world, and death by sin; and so death passed upon all men" through him, "for all have sinned" (Romans 5:12). Was it not to remedy this very thing that, "the Word was made flesh"? that, "as in Adam all die, so in Christ shall all be made alive"? Unless, then, *many* had been made sinners by the disobedience of one; by the obedience of one, *many* would not have been made righteous (verse 18). So there would have been no room for that amazing display of the Son of God's love to mankind. There would have been no occasion for His, "being obedient unto death, even the death of the cross." It could not then have been said, to the astonishment of all the hosts of heaven, "God so loved the world," yet, the ungodly world, which had no thought or desire of returning to Him, "that he gave his Son" out of His bosom, His only begotten Son, to the end "that whosoever believeth on him should not perish, but have everlasting life." Neither could we then have said, "God was in Christ reconciling the world to himself"; or that He "made him to be sin," that is, a sin offering "for us, who knew no sin; that we might be made the righteousness of God in him." There would have been no such occasion for such "an Advocate with the Father," as, "Jesus Christ the Righteous"; neither for His appearing, "at the right hand of God, to make intercession for us."

What is the necessary consequence of this? It is this: there could then have been no such thing as faith in God, thus loving the world, giving His only Son for us men and for our salvation. There could have been no such thing as faith in the Son of God, "as loving us and giving himself for us." There could have been no faith in the Spirit of God, as renewing the image of God in our hearts, as raising us from the death of sin unto the life of righteousness. Indeed, the whole privilege of justification by faith could have no existence; there could have been no redemption in the blood of Christ; neither could Christ have been "made of God unto us" either "wisdom, righteousness, sanctification, or redemption."

The same grand blank which was in our faith, must likewise have been in our love. We might have loved the Author of our being, the Father of angels and men, as our Creator and Preserver; we might have said, "O Lord our Lord, how excellent is thy name in all the earth!" But we could not have loved Him under the nearest and dearest relation, "as delivering up his Son for us all." We might have loved the Son of God, as being the, "brightness of his [Father's] glory, the express image of his person" (although this ground seems to belong rather to the inhabitants of heaven than earth). But we could not have loved Him as, bearing "our sins in his own body on the tree," and, by that one oblation of Himself once offered, making a full oblation, sacrifice, and satisfaction, for the sins of the whole world. We could not have been, "made conformable to his death" nor, "have known the power of his resurrection." We could not have loved the Holy Ghost as revealing to us the Father and Son, as opening the eyes of our understanding, bringing us out of the darkness into His marvelous light, renewing the image of God in our soul and sealing us unto the day of redemption. So that, in truth, what is now, "in the sight of God, even the Father," not of fallible men, "pure religion and undefiled," would then have had no being; inasmuch as it wholly depends on those grand principles, "By grace are ye saved through faith" and, "Jesus Christ is of God made unto us wisdom, and righteousness, and sanctification, and redemption."

We see then what unspeakable advantage we derive from the fall of our first parent with regard to faith: faith both in God the Father, who spared not His own Son, His only Son, but, "wounded him for our transgressions" and, "bruised him for our iniquities"; and in God the Son, who poured out His soul for us transgressors and washed us in His own blood. We see what advantage we derive therefrom with regard to the love of God, both of God the Father and God the Son. The chief ground of this love, as long as we remain in the body, is plainly declared by the apostle, "We love him, because he first loved us." But the greatest instance of His love had never been given, if Adam had not fallen.

As our faith, both in God the Father and the Son receives an unspeakable increase, if not its being, from this grand event, as does also our love both of the Father and the Son, so does the love of our neighbor also, our benevolence to all mankind, which cannot but increase in the same proportion with our faith and love of God. For who does not apprehend the force of that inference drawn by the loving Apostle, "Beloved, if God so loved us, we ought also to love one another." If God so loved us, observe, the stress of the argument lies on this point: so loved us! as to deliver up His only Son to die a cursed death for our salvation. "Beloved, what manner of love is this," wherewith God hath loved us? So as to give His *only Son!* In glory equal with the Father, in majesty coeternal! What manner of love is this wherewith the only begotten Son of God hath loved us, as to empty Himself, as far as possible, of His eternal Godhead; as to divest Himself of that glory, which He had with the Father before the world began; as to, "take upon him the form of a servant, being found in fashion as a man!" And then to humble Himself still further, "being obedient unto death, even the death of the cross!" If God so loved us, how ought we to love one another? But this motive to brotherly love had been totally wanting, if Adam had not fallen. Consequently we could not then have loved one another in so high a degree as we may now. Nor could there have been that height and depth in the command of our Blessed Lord, "As I have loved you, so love one another."

Such gainers may we be by Adam's fall, with regard both to the love of God and of our neighbor. But there is another grand point, which, though little adverted to, deserves our deepest consideration. By that one act of our first parent, not only, "sin entered into the world," but pain also, and was alike entailed on his whole posterity. Herein appeared, not only the justice, but the unspeakable goodness of God. For how much good does He continually bring out of this evil! How much holiness and happiness out of pain!

How innumerable are the benefits which God conveys to the children of men through the channel of sufferings! so that it might well be said, "What are termed afflictions in the language of men, are in the language of God styled blessings." Indeed had there been no suffering in the world, a considerable part of religion, yea, and in some respects, the most excellent part, could have had no place therein, since the existence of it depends on our suffering. Had there been no pain, it could have had no being. Upon this foundation, even our suffering, it is evident all our passive graces are built, yea, the noblest of all Christian graces: love enduring all things. Here is the ground for resignation to God, enabling us to say from the heart, in every trying hour, "It is the Lord: let him do what seemeth him good." "Shall we receive good at the hand of the Lord, and shall we not receive evil?" And what a glorious spectacle is this? Did it not constrain even a heathen to cry out, *"Ecce spectaculum Deo dignum!* See a sight worthy of God: a good man struggling with adversity and superior to it."

Here is the ground for confidence in God, both with regard to what we feel and with regard to what we should fear, were it not that our soul is calmly stayed on Him. What room could there be for trust in God, if there was no such thing as pain or danger? Who might not say then, "The cup which my Father hath given me, shall I not drink it?" It is by sufferings that our faith is tried, and, therefore, made more acceptable to God. It is in the day of trouble that we have occasion to say, "Though he slay me, yet will I trust in him." This is well pleasing to God, that we should own Him in the face of danger, in defiance of sorrow, sickness, pain, or death.

Again: had there been neither natural nor moral evil in the world, what must have become of patience, meekness, gentleness, long-suffering? It is manifest they could have had no being, seeing all these have evil for their object. If, therefore, evil had never entered into the world, neither could these have had any place in it. For who could have returned good for evil, had there been no evildoer in the universe? How had it been possible, on the supposition, to overcome evil with good? Well you say, "But all these graces might have been divinely infused into the hearts of men." Undoubtedly they might, but if they had, there would have been no use or exercise for them. Whereas in the present state of things we can never long want occasion to exercise them. The more they are exercised, the more all our graces are strengthened and increased. In the same proportion as our resignation, our confidence in God, our patience and fortitude, our meekness, gentleness, and long-suffering, together with our faith and love of God and man increase, must our happiness increase, even in the present world.

To sum up what has been said under this head: as the more holy we are upon earth, the more happy we must be (seeing there is an inseparable connection between holiness and happiness); as the more good we do to others, the more of present reward rebounds into our own bosom, even as our sufferings for God lead us to rejoice in Him, "with joy unspeakable and full of glory." Therefore, the fall of Adam, first, by giving us an opportunity of being far more holy; secondly, by giving us the occasions of doing innumerable good works, which otherwise could not have been done; and thirdly, by putting it into our power to suffer for God, whereby, "the Spirit of glory and of God rests upon us" may be of such advantage to the children of men, even in the present life, as they will not thoroughly comprehend till they attain life everlasting.

It is then we shall be enabled fully to comprehend, not only the advantages which accrue at the present time to the sons of men by the fall of their first parent, but the infinitely greater advantages which they may reap from it in eternity. In order to form some conception of this, we may remember the observation of the apostle, "As one star differeth from another star in glory, so also is the resurrection of the dead." The most glorious stars will undoubtedly be those who are the most holy, who bear most of that image of God wherein they were created. The next in glory to these will be those who have been most abundant in good works and next to them, those that have suffered most.

But what advantages in every one of these respects, will the children of God receive in heaven, by God's permitting the introduction of pain upon earth, in consequence of sin? By occasion of this they attained many holy tempers, which otherwise could have had no being: resignation to God, confidence in Him in times of trouble and danger, patience, meekness, gentleness, long-suffering and the whole train of passive virtues. On account of this superior holiness they will then enjoy superior happiness. Again: everyone will then, "receive his own reward, according to his own labor." Every individual will be "rewarded according to his work." But the Fall gave rise to innumerable good works, which could otherwise never have existed, such as ministering to the necessities of the saints, yea, relieving the distressed in every kind. Hereby innumerable stars will be added to their eternal crown.

Yet again: there will be an abundant reward in heaven, for suffering, as well as for doing, the will of God, "these light afflictions, which are but for a moment, work out for us a far more exceeding and eternal weight of glory." Therefore that event, which occasioned the entrance of suffering into the world, has thereby occasioned, to all the children of God, an increase of glory to all eternity. For although the sufferings themselves will be at an end, although:

> *The pain of life shall then be o'er*
> *The anguish and distracting care;*
> *The sighing grief shall weep no more;*
> *And sin shall never enter there.*

Yet the joys occasioned thereby shall never end, but flow at God's right hand forevermore.

There is one advantage more that we reap from Adam's fall, which is not unworthy our attention. Unless in Adam all had died, being in the loins of their first parent, every descendant of Adam, every child of man, must have personally answered for himself to God. It seems to be a necessary consequence of this, that if he had once fallen, once violated any command of God, there would have been no possibility of his rising again; there was no help, but he must have perished without remedy. For that covenant knew not to show mercy; the word was, "The soul that sinneth, it shall die." Who would not rather be on the footing he is now, under a covenant of mercy? Who would wish to hazard a whole eternity upon one stake? Is it not infinitely more desirable to be in a state wherein, though encompassed with infirmities, yet we do not run such a desperate risk, but if we fall, we may rise again? Wherein we may say:

My trespass is grown up to heaven!
  But, far above the skies,
In Christ abundantly forgiven,
  I see thy mercies rise!

In Christ! Let me entreat every serious person once more to fix his attention here. All that has been said, all that can be said, on these subjects, centers in this point. The fall of Adam produced the death of Christ! Hear, O heavens, and give ear, O earth! Yea:

Let earth and heaven agree,
  Angels and men be joined,
To celebrate with me
  The Saviour of mankind;
To adore the all-atoning Lamb,
And bless the sound of JESUS' Name!

If God had prevented the fall of man, the Word had never been made flesh; nor had we ever, "seen his glory, the glory as of the only begotten of the Father." Those mysteries had never been displayed, "which the very angels desire to look into." Methinks this consideration swallows up all the rest and should never be out of our thoughts. Unless, "by one man, judgment had come upon all men to condemnation," neither angels nor men could ever have known, "the unsearchable riches of Christ."

See then, upon the whole, how little reason we have to repine at the fall of our first parent, since herefrom we may derive such unspeakable advantages, both in time and eternity. See how small pretense there is for questioning the mercy of God in permitting that event to take place! Since, therein, mercy, by infinite degrees, rejoices over judgment! Where, then, is the man who presumes to blame God for not preventing

Adam's sin? Should we not rather bless Him from the ground of the heart for therein laying the grand scheme of man's redemption and making way for that glorious manifestation of His wisdom, holiness, justice, and mercy? If indeed God had decreed before the foundation of the world that millions of men should dwell in everlasting burnings, because Adam sinned, hundreds of thousands of years before they had a being, I know not who could thank Him for this, unless the Devil and his angels: seeing, on this supposition, all those millions of unhappy spirits would be plunged into hell by Adam's sin, without any possible advantage from it. But, blessed be God, this is not the case. Such a decree never existed. On the contrary, everyone born of a woman may be an unspeakable gainer thereby; and none ever was or can be a loser, but by his own choice.

We see here a full answer to that plausible account, "of the origin of evil," published to the world some years since and supposed to be unanswerable; that it, "necessarily resulted from the nature of matter, which God was not able to alter." It is kind in this sweet-tongued orator to make an excuse for God! But there is really no occasion for it: God hath answered for Himself. He made man in His own image, a spirit endued with understanding and liberty. Man abusing that liberty, produced evil, brought sin and pain into the world. This God permitted, in order to a fuller manifestation of His wisdom, justice and mercy, by bestowing on all who would receive it an infinitely greater happiness than they could possibly have attained if Adam had not fallen.

"O the depth of the riches both of the wisdom and knowledge of God!" Although a thousand particulars of, "his judgments, and of his ways are unsearchable" to us, and past our finding out, yet we may discern the general scheme, running through time into eternity. "According to the counsel of his own will," the plan He had laid before the foundation of the world, He created the parent of all mankind in His own image. He permitted all men to be made sinners by the disobedience of this one man, that by the obedience of one, all who receive the free gift may be infinitely holier and happier to all eternity!

William Carey
(1761—1834)

Remembered today as the "father of modern missions," William Carey was born in 1761 in Northamptonshire, England. At the age of fourteen he became a cobbler, but his life was redirected when he was converted in 1779. Soon after this, Carey began pastoring a church and running a school, while doing much study of his own. Although he lacked formal training, he taught himself Greek, Hebrew, and Latin, along with Dutch and French. It was during this time that he began reading about the voyages of Captain James Cook and was also greatly influenced by David Brainerd, a missionary to the Indians in America. Consequently, Carey became burdened for world missionary efforts and began praying for unevangelized regions of the world.

In 1786 Carey proposed a new missionary emphasis to a group of ministers but was told, "When God pleases to convert the heathen, He will do it without your aid or mine." He began some planning of his own which eventually led to the formation of the Baptist Missionary Society in 1792; he became its first missionary. He sailed for India in 1793 and used an indigo factory for a mission station. Carey immediately began translating the Bible into Bengali, a task that was completed in 1809. Before his death in 1834, he had translated all or parts of the Bible into twenty-four languages and dialects. In 1799 Carey went to Serampore and established a printing operation; he eventually published over 250,000 Bibles and Testaments, making the Scriptures available to more than 300 million people.

Although not known particularly as a great pulpiteer, Carey's pioneering work in India launched a new era in world missions. The following sermon is of great historical significance; it was originally published in 1792 in a pamphlet entitled "An Enquiry into the Obligation of Christians to Use Means for the Conversion of the Heathens." The "means" he had in mind were mission boards and organizations, and his Baptist Missionary Society became a prototype in a movement that changed the course of Christian history.

An Enquiry into the Obligation
of Christians to Use Means for the
Conversion of the Heathens
By William Carey

Go ye into all the world, and preach the gospel to every creature (Mark 16:15).

As our blessed Lord has required us to pray that His kingdom may come, and His will be done on earth as it is in heaven, it becomes us not only to express our desires of that event by word, but to use every lawful method to spread the knowledge of His name. In order to do this, it is necessary that we should become in some measure acquainted with the religious state of the world. As this is an object we should be prompted to pursue, not only by the gospel of our Redeemer but even by the feelings of humanity, so an inclination to conscientious activity therein would form one of the strongest proofs that we are the subject of grace and partakers of that spirit of universal benevolence and genuine philanthropy, which appear so eminent in the character of God Himself.

Sin was introduced among the children of men by the fall of Adam and has since been spreading its baneful influence. By changing its appearances to suit the circumstances of the times, it has grown up in ten thousand forms and constantly counteracted the will and designs of God. One would have supposed that the remembrance of the Deluge would have been transmitted from father to son and perpetually deterred mankind from transgressing the will of their Maker. But so blinded were they, that in the time of Abraham gross wickedness prevailed wherever colonies were planted, and the iniquity of the Amorites was great, though not yet full. After this, idolatry spread more and more, till the seven devoted nations were cut off with the most signal marks of divine displeasure. Still, however, the progress of evil was not stopped, but the

Israelites themselves too often joined with the rest of mankind against the God of Israel.

Yet God repeatedly made known His intention to prevail finally over all the power of the Devil, and to destroy all his works, and set up His own kingdom and interest among men, and extend it as universally as Satan had extended his. It was for this purpose that the Messiah came and died, that God might be just, and the justifier of all that should believe in Him. When He had laid down His life, and taken it up again, He sent forth His disciples to preach the good tidings to every creature and to endeavor by all possible methods to bring over a lost world to God. They went forth according to their divine Commission, and wonderful success attended their labours; the civilized Greeks, and uncivilized barbarians, each yielded to the Cross of Christ and embraced it as the only way of salvation. Since the apostolic age many other attempts to spread the gospel have been made, which have been considerably successful, notwithstanding which a very considerable part of mankind are still involved in all the darkness of heathenism. Some attempts are still being made, but they are inconsiderable in comparison to what might be done if the whole body of Christians entered heartily into the spirit of the divine command on this subject. Some think little about it, others are unacquainted with the state of the world, and others love their wealth better than the souls of their fellow creatures.

In order that the subject may be taken into more serious consideration, I shall: enquire whether the Commission given by our Lord to His disciples be not still binding on us; consider the practicability of doing something more than is done; and discuss the duty of Christians in general in this matter.

An Enquiry Whether the Commission Given by Our Lord to His Disciples Be Not Still Binding on Us

Our Lord Jesus Christ, a little before His departure, commissioned His apostles to "Go, and teach all nations"; or as another evangelist expresses it, "Go ye into all the world, and preach the gospel to every creature." This Commission was as extensive as possible and laid them under obligation to disperse themselves into every country of the habitable globe and preach to all the inhabitants, without exception or limitation. They accordingly went forth in obedience to the command, and the power of God evidently wrought with them. Many attempts of the same kind have been made since their day, which have been attended with various success; but the work has not been taken up or carried on in recent years (except by a few individuals) with that zeal and perseverance with which the primitive Christians went about it. It seems as if many thought the Commission was sufficiently put in execution by what the apostles and others have done; that we have enough to do to attend to the salvation of our own countrymen; and that, if God intends the salvation of the heathen, He will some way or other bring them to the gospel, or the gospel to them. It is thus that multitudes sit at ease and give themselves no concern about the far greater part of their fellow sinners, who to this day are lost in ignorance and idolatry. There seems also to be an opinion existing in the minds of some that because the apostles were extraordinary officers and have no proper successors, and because many things which were right for them to do would be utterly unwarrantable for us, therefore it may not be immediately binding on us to execute the Commission, though it was so upon them. To the consideration of such persons I would offer the following observations.

First, if the command of Christ to teach all nations be restricted to the apostles, or those under the immediate inspiration of the Holy Ghost, then that of baptizing should be so too; and every denomination of Christians, except the Quakers, do wrong in baptizing with water at all.

Secondly, if the command of Christ to teach all nations be confined to the apostles, then all such ordinary ministers who have endeavored to carry the gospel to the heathens have acted without a warrant and run before they were sent. Yea, and though God has promised the most glorious things to the heathen world by sending His gospel to them, yet whoever goes first, or indeed at all, with that message, unless he have a new and special commission from heaven, must go without any authority for so doing.

Thirdly, if the command of Christ to teach all nations extend only to the apostles, then, doubtless, the promise of the divine presence in this work must be so limited; but this is worded in such a manner as expressly precludes such an idea. "Lo, I am with you alway, even unto the end of the world."

It has been said that we ought not to force our way but to wait for the openings and leading of Providence; but it might with equal propriety be answered in this case, neither ought we to neglect embracing those openings in Providence which daily present themselves to us. What openings of Providence do we wait for? We can neither expect to be transported into the heathen world without ordinary means, nor to be endowed with the gift of tongues, and so forth, when we arrive there. These would not be providential interpositions, but miraculous ones. Where a command exists nothing can be necessary to render it binding but a removal of those obstacles which render obedience impossible, and these are removed already. Natural impossibility can never be pleaded so long as facts exist to prove the contrary.

It has been objected that there are multitudes in our own nation, and within our immediate spheres of action, who are ignorant as the South-

Sea savages, and that therefore we have work enough at home, without going into other countries. That there are thousands in our own land as far from God as possible, I readily grant, and that this ought to excite us to tenfold diligence to our work and in attempts to spread divine knowledge among them is a certain fact; but that it ought to supersede all attempts to spread the gospel in foreign parts seems to want proof. Our own countrymen have the means of grace and may attend on the Word preached if they choose it. They have the means of knowing the truth, and faithful ministers are placed in almost every part of the land, whose spheres of action might be much extended if their congregations were but more hearty and active in the cause. But with the heathen the case is widely different. They have no Bible, no written language, no ministers, no good civil government, nor any of those advantages which we have. Pity therefore, humanity, and much more Christianity; call loudly for every possible exertion to introduce the gospel among them.

The Practicability of Something Being Done, More Than What Is Done, for the Conversion of the Heathen

The impediments in the way of carrying the gospel among the heathen must arise, I think, from one or other of the following things: their distance from us, their barbarous and savage manner of living, the danger of being killed by them, the difficulty of procuring the necessities of life, or the unintelligibleness of their languages.

As to their distance from us, whatever objections might have been made on that account before the invention of the mariner's compass, nothing can be alleged for it, with any color of plausibility in the present age. Men can now sail with as much certainty through the Great South Sea as they can through the Mediterranean, or any lesser sea. Yea, and Providence seems in a manner to invite us to the trial, as there are to our knowledge trading companies, whose commerce lies in many of the places where these barbarians dwell.

As to their uncivilized and barbarous way of living, this can be no objection to any, except those whose love of ease renders them unwilling to expose themselves to inconveniences for the good of others.

It was no objection to the apostles and their successors, who went among the barbarous Germans and Gauls, and still more barbarous Britons! They did not wait for the ancient inhabitants of these countries to be civilized before they could be Christianized but went simply with the doctrine of the Cross, and Tertullian could boast that "those parts of Britain which were proof against the Roman armies were conquered by the gospel of Christ." It was no objection to an Elliot, or a Brainerd, in later times. They went forth, and encountered every difficulty of the kind, and found that a cordial reception of the gospel produced those happy effects which the longest intercourse with Europeans without it could never accomplish. It *is* no objection to commercial men. It only requires that we should have as much love to the souls of our fellow creatures and fellow sinners as they have for the profits arising from a few otter skins, and all these difficulties would be easily surmounted.

After all, the uncivilized state of the heathen, instead of affording an objection *against* preaching the gospel to them, ought to furnish an argument *for* it. Can we as men, or as Christians, hear that a great part of our fellow creatures, whose souls are as immortal as ours, and who are as capable as ourselves of adorning the gospel and contributing by their preaching, writings, or practices to the glory of our Redeemer's name and the good of His church, are enveloped in ignorance and barbarism? Can we hear that they are without the gospel, without government, without laws, and without arts and sciences, and not exert ourselves to introduce among them the sentiments of men, and of Christians? Would not the spread of the gospel be the most effectual means of their civilization? Would not that make them useful members of society? We know that such effects did in a measure follow the aforementioned efforts of Elliot, Brainerd, and others among the American Indians; and if similar attempts were made in other parts of the world, and succeeded with a divine blessing (which we have every reason to think they would), might we not expect to see able divines, or read well-conducted treatises in defence of the truth, even among those who at present seem to be scarcely human?

In respect to the danger of being killed by them, it is true that whoever does go must put his life in His hand, and not consult with flesh and blood. But do not the goodness of the cause; the duties incumbent on us as the creatures of God, and Christians; and the perishing state of our fellow men loudly call upon us to venture all and use every warrantable exertion for their benefit? Paul and Barnabas, who *hazarded their lives for the name of our Lord Jesus Christ*, were not blamed as being rash but commended for so doing, while John Mark, who through timidity of mind deserted them in their perilous undertaking, was branded with censure. After all, as has been already observed, I greatly question whether most of the barbarisms practiced by the savages upon those who have visited them have not originated in some real or supposed affront, and were therefore, more properly, acts of self-defense rather than proofs of ferocious dispositions. This is no wonder, if the imprudence of sailors should prompt them to offend the simple savage, and the offence be resented; but Elliot, Brainerd, and the Moravian missionaries, have been very seldom molested. Nay, in general the heathen have showed a willingness to hear the Word, and have principally expressed their hatred of Christianity on account of the vices of nominal Christians.

As to the difficulty of procuring the necessaries of life, this would not be so great as may appear at first sight; for though we could not procure European food, yet we might procure such as the natives of those countries which we visit subsist upon themselves. And this would only be passing through what we have virtually engaged in by entering on the ministerial office. A Christian minister is a person who in a peculiar sense is *not his own*; he is the *servant* of God and therefore ought to be wholly devoted to Him. By entering on that sacred office he solemnly undertakes to be always engaged, as much as possible, in the Lord's work and not to choose his own pleasure or employment, or pursue the ministry as something that is to subserve his own ends or interest, or as a kind of bye-work. He engages to go where God pleases, and to do or endure what He·sees fit to command, or call him to, in the exercise of His function.

It might be necessary, however, for at least two to go together. In general I should think it best that they should be married men, and to prevent their time from being employed in procuring necessaries, two or more other persons, with their wives and families, might also accompany them, who should be wholly employed in providing for them. In most countries it would be necessary for them to cultivate a little spot of ground just for their support, which would be a resource to them whenever their supplies failed. Indeed a variety of methods may be thought of, and when once the work is undertaken many things will suggest themselves to us, of which we at present can form no idea.

As to learning their languages, the same means would be found necessary here as in trade between different nations. In some cases interpreters might be obtained, who might be employed for a time; and where these were not to be found, the missionaries must have patience and mingle with the people till they have learned so much of their language as to be able to communicate their ideas to them in it. It is well known to require no very extraordinary talents to learn, in the space of a year, or two at the most, the language of any people upon earth, so much of it at least, as to be able to convey any sentiments we wish to their understandings.

An Enquiry into the Duty of Christians in General, and What Means Ought to Be Used, in Order to Promote This Work

If the prophecies concerning the increase of Christ's kingdom be true, and if what has been advanced concerning the Commission given by Him to His disciples being obligatory on us be just, it must be inferred that all Christians ought heartily to concur with God in promoting His glorious designs, for "he that is joined unto the Lord is one spirit."

One of the first and most important of those duties which are incumbent upon us is *fervent* and *united prayer*. However the influence of the Holy Spirit may be set at nought, and run down by many, it will be found upon trial that all means which we can use, without it, will be ineffectual. If a temple is raised for God in the heathen world, it will not be "by might, nor by power," nor by the authority of the magistrate, or the eloquence of the orator; "but by my Spirit, saith the Lord of hosts." We must therefore be in real earnest in supplicating His blessing upon our labors.

The most glorious works of grace that have ever taken place have been in answer to prayer; and it is in this way, we have the greatest reason to suppose, that the glorious outpouring of the Spirit, which we expect at last, will be bestowed.

Many can do nothing but pray, and prayer is perhaps the only thing in which Christians of all denominations can cordially and unreservedly unite; but in this we may all be one, and in this strictest unanimity ought to prevail.

We must not be contented however with praying, without exerting ourselves in the use of means for the obtaining of those things we pray for. Were the children of light but as wise in their generation as the children of this world, they would stretch every nerve to gain so glorious a prize, nor ever imagine that it was to be obtained in any other way.

When a trading company have obtained their charter they usually go to its utmost limits; and their stocks, their ships, their officers, and men are so chosen and regulated as to be likely to answer to their purpose. But they do not stop here, for encouraged by the prospect of success, they use every effort, cast their bread upon the waters, cultivate friendship with every one from whose information they expect the least advantage. They cross the widest and most tempestuous seas and encounter the most unfavorable climates. They introduce themselves into the most barbarous nations and sometimes undergo the most affecting hardships. Their minds continue in a state of anxiety and suspense, and a longer delay then usual in the arrival of their vessels agitates them with a thousand changeful thoughts. Foreboding apprehensions continue till the rich returns are safe arrived in port. But why these fears? Whence all these disquietudes and this labor? Is it not because their souls enter into the spirit of the project and their happiness in a manner depends on its success? Christians are a body whose truest interest lies in the exaltation of the Messiah's kingdom. Their charter is very extensive, their encouragements exceeding great, and the return promised infinitely superior to all the gains of the most lucrative fellowship. Let then every one in his station consider himself as bound to act with all his might and in every possible way for God.

Suppose a company of serious Christians, ministers and private persons, were to form themselves into a society and make a number of rules respecting the regulation of the plan, the persons who are to be employed as missionaries, the means of defraying the expense, and so on. This society must consist of persons whose hearts are in the work, men of serious religion who possess a spirit of perseverance. There must be a determination not to admit any person who is not of this description or to retain him longer than he answers to it.

From such a society a *committee* might be appointed, whose business it should be to procure all the information they could upon the subject; to receive contributions; to enquire into the characters, tempers, abilities, and religious views of the missionaries; and also to provide them with necessaries for their undertakings.

If there is any reason for me to hope that I shall have any influence upon any of my brethren and fellow Christians, probably it may be more especially among them of my own denomination. I would therefore propose that such a society and committee should be formed among the *Particular Baptist Denomination.*

I do not mean by this, in any wise to confine it to one denomination of Christians. I wish with all my heart that everyone who loves our Lord Jesus Christ in sincerity would in some way or other engage in it. But in the present divided state of Christendom, it would be more likely for good to be done by each denomination engaging separately in the work than if they were to embark in it conjointly.

We are exhorted "to lay up treasures in heaven, where neither moth nor rust doth corrupt, and where thieves do not break through nor steal." It is also declared that "whatsoever a man soweth, that shall he also reap." These Scriptures teach us that the enjoyments of the life to come bear a near relation to that which now is a relation similar to that of the harvest and the seed. It is true all the reward is of mere grace, but it is nevertheless encouraging what a *treasure,* what a *harvest* must await such characters as Paul, and Elliot, and Brainerd, and others, who have given themselves wholly to the work of the Lord. What a heaven will it be to see the many myriads of poor heathens, of Britons among the rest, who by their labors have been brought to the knowledge of God. Surely a *crown of rejoicing* like this is worth aspiring to. Surely it is worthwhile to lay ourselves out with all our might in promoting the cause and kingdom of Christ.

Christmas Evans
(1766—1838)

This great preacher got his unusual name because he was born on December 25, 1766, in South Wales. His father died when he was nine years old, and he went to live with his cruel and godless uncle. Christmas Evans was an illiterate farm laborer until he was converted at age seventeen. He learned to read because of his desire to study the Bible.

Evans was ordained into the ministry at age twenty-four and began preaching in churches, coal mines, and surrounding fields. At twenty-six he went to the island of Anglesea, where he labored for twenty years. As Evans traveled Wales, unusual manifestation of Holy Spirit power accompanied his preaching, and revival began to sweep the country. People fell under conviction, mourned over sin, and repented in wholesale fashion. This became known as the "Welch Revival," and its fame spread around the world.

A remarkably powerful preacher, Christmas Evans possessed a commanding stature and authoritative presence. He was also called "the one-eyed apostle" because after he was saved, former companions beat him, causing him to lose one eye. Oddly enough, the deformity notably assisted his efforts.

Evans was a great natural preacher who combined splendid allegory with a lively imagination that held his congregations spellbound. His wonderful descriptive ability and pictorial powers earned him the title: "John Bunyan of Wales." The forgiveness of sin and the grace of God were his constant themes. Evans died in 1838.

5

The Triumph of Calvary
By Christmas Evans

Who is this that cometh from Edom, with dyed garments from Bozrah? this that is glorious in his apparel, travelling in the greatness of his strength? I that speak in righteousness, mighty to save. Wherefore art thou red in thine apparel and thy garments like him that treadeth in the winevat? I have trodden the winepress alone; and of the people there was none with me: for I will tread them in mine anger, and trample them in my fury; and their blood shall be sprinkled upon my garments, and I will stain all my raiment. For the day of vengeance is in mine heart, and the year of my redeemed is come. And I looked, and there was none to help; and I wondered that there was none to uphold: therefore mine own arm brought salvation unto me: and my fury, it upheld me. And I will tread down the people in mine anger, and make them drunk in my fury, and I will bring down their strength to the earth (Isa. 63:1-6).

This passage is one of the sublimest in the Bible. Not more majestic and overwhelming is the voice of God issuing from the burning bush. It represents "the Captain of our salvation," left alone in the heat of battle, marching victoriously through the broken columns of the foe, bursting the bars asunder, bearing away the brazen gates, and delivering by conquest the captives of sin and death. Let us first determine the events to which our text relates, and then briefly explain the questions and answers which it contains.

1. We have here a wonderful victory, obtained by Christ, in the city of Bozrah, in the land of Edom. Our first inquiry concerns the time and the place of that achievement.

Some of the prophecies are literal and others are figurative. Some of them are already fulfilled and others in daily process of fulfillment. Respecting this prophecy, divines disagree. Some think it is a description of Christ's conflict and victory, without the gates of Jerusalem, eighteen centuries ago; and others understand it as referring to the great battle of

48

Armageddon, predicted in the Apocalypse, and yet to be consummated before the end of the world.

I am not willing to pass by mount Calvary, and Joseph's new tomb, on my way to the field of Armageddon; nor am I willing to pause at the scene of the Crucifixion and the Ascension, without going farther on to the final conquest of the foe. I believe divine inspiration has included both events in the text—the victory already won on Calvary, and the victory yet to be accomplished in Armageddon—the finished victory of Messiah's passion, and the progressive victory of His gospel and His grace.

The former part of the text has reference to the victory of Calvary; the latter part anticipates the battle and triumph of Armageddon, mentioned in Revelation. The victory of Calvary is consummated on the morning of the third day after the Crucifixion. The Conqueror comes up from the earth, exclaiming:—"I have trodden the winepress alone on Calvary; and I will tread them in mine anger, and make them drunk in my fury, at the battle of Armageddon. I will overtake and destroy the beast, and the false prophet, and that old serpent the Devil, with all their hosts."

When the tide of battle turned, on the field of Waterloo, the Duke of Wellington mounted his horse and pursued the vanquished foe. So Isaiah's Conqueror, having routed the powers of hell on Calvary, pursues and destroys them on the field of Armageddon. Here He is represented as a hero on foot, a prince without an army; but John, the revelator, saw Him riding on a white horse, and followed by the armies of heaven, all on white horses, and not a footman among them.

The victory of Calvary is like the blood of atonement in the sanctuary. The cherubim were some of them looking one way, and some the other, but all were looking on the atoning blood. Thus all the great events of time—all the trials and triumphs of God's people—those which happened before, those which have happened since, and those which are yet to happen, are all looking toward the wrestling of Gethsemane, the conflict of Golgotha, and the triumph of Olivet. The escape from Egypt and the return from Babylon looked forward to the cross of Christ; and the faith of the perfect man of Uz hung on a risen Redeemer. The Christian martyrs overcame by the blood of the Lamb, and all their victories were in virtue of one great achievement. The tomb of Jesus is the birthplace of His people's immortality, and the power which raised Him from the dead shall open the sepulchers of all His saints. "Thy dead men shall live, together with my dead body shall they arise. Awake and sing, ye that dwell in the dust: for thy dew is as the dew of herbs, and the earth shall cast out the dead."

Christ offered Himself a sacrifice for us and drank the cup of God's righteous indignation in our stead. He was trodden by almighty justice, as a cluster of grapes in the winepress of the law, till the vessels of mercy overflowed with the wine of peace and pardon, which has made thousands of contrite and humble spirits "rejoice with joy unspeakable and full of glory." He suffered for us, that we might triumph with Him. But our text describes Him as a king and a conqueror. He was, at once, the dying victim and the immortal victor. In "the power of an endless life," He was standing by the altar when the sacrifice was burning. He was alive in His sacerdotal vestments, with His golden censer in His hand. He was alive in His kingly glory, with His sword and His scepter in His hand. He was alive in His conquering prowess, and had made an end of sin, and bruised the head of the serpent, and spoiled the principalities and powers of hell, and turned the vanquished hosts of the prince of darkness down to the winepress of the wrath of Almighty God. Then, on the morning of the third day, when He arose from the dead and made a show of them openly—then began the year of jubilee with power!

After the prophets of ancient times had long gazed through the mists of futurity, at the sufferings of Christ and the glory that should follow, a company of them were gathered together on the summit of Calvary. They saw a host of enemies ascending the hill, arrayed for battle, and most terrific in their aspect. In the middle of the line was the law of God, fiery and exceeding broad, and working wrath. On the right wing, was Beelzebub with his troops of infernals; and on the left Caiaphas with his Jewish priests, and Pilate with his Roman soldiers. The rear was brought up by Death, the last enemy. When the holy seers had spied this army and perceived that it was drawing nigh, they started back and prepared for flight. As they looked around they saw the Son of God advancing with intrepid step, having His face fixed on the hostile band. "Seest thou the danger that is before thee," said one of the men of God.

"I will tread them in mine anger," He replied, "and trample them in my fury."

"Who art thou?" said the prophet.

He answered: "I that speak in righteousness, mighty to save."

"Wilt thou venture to the battle alone?" asked the seer.

The Son of God replied: "I looked, and there was none to help; and I wondered there was none to uphold; therefore mine own arm shall bring salvation unto me; and my fury it upheld me."

"At what point wilt thou commence thy attack?" inquired the anxious prophet.

"I will first meet the Law," He replied, "and pass under its curse: for lo! I come to do thy will, O God. When I shall have succeeded at the center of the line, the colors will turn in my favor." So saying he moved forward. Instantly the thunderings of Sinai were heard, and the whole band of prophets quaked with terror. But He advanced, undaunted, amidst the gleaming lightnings. For a moment He was concealed from view, and the banner of wrath waved about in triumph. Suddenly the scene was changed. A stream of blood poured forth from His wounded side and put out all the fires of Sinai. The flag of peace was now seen unfurled and consternation filled the ranks of His foes. He then crushed, with His bruised heel, the old Serpent's head; and put all the infernal powers to flight. With His iron rod He dashed to pieces the enemies on the left wing, like a potter's vessel. Death still remained, who thought himself invincible, having hitherto triumphed over all. He came forward, brandishing his sting, which he had whetted on Sinai's tables of stone. He darted it at the Conqueror, but it turned down and hung like the flexible lash of a whip. Dismayed, he retreated to the grave, his palace, into which the Conqueror pursued. In a dark corner of his den, he sat on his throne of moldering skulls, and called upon the worms, his hitherto faithful allies, to aid him in the conflict; but they replied—"His flesh shall see no corruption." The scepter fell from his hand. The Conqueror seized him, bound him, and condemned him to the lake of fire; and then rose from the grave, followed by a band of released captives, who came forth after His Resurrection to be witnesses of the victory which He had won.

John in the Apocalypse did not look so far back as the treading of this winepress; but John saw Him on His white horse, decked with His many crowns, His eyes like flames of fire, a two-edged sword in His hand, in the van of the armies of heaven, going forth conquering and to conquer. This is the fulfillment of His declaration in our text:—"For I will tread them in mine anger, and trample them in my fury." This is the beginning of the jubilee, the battle of Armageddon, wherein all heathen idolatry and superstition shall be overthrown, and the beast and the false prophet shall be discomfited, and the devil and his legions shall be taken prisoners by Emmanuel and shut up in the bottomless pit. He who hath conquered principalities and powers on Calvary will not leave the field till He make all His enemies His footstool and sway His scepter over a subject universe. Having sent forth the gospel from Jerusalem, He accompanies it with the grace of His Holy Spirit; and it shall not return unto Him void, but shall accomplish that which He pleaseth, and prosper in the thing whereto He hath sent it.

The victory of Armageddon is obtained by virtue of the victory of Calvary. It is but the consummation of the same glorious campaign; and the first decisive blow dealt on the prince of darkness is a sure precursor of the final conquest. "I will meet thee again at Philippi!" said the ghost of Julius Caesar to Brutus. "I will meet thee again at Armageddon," saith the Son of God to Satan on Calvary—"I will meet thee in the engagement between good and evil, grace and depravity, in every believer's heart; in the contest of Divine Truth with human errors, of the religion of God with the superstitions of men; in every sermon, every revival, every missionary enterprise; in the spread and glory of the gospel in the latter day, I will meet thee; and the heel which thou hast now bruised shall crush thy head forever!"

This campaign is carried on at the expense of the government of heaven. The treasury is inexhaustible; the arms are irresistible; therefore the victory is sure. The Almighty King has descended; He has taken the city of Bozrah; He has swayed His scepter over Edom; He has risen victoriously, and gone up with a shout, as the leader of all the army. This is but the pledge and the earnest of His future achievements. In the battle of Armageddon, He shall go forth as a mighty man; He shall stir up jealousy as a man of war; and He shall prevail against His enemies. They shall be turned back—they shall be greatly ashamed, that trust in graven images—that say unto molten images, "Ye are our gods!" Then He will open the blind eyes, and bring the prisoners from the prison, and them that sit in darkness out of the prison-house. He will make bare His holy arm—He will show the sword in that hand which was hidden under the scarlet robe—He will manifest His power in the destruction of His enemies, and the salvation of His people. As certainly as He hath shed His blood on Calvary, shall He stain all His raiment with the blood of His foes on the field of Armageddon. As certainly as He hath drained the cup of wrath, and received the baptism of suffering, on Calvary, shall He wield the iron rod of justice, and sway the golden scepter of mercy, on the field of Armageddon. Already the sword is drawn, and the decisive blow is struck, and the helmet of Apollyon is cleft, and the bonds of iniquity are cut asunder. Already the fire is kindled, and all the powers of hell cannot quench it. It has fallen from heaven; it is consuming the camp of the foe; it is inflaming the hearts of men; it is renovating the earth, and purging away the curse. "The bright and morning star" has risen on Calvary; and soon "the Sun of righteousness" shall shine on the field of Armageddon; and the darkness that covers the earth, and the gross darkness that covers the people, shall melt away; and Mohammedanism, and Paganism, and Popery, with their prince, the Devil, shall seek shelter in the bottomless pit!

After a battle, we are anxious to learn who is dead, who is wounded, and who is missing from the ranks. In the engagement of Messiah with Satan and his allies on Calvary, Messiah's heel was bruised, but Satan and his allies received a mortal wound in the head. The head denotes wisdom, cunning, power, government. The Devil, sin, and death have lost their dominion over the believer in Christ, since the achievement of

Calvary. There is no condemnation, no fear of hell. But the Serpent, though his head is bruised, may be able to move his tail and alarm those of little faith. Yet it cannot last long. The wound is mortal and the triumph sure. On Calvary the Dragon's head was crushed by the Captain of our salvation; after the battle of Armageddon, his tail shall shake no more!

There is no discharge in this war. He that enlisteth under the banner of the Cross must endure faithful until death—must not lay aside his arms till death is swallowed up in victory. Then shall every conqueror bear the image of the heavenly, and wear the crown instead of the cross, and carry the palm instead of the spear. Let us be strong in the Lord, and in the power of his might, that we may be able to stand in the evil day; and after all the war is over, to stand accepted in the Beloved, that we may reign with Him forever and ever.

2. It remains for us to explain, very briefly, the glorious colloquy in the text—the interrogatives of the church, and the answers of Messiah.

How great was the wonder and joy of Mary, when she met the Master at the tomb, clothed in immortality, where she thought to find Him shrouded in death! How unspeakable was the astonishment and rapture of the disciples, when their Lord, whom they had so recently buried, came into the house where they were assembled, and said,"Peace be unto you!" Such are the feelings which the church is represented as expressing in this sublime colloquy with the Captain of her salvation. He has traveled into the land of tribulation; He has gone down to the dust of death; but lo, He returns a conqueror, the golden scepter of love in His left hand, the iron rod of justice in His right, and on His head a crown of many stars. The church beholds Him, with great amazement and delight. She lately followed Him, weeping, to the Cross, and mourned over His body in the tomb; but now she beholds Him risen indeed, having destroyed death, and Him that had the power of death—that is, the Devil. She goes forth to meet Him with songs of rejoicing, as the daughters of Israel went out to welcome David when he returned from the valley with the head of the giant in his hand and the blood running down upon his raiment. The choir of the church is divided into two bands; which chant to each other in alternate strains. The right hand division begins the glorious colloquy—"Who is this that cometh from Edom?" and the left takes up the interrogative and repeats it with a variation—"with dyed garments from Bozrah?" "This that is glorious in His apparel?" resumes the right-hand company—"glorious not withstanding the tribulations He hath endured?" "Traveling in the greatness of His strength?" responds the left—"strength sufficient to unbar the gates of the grave, and liberate the captives of corruption?" The celestial Conqueror pauses, and casts upon the company of the daughters of Zion a look of infinite benignity; and with a voice of angel melody, and more than angel majesty, He replies—"I that speak in righteousness, mighty to save!" Now bursts the song again, like the sound of many waters, from the right—"Wherefore art thou red in thine apparel?" and the response rolls back in melodized thunder from the left—"And thy garments like Him that treadeth in the winevat?" The divine hero answers:—"I have trodden the winepress alone; and of the people there was none with me. Even Peter has left me, with all his courage and affection; and as for John, to talk of love is all that he can do. I have triumphed over principalities and powers. I am wounded, but they are vanquished. Behold the blood which I have lost! Behold the spoils which I have won! Now will I mount my white horse, and pursue after Satan, and demolish his kingdom, and send him back to the land of darkness in everlasting chains, and all his allies shall be exiles with him forever. My own arm, which has gained the victory on Calvary, and brought salvation to all my people from the sepulcher, is still strong enough to wield the golden scepter of love, and break my foes on the field of Armageddon. I will destroy the works of the Devil, and demolish all his hosts; I will dash them in pieces like a potter's vessel. For the day of vengeance is in my heart, and the year of my redeemed is come. My compassion is stirred for the captives of sin and death; my fury is kindled against the tyrants that oppress them.

"It is time for me to open the prisons and break off the fetters. I must gather my people to myself. I must seek that which was lost, and bring again that which was driven away. I must bind up that which was broken, and strengthen that which was weak; but I will destroy the fat and the strong; I will feed them with judgment; I will tread them in mine anger, and trample them in my fury, and bring down their strength to the earth, and stain all my raiment with their blood!"

Let us flee from the wrath to come! Behold, the sun is risen high on the day of vengeance! Let us not be found among the enemies of Messiah, lest we fall a sacrifice to His righteous indignation on the field of Armageddon! Let us escape for our lives, for the fire-storm of His anger will burn to the lowest hell! Let us pray for grace to lay hold on the salvation of His redeemed! It is a free, full, perfect, glorious and eternal salvation. Return, ye ransomed exiles from happiness, return to your forfeited inheritance! Now is the year of jubilee. Come to Jesus, that your debts may be canceled, your sins forgiven, and your persons justified! Come, for the Conqueror of your foes is on the throne! Come, for the trumpets of mercy are sounding! Come, for all things are now ready!

Robert Murray McCheyne
(1813—1843)

Born in Edinburgh, Scotland, in 1813, this great Scottish preacher grew up in a Christian environment with godly parents. McCheyne displayed outstanding intellectual skills as a child and could recite the Greek alphabet at the age of four. He later used a remarkable memory to memorize long passages of Scripture. Attending the University of Edinburgh, he was greatly influenced by Thomas Chalmers; he graduated in 1830. Having been licensed to preach when he was twenty-two, McCheyne was ordained a year later and began pastoring in Dundee, Scotland.

As pastor of St. Peter's Church (of the Church of Scotland), McCheyne pastored a congregation of over one thousand members. In 1839 he visited Palestine concerning future evangelizaton of the Jewish people. While there, he prayed fervently for his congregation back home. Upon his return he found that a spiritual awakening was in progress. His preaching consequently made a significant contribution to the revival and helped it spread across Scotland to northern England. He used his intellectual ability to design sermons that had a tremendous persuasion upon the unconverted. He was only thirty when he died in 1843, reportedly of typhoid fever.

Few men have had the impact in a long lifetime that Robert Murray McCheyne had in his thirty years. Though his ministry lasted only seven years, it had a profound impact upon many notable preachers of his day. His was a daily walk with God, and it was perhaps his Christlike dependence upon God's Spirit that left such a deep impression on men's lives. After hearing him preach, one Scottish evangelist reportedly said, "He preached with eternity stamped upon his brow. I trembled, and never felt God so near." McCheyne's life undoubtedly exemplified the words he so often repeated: "Live so as to be missed."

6

The Pilgrim's Staff
By Robert Murray McCheyne

I will never leave thee, nor forsake thee (Heb. 13:5).

My beloved friends, let us notice, in the first place, the history of this remarkable promise: "I will never leave thee, nor forsake thee." These words have been a staff in the hand of believers throughout all ages; and they will be so to you, if you lean upon them.

I. First of all, let us trace *the history of this promise*. You will notice that it is not put into this epistle for the first time—it is a borrowed promise. First of all, I think, it is borrowed from what God said to Jacob in Genesis 28:15: "Behold, I am with thee, and will keep thee in all places whither thou goest, and will bring thee again into this land; for *I will not leave thee*, until I have done that which I have spoken to thee of." There is another place from which I think it is borrowed, 1 Chronicles 28:20: "And David said to Solomon his son, Be strong and of good courage, and do it; fear not, nor be dismayed: for the Lord God, even my God, will be with thee; *He will not fail thee, nor forsake thee.*" Now, you see, here is the promise again—"He will not fail thee, nor forsake thee." There is still another place where the same staff is put into a believer's hand, Joshua 1:5: "There shall not any man be able to stand before thee all the days of thy life: As I was with Moses, so I will be with thee: *I will not fail thee, nor forsake thee.*" Now, turn back again to Hebrews, and observe how Paul brings it in—"Be content with such things as ye have: *for* he hath said, I will never leave thee, nor forsake thee." Now, a believer may ask this question—"When did He say that to me?" Ah! but He said it to Jacob, and Solomon, and Joshua, and therefore it is said to you. Observe, brethren, what a blessed principle this brings out: What God speaks to one believer, He says to me. You will observe that this promise in the Old Testament is special—that is, it is addressed to one individual,

58

but in the New Testament it is general. Some, when they read the Old Testament, say, "This is addressed to Abraham," or "This is addressed to Jacob, but it is not said to me." But what was said to Abraham, or Jacob, or Joshua, is spoken to you. The special promise to Joshua is to all believing Joshuas to the end of the world—"I will never leave thee, nor forsake thee." I do not know if you understand what I mean, but from this little verse we know that the special promises in the Old Testament are to all believers. God said to Abraham—"I will bless thee, and make thy name great; and thou shalt be a blessing." So He says to all that are children of Abraham. And there is a sweet promise in the forty-third of Isaiah—"Fear not: for I have redeemed thee, I have called thee by my name; thou art mine." That promise was special to Israel, and yet it belongs to me. And there is another sweet promise in the fifty-fourth chapter—"For a small moment have I forsaken thee; but with great mercies will I gather thee." Now, if you were reading this promise, you might say, "Ah! that does not belong to me." But by turning to the thirteenth of Hebrews, we know that it belongs to all believers. There are two reasons I would give why this is true, because to some it may appear wonderful. The first is, God is the same yesterday, today, and forever—"I am the Lord; I change not." Ah! the unchangeableness of God explains it—"I am the Lord; I change not." Jesus Christ is the same yesterday, today, and forever. And there is another reason why this promise of Scripture belongs to believers now; it is that all believers are one body, and therefore whatever belongs to one, belongs to all. All believers are branches of one vine; and therefore if God say to one branch, "I will never leave thee, nor forsake thee," He says so to all. And therefore, for these two reasons, all the promises made to Jacob or Solomon or Joshua are made to me. And this makes the Bible not a book written for one, but a Book written to me—a letter by the Lord, and directed to me: and therefore every word of divine love and tenderness that He has written in this Book belongs to me.

II. And now, dear brethren, I would speak, in the second place, of *the person here spoken of*—"I will never leave thee, nor forsake thee." It is quite evident that it is not the language of a creature. Our parents will leave us, and our friends will leave us. These are not the words of a creature, then—"I will never leave thee, nor forsake thee." Observe, then, dear brethren, I entreat you, whose word it is—"*He* hath said, I will never leave thee, nor forsake thee." It is the word of the three-one God. You may take each of the persons of the Godhead, and apply this word to Him—"I will never leave thee, nor forsake thee." You may take it as the word of Immanuel. You remember what Christ said to His disciples—"Lo, I am with you alway, even unto the end of the world." This is the same promise. Brethren, when the Lord Jesus comes to you, and covers you with His garment, and says, "Fear not," He will never forsake that soul. A mother may forsake—"Can a woman forget her sucking child, that she should not have compassion on the son of her womb? Yea, she may forget; yet will I not forget thee." Observe, brethren, that when once the Lord Jesus comes to a sinner to be his righteousness, He will never leave him—"I am with you alway." Oh! it is this that makes him a friend that sticketh closer than a brother. Why will He never leave us? The first reason is, His love is everlasting love. It is not like the love of a creature—it is unchangeable. Another reason is, He has died for that soul: He has borne all for that soul. Will He ever leave a soul that He has died for?

Again, you may take these words as those of the Spirit, and then they are like those words in the fourteenth of John—"I will pray the Father, and he shall give you another Comforter, that he may abide with you for ever"—to abide with you forever. It is the same as these words—"I will never leave thee, nor forsake thee." When God the Holy Spirit comes to a soul, He will never leave it. Some may often be made to say, "I think the Spirit will go away from me." But, observe, He says, "I will never leave thee, nor forsake thee." David cried out in the bitterness of his soul. "Take not thy holy spirit from me." Here is the answer—"I will never leave thee, nor forsake thee." God will never forsake the temple in which He dwells. He forsook the tabernacle in the wilderness, and He forsook the temple at Jerusalem, but He will never forsake the living temple.

Or, you may take these words, and apply them to God the Father. And here they come to be very much the words God gave to Abraham: He said, "Fear not, Abram: I am thy shield, and thy exceeding great reward." He had returned from the slaughter of Chedorlaomer, and of the kings that were with him. The king of Sodom came out to meet him, and said unto him, "Give me the persons, and take the goods to thyself." But Abraham said, "I have lifted up mine hand unto the Lord, the most high God, the possessor of heaven and of earth, that I will not take from a thread even to a shoelatchet, and that I will not take any thing that is thine, lest thou shouldest say, I have made Abram rich." And, immediately after, God appeared to him, and said: "Fear not, Abram: I am thy shield, and thy exceeding great reward." This is what Asaph felt. He says, in the seventy-third Psalm, "My flesh and my heart faileth: but God is the strength of my heart, and my portion for ever." Ah, brethren, this is a sweet word to a poor soul who is mourning over the broken pots at his feet. This is a sweet word to those of you who are mourning over the dead. O brethren! is this your portion? Can you look up to a three-one God, Father, Son, and Spirit, standing on these broken shreds at your feet, and say, "Thou wilt never leave me, nor forsake me?" This is happiness. Well, well did the Lord say, "Mary hath chosen that good part, which shall never be taken away from her." Ah, poor souls! that have chosen the world as your portion—that have chosen the portion that will be taken from you. Ah, brethren! be you wiser.

Let me mention now some of the times when we should remember these words.

1. *A time of guilt.* O the dark hour, when guilt is on the conscience, and when a frown looks down from heaven upon us. O in such an hour remember these words—"I will never leave thee, nor forsake thee." "Thou hast played the harlot with many lovers; yet return unto me." Thy redeeming God calls out, "I will never leave thee, nor forsake thee." "Jesus Christ, the same yesterday, today, and forever." Thy redeeming God calls out, "I will never leave thee, nor forsake thee." "Turn, O backsliding children, said the Lord; for I am married unto you." O there is a deceitfulness in sin! When Satan has got you down, he tries to make you think God has forsaken you.

2. *A time of danger.* There is no time when you may be more inclined to think God has forsaken you than when sin and Satan are raging. There is a difference from sin raging and sin reigning, though the soul may not see it. In such a time, remember these words—"I will never leave thee, nor forsake thee." In a time of temptation, the believer should remember this promise. Jacob rested on it; Solomon rested on it: yea, it is a staff which has been leaned on by many believers, and you may lean on it too.

3. *When creatures leave you.* Some of you may be *bereft* of your substance, but remember, "I will never leave thee, nor forsake thee." Some of you may be called upon—some have been called upon—to part with those who are dear to you. Some of you may be called upon to part with your teachers; but remember—and, Oh! it is hard to remember—that He that makes the creatures pleasant, still lives. Brethren, I do not know a lesson in the world that is harder to learn than this. It was God that gave me the creatures; and, now that He has taken them away, in Himself I can find all that I had in them. O then! remember this—"I will never leave thee, nor forsake thee." Bereavements come suddenly, they come like the whirlwind; but O remember that He comes and says, "I will never leave thee, nor forsake thee." And, O brethren! that the word "never" reaches to death—it reaches to the judgment seat. You may lay hold of that word there—"I will never leave thee, nor forsake thee." And when the judgment is past, these words will be the eternal solace of all those here who have believed—"I will never leave thee, nor forsake thee." Eternity alone will unfold the riches of this promise. He who died for us will be our eternal friend; and He who sanctifies us will forever dwell in us; and then God,

who loved us, will be ever with us. Then will we get into the meaning of His promise—"I will never leave thee, nor forsake thee." Amen.

Charles G. Finney
(1792—1875)

Born in Warren, Connecticut, in 1792, Charles Grandison Finney moved to New York with his parents at the age of two. With little formal education, he became an avid reader on his own and was largely self-educated. Although he had no earned degrees, Finney taught himself Greek, Hebrew, and Latin but later began studying law. It was during this period of his life that he became interested in religious matters and was converted in 1821. It is said that Finney led several to Christ, including his parents, the very day of his conversion.

Shortly after his salvation experience, Finney left his law career for the gospel ministry. He began doing home mission work for the Presbyterian church in 1824 and a great revival broke out in the area. This began his great revival ministry and he subsequently held meetings in many larger cities. After short pastorates (1832-1835) Finney went to Oberlin College in Ohio as a professor. He later became president of the college, and it was during this time that he wrote several treatises, including *Lectures on Revivals.*

Finney's primary efforts centered around mass evangelism and revival lectures, which took him to many parts of America and Great Britain. He played a significant role in the Great Revival of 1868-69, in which over one-half million people were converted.

Few preachers have ever ministered with such power and conviction. It was a common occurrence for men and women to fall prostrate under Holy Spirit conviction as he preached. Once as Finney walked through a factory, revival swept through the building as workers fell under conviction due to his very presence. He was a dedicated man who fasted often and held long prayer vigils. Finney was highly intelligent, and his legal experience was seen in the logic of his preaching. He pressed his audience for a "verdict," and made use of the public invitation, a rare event in his day. The protracted revival meetings of later years were also largely an outgrowth of his ministry. This great American revivalist died in 1875 at the age of eighty-three.

7

Stewardship
By Charles G. Finney

Give an account of thy stewardship (Luke 16:2).

A steward is one who is employed to transact the business of another, as his agent or representative in the business in which he is employed.

His duty is to promote, in the best possible manner, the interest of his employer. He is liable, at any time, to be called to an account for the manner in which he has transacted his business, and to be removed from his office at the pleasure of his employer.

One important design of the parable of which the text is a part is to teach that all men are God's stewards. The Bible declares that the silver and the gold are His, and that He is, in the highest possible sense, the proprietor of the universe. Men are mere stewards, employed by Him for the transaction of His business, and required to do all they do for His glory. Even their eating and drinking are to be done for His glory, that they be strengthened for the best performance of His business.

1. If men are God's stewards, they are bound to account to Him for their *time.* God has created them and keeps them alive and their time is His. Hearer, should you employ a steward and pay him for his time, would you not expect him to employ that time in your service? Would you not consider it fraud and dishonesty, for him, while in your pay, to spend his time in idleness, or in promoting his private interests? Suppose he were often idle; that would be bad enough. But suppose that he *wholly* neglected your business, and that, when called to an account and censured for not doing his duty, he should say, "Why, what have I done?" Would you not suppose that for him to have done *nothing,* and let your business suffer, was great wickedness, for which he deserved to be punished?

Now, you are God's steward, and if you are an impenitent sinner, you have wholly neglected God's business, and have remained idle in His vineyard, or have been only attending to your own private interest; and now you are ready to ask what you have done? Are you not a knave, thus to neglect the business of your great employer and go about your own private business, to the neglect of all that justice and duty and God require of you?

2. Stewards are bound to give an account of their *talents*. By talents, I mean here the powers of their minds. Suppose you should educate a man to be your steward, should support him during the time that he was engaged in study, and be at all the expense of his education, and that then he should either neglect to employ his mind in your service, or should use the powers of his cultivated intellect for the promotion of his own interests; would you not consider this as fraud and villany? Now, God created your minds, and has been at the expense of your education, and has trained you up for His service; and do you either let your mind remain in idleness, or pervert the powers of your cultivated intellect, to the promotion of your own private interest, and then ask what you have done to deserve the wrath of God?

3. A steward is bound to give an account for the *influence he exerts* upon mankind around him.

Suppose you should employ a steward, should educate him until he possessed great talents, should put a large capital into his hands, should exalt him high in society, and place him in circumstances to exert an immense influence in the commercial community, and that then he should refuse or neglect to exert this influence in promoting your interest; would you not consider this default a perpetual fraud practiced upon you?

But suppose he should exert all this influence against you, and array himself with all his weight of character and talent and influence, and even employ the capital with which he was intrusted, in *opposing* your interest—what language, in your estimation, could then express your sense of his guilt?

Hearer, whatever influence God has given you, if you are an impenitent sinner, you are not only neglecting to use it for God, to build up His kingdom, but you are employing it in *opposition* to His interest and glory; and for this, do you not deserve the damnation of hell? Perhaps you are rich, or learned, or have, on other accounts, great influence in society, and are refusing to use it to save the souls of men, but are bringing all your weight of character and talents and influence and example, to drag all who are within the sphere of your influence, down to the gates of hell.

4. You must give an account for the manner in which you use *the property in your possession*. Suppose your steward should refuse to employ the capital with which you entrusted him for the promotion of your interest. Or suppose he were to account it his own, and to use it for his own

private interest, or apply it to the gratification of his lusts, or the aggrandizement of his family—in bestowing large portions upon his daughters or in ministering to the lusts and pride of his sons—while at the same time your business was suffering for the want of this very capital. Or suppose that this steward held the purse-strings of your wealth, and that you had multitudes of other servants, whose necessities were to be supplied out of the means in his hands, and that their welfare, and even their lives, depended on these supplies; and yet this steward should minister to his own lusts, and those of his family, and suffer those, your other servants, to perish—what would you think of such wickedness? You entrusted him with your money and enjoined him to take care of your other servants, and, through his neglect, they were all dead men.

Now, you have God's money in your hands and are surrounded by God's children, whom He commands you to love as you do yourself. God might, with perfect justice, have given His property to them instead of you. The world is full of poverty, desolation, and death; hundreds and millions are perishing, body and soul; God calls on you to exert yourself as His steward for their salvation; to use all the property in your possession so as to promote the greatest possible amount of happiness among your fellow creatures. The Macedonian cry comes from the four winds of heaven, "Come over and help us," and yet you refuse to help; you hoard up the wealth in your possession, live in luxury, and let your fellowmen go down to hell. What language can describe your guilt?

5. You must give an account of your *soul.* You have no right to go to hell. God has a right to your soul; your going to hell would injure the whole universe. It would injure hell, because it would increase its torments. It would injure heaven, because it would wrong it out of your services. Who shall take the harp in your place, in singing praises to God? Who shall contribute your share to the happiness of heaven?

Suppose you had a steward to whom you had given life, and educated him at a great expense, and then he should willfully throw that life away; has he a right thus to dispose of a life of so much value to you? Is it not as just as to rob you of the same amount of property in anything else? God has made your soul, sustained and educated you, till you are now able to render Him important services, and to glorify Him forever; and have you a right to go to hell, and throw away your soul, and thus rob God of your service? Have you a right to render hell more miserable, and heaven less happy, and thus injure God and all the universe?

Do you still say, What if I do lose my soul, it is nobody's business but my own? That is false; it is everybody's business. Just as well might a man bring a contagious disease into a city, and spread dismay and death all around, and say it was nobody's business but his own.

6. You must give an account for the *souls of others.* God commands

you to be a co-worker with Him in converting the world. He needs your service, for He saves souls only through the agency of men. If souls are lost, or the gospel is not spread over the world, sinners charge all the blame upon Christians, as if they only were bound to be active in the cause of Christ, to exercise benevolence, to pray for a lost world, to pull sinners out of the fire. I wonder who has absolved *you* from these duties? Instead of doing your duty, you lie as a stumbling-block in the way of other sinners. Thus, instead of helping to save a world, all your actions help to send souls to hell.

7. You are bound to give an account of the *sentiments you entertain and propagate*. God's kingdom is to be built up by truth and not by error. Your sentiments will have an important bearing upon the influence you exert over those around you.

Suppose the business in which your steward was employed required that he should entertain right notions concerning the manner of doing it, and the principle involved in it, of your will and of his duty. And suppose you had given him, in writing, a set of rules for the government of his conduct, in relation to all the affairs with which he was entrusted. Then if he should neglect to examine those rules, or should pervert their plain meaning, and should thus pervert his own conduct, and be instrumental in deceiving others, leading them in the way of disobedience, would you not look upon this as criminal and deserving the severest reprobation?

God has given you rules for the government of your conduct. In the Bible you have a plain revelation of His will in relation to all your actions. And now, do you either neglect or pervert it, and thus go astray yourself, and lead others with you in the way of disobedience and death, and then call yourself an honest man? For shame!

8. You must give an account of your *opportunities of doing good*.

If you employ a steward to transact your business, you expect him to take advantage of the state of the market and of things in general, to improve every opportunity to promote your interest. Suppose at the busy seasons of the year, he should spend his time in idleness, or in his own private affairs, and not have an eye at all to the most favorable opportunities of promoting your interest. Would you not soon say to him, "Give an account of thy stewardship; for thou mayest be no longer steward"? Now, sinner, you have always neglected opportunities of serving God, of warning your fellow sinners, of promoting revivals of religion, and of advancing the interests of truth. You have been diligent merely to promote your own private interests and have entirely neglected the interests of your great Employer; and are you not a wretch, and do you not deserve to be put out of the stewardship, as a dishonest man, and to be sent to the state prison of the universe? How can you escape the damnation of hell?

Remarks. From this subject you can see why the business of this world is a snare that draws men's souls in destruction and perdition.

Sinners transact business to promote their own private interests, and not as God's stewards, and thus act dishonestly, defraud God, grieve the Spirit, and promote their own sensuality, pride, and death. If men considered themselves as God's clerks, they would not lie, and overreach, and work on the Sabbath, to make money for *Him;* they would be sure that such conduct would not please Him. God never created this world to be a snare to men—it is abused; He designed it to be a delightful abode for them—but how perverted!

Suppose a mother, whose son was in a distant land, was busy all day in putting up clothes, and books, and necessaries for him, continually questioning, how will this please him? and how will that please him? Would that employment have a tendency to divert her mind from her absent son? Now if you consider yourself as God's steward, doing His business; if you are in all things consulting His interests and His glory, and consider all your possessions as His, your time and your talents; the more busily you are engaged in His service, the more will God be present to all your thoughts.

You see why idleness is a snare to the soul. A man that is idle is dishonest, forgets his responsibility, refuses to serve God, and gives himself up to the temptations of the Devil. Nay the idle man tempts the Devil to tempt him.

You see the error of the maxim, that men cannot attend to business and religion at the same time. A man's business ought to be a part of his religion. He cannot be religious in idleness. He must have some business, to be religious at all, and if it is performed from a right motive, his lawful and necessary business is as much a necessary part of religion as prayer, or going to church, or reading his Bible. Anyone who pleads this maxim is a knave by his own confession, for no man can believe that an honest employment, and pursued for God's glory, is inconsistent with religion. The objection supposes in the face of it that he considers his business either as unlawful in itself, or that he pursues it in a dishonest manner. If this be true, he cannot be religious while thus pursuing his business; if his employment be wicked, he must relinquish it; or if honest and pursued in an unlawful manner, he must pursue it lawfully; or in either case he will lose his soul. But if his business is lawful, let him pursue it honestly, and from right motives, and he will find no difficulty in attending to his business and being religious at the same time. A life of business is best for Christians, as it exercises their graces and makes them strong.

That most men do not account themselves as God's stewards is evident from the fact that they consider the losses they sustain in business as their own losses. Suppose that some of your debtors should fail, and your clerks should speak of it as their loss, and say they had met with great losses, would you not look upon it as ridiculous in the extreme? And is it not quite as ridiculous for you, if any of your Lord's debtors fail, to make yourself very uneasy and unhappy about it? Is it your loss, or His? If you have done your duty, and taken suitable care of His property, and a loss is sustained, it is not your loss, but His. You should look at your sins and your duty, and not be frightened lest God should become bankrupt. If you acted as God's steward or as His clerk, you would not think of speaking of the loss as your own loss. But if you have considered the property in your possession as your own, no wonder that God has taken it out of your hands.

You see the wickedness of laying up money for your children, and why money so laid up is a *curse* to them. Suppose your steward should lay up your money for his children, would you not consider him a knave? How then dare you take God's money and lay it up for your children, while the world is sinking down to hell? But will you say, Is it not my duty to provide for my "own household"? Yes, it is your duty *suitably* to provide for them, but what is a suitable provision? Give them the best education you can for the service of God. Make all *necessary* provision for the supply of their *real* wants, "till they become of sufficient age to provide for themselves"—and then if you see them disposed to do good in serving God and their generation, give them all the advantages for *doing this* in your power. But to make them rich—to gratify their pride—to enable them to live in luxury or ease—or to provide that they may become rich—to give your daughters what is called a genteel education—to allow them to spend their time in dress, idleness, gossiping, and effeminacy, you have no right—it is defrauding God, ruining your own soul, and greatly endangering theirs.

Impenitent sinners will be finally and eternally disgraced. Do you not account it a disgrace to a man, to be detected in fraud and every species of knavery in transacting the business of his employer? Is not such a man deservedly thrown out of business; is he not a disgrace to himself and his family; can anybody trust him? How then will you appear before an injured God and an injured universe—a God whose laws and rights you have despised—a universe with whose interests you have been at war? How will you, in the solemn judgment, be disgraced, your name execrated, and you become the hissing and contempt of hell, for the numberless frauds and villainies you have practiced upon God and upon His creatures! But perhaps you are a professor of religion: Will your profession cover up your selfishness and vile hypocrisy, while you have defrauded God, spent His money upon your lusts, and accounted those as beggars who came with drafts upon you to pay over into His treasury?

How will you hold up your head in the face of heaven? How dare you now pray; how dare you sit at the communion table; how dare you profess the religion of Jesus Christ, if you have set up a private interest, and do not consider all that you have as His, and use it for all His glory?

We have here a true test of Christian character. True Christians *consider themselves* as God's stewards: they act for Him, live for Him, transact business for Him, eat and drink for His glory, live and die to please Him. But sinners and hypocrites live for themselves; account for their time, their talents, their influence, as their own; and dispose of them all for their own private interest and thus drown themselves in destructon and perdition.

At the judgment, we are informed that Christ will say to those who are accepted, "Well done, good and faithful servants." Hearer! could He truly say this of you, "Well done, good and faithful servant; thou hast been faithful over a few things," *i.e.* over the things committed to your charge. He will pronounce no false judgment, put no false estimate upon things; and if He cannot say this truly, "Well done, good and faithful servant," you will not be accepted, but will be thrust down to hell. Now, what is your character, and what has been your conduct? God will soon call you to give an account of your stewardship. Have you been faithful to God, faithful to your own soul, and the souls of others? Are you ready to have your accounts examined, your conduct scrutinized, and your life weighed in the balance of the sanctuary? Are you interested in the blood of Jesus Christ? If not, repent, *repent now,* of all your wickedness, and lay hold upon the hope that is set before you; for, hark! a voice cries in your ears, "Give an account of thy stewardship, for thou mayest be no longer steward."

Charles Haddon Spurgeon
(1834—1892)

Perhaps the greatest preacher in English history, this "prince of preachers" was born in 1834 in Kelvedon, Essex, England. Converted at the age of sixteen, Charles Haddon Spurgeon bypassed college; like his father and grandfather, he became a preacher. Before reaching twenty he had pastored the Waterbeach Baptist Chapel for three years.

In 1854 he became the pastor of New Park Street Chapel in London. His first Sunday only 100 people were present, but soon the building was too small to accommodate the crowds. By the time Spurgeon was twenty-two years old, he was the most popular preacher in the world, preaching weekly to crowds of over 10,000. The 6,000-seat Metropolitan Tabernacle, built for him and opened in 1861, was packed twice each Sunday to hear him preach, until his death in 1892. A record crowd of over 23,000 came to hear him preach at the Crystal Palace in London.

Spurgeon combined a vivid imagination with a beauty of expression that many feel is unequalled in English literature. He preached without notes after much prayer and study alone. Asked the secret of his success, he replied without hesitation: "Day after day, thousands of God's people ask for His blessing on me and my sermons."

In addition to pastoring the Metropolitan Tabernacle, Spurgeon established the Pastors' College in 1857, and the Stockwell Orphanage in 1867. During his ministry his sermons were distributed worldwide and were read weekly by millions of people. Over 3,500 of them are in print today. Spurgeon is still read by more people than any other preacher in history.

The Cross Our Glory
By Charles Haddon Spurgeon

But God forbid that I should glory, save in the cross of our Lord Jesus Christ, by whom the world is crucified unto me, and I unto the world (Gal. 6:14).

Almost all men have something wherein to glory. Every bird has its own note of song. It is a poor heart that never rejoices; it is a dull packhorse that is altogether without bells. Men usually rejoice in something or other, and many men so rejoice in that which they choose that they become boastful and full of vain glory. It is very sad that men should be ruined by their glory, and yet many are so. Many glory in their shame, and more glory in that which is mere emptiness. Some glory in their physical strength, in which an ox excels them; or in their gold, which is but thick clay; or in their gifts, which are but talents with which they are entrusted. The pounds entrusted to their stewardship are thought by men to belong to themselves, and therefore they rob God of the glory of them. O my hearers, hear ye the voice of wisdom, which crieth, "He that glorieth, let him glory in the Lord." To live for personal glory is to be dead while we live. Be not so foolish as to perish for a bubble. Many a man has thrown his soul away for a little honor, or for the transient satisfaction of success in trifles. O men, your tendency is to glory in somewhat; your wisdom will be to find a glory worthy of an immortal mind.

Brethren, notice that Paul does not here say that he gloried in Christ, though he did so with all his heart; but he declares that he gloried most in "the cross of our Lord Jesus Christ," which in the eyes of men was the very lowest and most inglorious part of the history of the Lord Jesus. He could have gloried in the incarnation: angels sang of it, wise men came from the far East to behold it. Did not the newborn King awake the song from heaven of "Glory to God in the highest"? He might have gloried in the life of Christ: was there ever such another, so benevolent and blameless? He might have gloried in the Resurrection of Christ: it is the world's great hope concerning those that are asleep. He might have gloried in our Lord's ascension; for He "led captivity captive," and all His followers glory in His victory. He might have gloried in His Second Advent, and I doubt not that he did; for the Lord shall soon descend from heaven with a shout, with the voice of the archangel and the trump of God, to be admired in all them that believe. Yet the apostle selected beyond all these that the center of the Christian system, that point which is most assailed by its foes, that focus of the world's derision—the Cross; and, putting all else somewhat into the shade, he exclaims, "God forbid that I should glory, save in the cross of our Lord Jesus Christ." Learn, then, that the highest glory of our holy religion is the Cross. The history of grace begins earlier and goes on later, but in its middle point stands the Cross. Of two eternities this is the hinge: of past decrees and future glories this is the pivot. Let us come to the Cross this morning, and think of it, till each one of us, in the power of the Spirit of God, shall say, "God forbid that I should glory, save in the cross of our Lord Jesus Christ."

1. First, as the Lord shall help me (for who shall describe the cross without the help of Him that did hang upon it?) WHAT DID PAUL MEAN BY THE CROSS? Did he not include under this term, first, the fact of the Cross: secondly, the doctrine of the Cross: and thirdly, the cross of the doctrine?

I think he meant, first of all, *the fact of the Cross.* Our Lord Jesus Christ did really die upon a gibbet, the death of a felon. He was literally put to death upon a tree, accursed in the esteem of men. I beg you to notice how the apostle puts it—"the cross of our Lord Jesus Christ." In his epistles he sometimes said "Christ," at another time "Jesus," frequently, "Lord," oftentimes, "our Lord"; but here he saith "our Lord Jesus Christ." There is a sort of pomp of words in this full description, as if in contrast to the shame of the Cross. The terms are intended in some small measure to express the dignity of Him who was put to so ignominious a death. He is Christ the anointed, and Jesus the Savior; He is the Lord, the Lord of all, and He is "our Lord Jesus Christ." He is not a Lord without subjects, for He is "our Lord"; nor is He a Savior without saved ones, for He is "our Lord Jesus"; nor has He the anointing for Himself alone, for all of us have a share in Him as "our Christ": in all He is ours, and was so upon the cross. When they bury a great nobleman, a herald stands at the head of the grave and proclaims his titles. "Here lieth the body of William Duke of this, and Earl of that, and Count of the other, Knight of this order, and commander of the other." Even thus, in deep solemnity, with brevity and fullness, Paul proclaims beneath the bitter tree the names and titles of the Savior of men, and styles Him "our Lord Jesus Christ."

I declare this fact to you in words, but I think them poor, dumb things; I wish I could speak this matchless truth in fire-flakes! The announcement that the Son of God died upon the cross to save men deserves the accompaniment of angelic trumpets and of the harps of the redeemed.

But, next, I said that Paul gloried in *the doctrine of the Cross;* and it was so. What is that doctrine of the Cross, of which it is written that it is "to them that perish foolishness; but unto us which are saved it is the power of God"? In one word, it is the doctrine of the atonement, the doctrine that the Lord Jesus Christ was made sin for us, that Christ was once offered to bear the sins of many, and that God hath set Him forth to be the propitiation for our sins. Paul saith, "When we were yet without strength, in due time Christ died for the ungodly." And again, "Now once in the end of the world hath he appeared to put away sin by the sacrifice of himself." The doctrine of the Cross is that of sacrifice for sin: Jesus is "the Lamb of God which taketh away the sin of the world." "God so loved the world, that he gave his only begotten Son, that whosoever believeth in him should not perish, but have everlasting life." The doctrine is that of a full atonement made, and the utmost ransom paid. "Christ hath redeemed us from the curse of the law, being made a curse for us: for it is written, Cursed is every one that hangeth on a tree." In Christ upon the cross we see the Just dying for the unjust, that He might bring us to God; the innocent bearing the crimes of the guilty, that they might be forgiven and accepted. That is the doctrine of the Cross, of which Paul was never ashamed.

But the apostle also gloried in the *cross of the doctrine,* for the death of the Son of God upon the cross is the *crux* of Christianity. Here is the difficulty, the stumbling block, and rock of offence. The Jew could not endure a crucified Messiah: he looked for pomp and power. Multitudinous ceremonies and divers washings and sacrifices, were these all to be put away and nothing left but a bleeding Savior? At the mention of the cross the philosophic Greek thought himself insulted, and vilified the preacher as a fool. In effect he said, "You are not a man of thought and intellect; you are not abreast of the times but are sticking in the mire of antiquated prophecies. Why not advance with the discoveries of modern thought?" The apostle, teaching a simple fact which a child might comprehend, found in it the wisdom of God. Christ upon the cross working out the salvation of men was more to him than all the sayings of the sages. As for the Roman, he would give no heed to any glorying in a dead Jew, a crucified Jew! Crushing the world beneath his iron heel, he declared that such romancing should never win him from the gods of his fathers. Paul did not pale before the sharp and practical reply of the conquerors of the world. He trembled not before Nero in his palace. Whether to Greek or Jew, Roman or barbarian, bond or free, he was not ashamed of the gospel of Christ, but gloried in the cross. Though the testimony that the one all-sufficient atonement was provided on the cross stirs the enmity of man, and provokes opposition, yet Paul was so far from attempting to mitigate that opposition, that he determined to know nothing save Jesus Christ and Him crucified. His motto was "We preach Christ crucified." He had the Cross for his philosophy, the Cross for his tradition, the Cross for his gospel, the Cross for his glory, and nothing else.

2. But, secondly, WHY DID PAUL GLORY IN THE CROSS? He did not do so because he was in want of a theme; for, as I have shown you, he had a wide field for boasting if he had chosen to occupy it. He gloried in the Cross from solemn and deliberate choice. He had counted the cost, he had surveyed the whole range of subjects with eagle eye, and he knew what he did and why he did it. He was master of the art of thinking. As a metaphysician, none could excel him; as a logical thinker, none could have gone beyond him. He stands almost alone in the early Christian church, as a mastermind. Others may have been more poetic, or more simple, but none were more thoughtful or argumentative than he. With decision and firmness Paul sets aside everything else, and definitely declares throughout his whole life, "I glory in the cross." He does this exclusively saying, "God forbid that I should glory, save in the cross." There are many other precious things, but he puts them all up on the shelf in comparison with the Cross. He will not even make his chief point any of the great scriptural doctrines, nor even an instructive and godly ordinance. No, the Cross is to the front. This constellation is chief in Paul's sky. The choice of the Cross he makes devoutly, for although the expression used in our English version may not stand, yet I do not doubt that Paul would have used it, and would have called upon God to witness that he abjured all other ground of glorying save the atoning sacrifice.

> *Forbid it, Lord, that I should boast,*
> *Save in the death of Christ my God:*
> *All the vain things that charm me most,*
> *I sacrifice them to His blood.*

He would have called God to witness that he knew no ambition save that of bringing glory to the Cross of Christ. As I think of this I am ready to say, "Amen" to Paul, and bid you sing that stirring verse—

> *It is the old cross still,*
> > *Hallelujah! hallelujah!*
> *Its triumphs let us tell,*
> > *Hallelujah! hallelujah!*

The grace of God here shone
  Through Christ, the blessed Son,
Who did for sin atone;
  Hallelujah for the cross!

Why did Paul thus glory in the Cross? You may well desire to know,
for there are many nowadays who do not glory in it, but forsake it. Alas
that it should be so! But there are ministers who ignore the atonement;
they conceal the Cross, or say but little about it. You may go through
service after service and scarce hear a mention of the atoning blood, but
Paul was always bringing forward the expiation for sin; Paul never tried
to explain it away. Oh the number of books that have been written to
prove that the Cross means an example of self-sacrifice, as if every martyrdom did not mean that. They cannot endure a real substitutionary
sacrifice for human guilt and an effectual purgation of sin by the death of
the Great Substitute. Yet the Cross means that or nothing. Paul was very
bold. Although he knew that this would make him many enemies, you
never find him refining and spiritualizing; the Cross and the atonement
for sin is a plain matter of fact to him. Neither does he attempt to
decorate it by adding philosophical theories. No, to him it is the bare,
naked, cross, all blood-bestained, and despised. In this he glories, and in
none of the wisdom of words with which others vexed him. He will have
the Cross, the Cross, and nothing but the Cross. He pronounces an
anathema on all who propose a rival theme—"But though we, or an
angel from heaven, preach any other gospel unto you than that which we
have preached unto you, let him be accursed."

I take it that this was so, first, because Paul saw in the cross *a vindication of divine justice.* Where else can the justice of God be seen so clearly as
in the death of God Himself, in the person of His dear Son? If the Lord
Himself suffers on account of broken law, then is the majesty of the law
honored to the full. Some time ago, a judge in America was called upon
to try a prisoner who had been his companion in his early youth. It was a
crime for which the penalty was a fine, more or less heavy. The judge did
not diminish the fine; the case was clearly a bad one, and he fined the
prisoner to the full. Some who knew his former relation to the offender
thought him somewhat unkind thus to carry out the law, while others admired his impartiality. All were surprised when the judge quitted the
bench and himself paid every farthing of the penalty. He had both shown
his respect for the law and his goodwill to the man who had broken it; he
exacted the penalty, but he paid it himself. So God hath done in the Person of His dear Son. He has not remitted the punishment, but He has
Himself endured it. His own Son, who is none other than God
Himself—for there is an essential union between them—has paid the
debt which was incurred by human sin. I love to think of the vindication

of divine justice upon the cross; I am never weary of it. Some cannot bear the thought; but to me it seems inevitable that sin must be punished, or else the foundations of society would be removed. If sin becomes a trifle, virtue will be a toy. Society cannot stand if laws are left without penal sanction, or if that sanction is to be a mere empty threat. Men in their own governments every now and then cry out for greater severity. When a certain offense abounds, and ordinary means fail, they demand exemplary punishment; and it is but natural that they should do so; for deep in the conscience of every man there is the conviction that sin must be punished to secure the general good. Justice must reign; even benevolence demands it. If there could have been salvation without an atonement it would have been a calamity; righteous men, and even benevolent men, might deprecate the setting aside of law in order to save the guilty from the natural result of their crimes.

But we glory because on the cross we have an unexampled *display of God's love.* "God commendeth his love toward us, in that, while we were yet sinners, Christ died for us." Oh to think of it, that He who was offended takes the nature of the offender, and then bears the penalty due for wanton transgression. He who is infinite, thrice holy, all glorious, forever to be worshiped, yet stooped to be numbered with the transgressors and to bear the sin of many. The mythology of the gods of high Olympus contains nothing worthy to be mentioned in the same day with this wondrous deed of supreme condescension and infinite love. The ancient Shasters and Vedas have nothing of the kind. The death of Jesus Christ upon the cross cannot be an invention of men; none of the ages have produced aught like it in the poetic dreams of any nation. If we did not hear of it so often, and think of it so little, we should be charmed with it beyond expression. If we now heard of it for the first time, and seriously believed it, I know not what we should not do in our glad surprise; certainly we should fall down and worship the Lord Jesus, and continue to worship Him forever and ever.

I believe again, thirdly, that Paul delighted to preach the Cross of Christ as *the removal of all guilt.* He believed that the Lord Jesus on the cross finished transgression, made an end of sin, and brought in everlasting righteousness. He that believes in Jesus is justified from all things from which he could not be justified by the law of Moses. Since sin was laid on Jesus, God's justice cannot lay it upon the believing sinner. The Lord will never punish twice the same offense. If He accepts a Substitute for me, how can He call me to His bar and punish me for that transgression, for which my substitute endured the chastisement? Many a troubled conscience has caught at this and found deliverance from despair. Wonder not that Paul gloried in Christ, since it is written, "In the Lord shall all the seed of Israel be justified, and shall glory." This is the method of salvation which completely and eternally absolves the sinner and makes the blackest offender white as snow. Transgression visited upon Christ has ceased to be, so far as the believer is concerned. Doth not faith cry, "Thou wilt cast all their sins into the depths of the sea"? O sirs, there is something to glory in, in this, and those who know the sin-removing power of the Cross will not be hindered in this glorying by all the powers of earth or hell.

He glories in it, again, *as a marvel of wisdom.* It seemed to him the sum of perfect wisdom and skill. He cried, "O the depth of the riches both of the wisdom and knowledge of God!" The plan of salvation by vicarious suffering is simple, but sublime. It would have been impossible for human or angelic wisdom to have invented it. Men already so hate it and fight against it that they never would have devised it. God alone out of the treasury of His infinite wisdom brought forth the matchless project of salvation for the guilty through the substitution of the innocent. The more we study it, the more we shall perceive that it is full of teaching. It is only the superficial thinker who regards the Cross as a subject soon to be comprehended and exhausted: the most lofty intellects will here find ample room and verge enough. The profoundest minds might lose themselves in considering the splendid diversities of light which compose the pure white light of the Cross. Everything of sin and justice, of misery and mercy, of folly and wisdom, of force and tenderness, of rage and pity, on the part of man and God, may be seen here. In the Cross may be seen the concentration of eternal thought, the focus of infinite purpose, the outcome of illimitable wisdom. Of God and the Cross we may say:

> *Here I behold His inmost heart,*
> > *Where grace and vengeance strangely join;*
> *Piercing His Son with sharpest smart*
> > *To make the purchased pleasures mine.*

I believe that Paul gloried in the Cross, again, because it is *the door of hope,* even to the vilest of the vile. The world was very filthy in Paul's time. Roman civilization was of the most brutal and debased kind, and the masses of the people were sunken in vices that are altogether unmentionable. Paul felt that he could go into the darkest places with light in his hand when he spoke of the Cross. To tell of pardon bought with the blood of the Son of God is to carry an omnipotent message. The Cross uplifts the fallen and delivers the despairing. Today, my brethren, the world's one and only remedy is the Cross. Go, ye thinkers, and get up a mission to the fallen in London, leaving out the Cross! Go, now, ye wise men, reclaim the harlots, and win to virtue the degraded by your perfumed philosophies! See what you can do in the slums and alleys without the Cross of Christ! Go talk to your titled reprobates, and win them from their abominations by displays of art! You will fail, the most cultivated of you, even to win the rich and educated to anything like purity, unless your themes be drawn from Calvary and the love which there poured out its heart's blood. This hammer breaks rocky hearts, but no other will do it. Pity itself stands silent. Compassion bites her lip and inwardly groans, she has nothing to say till she has learned the story of the Cross; but, with that on her tongue, she waxes eloquent; with tears she entreats, persuades, prevails. She may but stammer in her speech; like Moses, she may be slow of utterance; but the cross is in her hand, as the rod of the prophet. With this she conquers the Pharaoh of tyrannic sin; with this she divides the Red Sea of guilt; with this she leads the host of God out of the house of bondage into the land of promise which flows with milk and honey. The cross is the standard of victorious grace. It is the lighthouse whose cheering ray gleams across the dark waters of despair and cheers the dense midnight of our fallen race, saving from eternal shipwreck, and piloting into everlasting peace.

Again, Paul, I believe, gloried in the Cross, as I often do, because it was *the source of rest* to him and to his brethren. I make this confession, and I make it very boldly, that I never knew what rest of heart truly meant till I understood the doctrine of the substitution of our Lord Jesus Christ. Now, when I see my Lord bearing away my sins as my scapegoat, or dying for them as my sin-offering, I feel a profound peace of heart and satisfaction of spirit. The Cross is all I want for security and joy. Truly, this bed is long enough for a man to stretch himself on it. The Cross is a chariot of salvation, wherein we traverse the high road of life without fear. The pillow of atonement heals the head that aches with anguish. Beneath the shadow of the Cross I sit down with great delight, and its fruit is sweet unto my taste. I have no impatience even to haste to heaven while resting beneath the Cross, for our hymn truly says:

> Here it is I find my heaven,
> While upon the cross I gaze.

Here is perfect cleansing, and hence a divine security, guarded by the justice of God, and hence a "peace of God, which passeth all understanding." To try to entice me away from the truth of substitution is labor in vain. Seduce me to preach the pretty nothings of modern thought! This child knows much better than to leave the substance for the shadow, the truth for the fancy. I see nothing that can give to my heart a fair exchange for the rest, peace, and unutterable joy which the old-fashioned doctrine of the Cross now yields me. Will a man leave bread for husks, and quit the home of his love to dwell in a desolate wilderness? I dare not renounce the truth in order to be thought cultured. I am no more a fool than the most of my contemporaries, and if I could see anything better than the Cross I would as willingly grasp it as they; for it is a flattering thing to be thought a man of light and leading; but whither shall I go if I quit the rock of the atoning sacrifice? I cannot go beyond my simple faith that Jesus stood in my stead, and bore my sin, and put my sin away. This I must preach; I know nothing else. God helping me I will never go an inch beyond the Cross, for me all else is vanity and vexation of spirit. Return unto thy rest, O my soul! Where else is there a glimpse of hope for thee but in Him who loved thee and gave Himself for thee?

3. One of Paul's great reasons for glorying in the Cross was its action upon himself. WHAT WAS ITS EFFECT UPON HIM? The cross is never without influence. Come where it may, it worketh for life or for death. Wherever there is Christ's Cross there are also two other crosses. On either side there is one, and Jesus is in the midst. Two thieves are crucified with Christ; and Paul tells us their names in his case: "the world is crucified to me, and I unto the world." Self and the world are both crucified when Christ's Cross appears and is believed in. Beloved, what does Paul mean? Does he not mean just this—that ever since he had seen Christ he looked upon the world as a crucified, hanged up, gibbeted thing, which had no charms for him, whose frown he did not fear, whose love he did not court. The world had no more power over Paul than a criminal hanged upon a cross. What power has a corpse on a gibbet? Such power had the world over Paul. The world despised him, and he could not go after the world if he would, and would not go after it if he could. He was dead to it, and it was dead to him; thus there was a double separation.

How does the Cross do this? To be under the dominion of this present evil world is horrible; how does the Cross help us to escape? Why, brethren, he that has ever seen the Cross looks upon the world's pomp and glory as a vain show. The pride of heraldry and the glitter and honor fade into meanness before the Crucified One. O ye great ones, what are your silks, and your furs, and your jewelry, and your gold, your stars and your garters, to one who has learned to glory in Christ crucified! The old clothes which belong to the hangman are quite as precious. The world's light is darkness when the Sun of Righteousness shines from the tree. What care we for all the kingdoms of the world and the glory thereof when once we see the thorn-crowned Lord? There is more glory about one nail of the cross than about all the sceptres of all kings. Let the knights of the Golden Fleece meet in chapter, and all the Knights of the Garter stand in their stalls, and what is all their splendor? Their glories wither before the inevitable hour of doom, while the glory of the Cross is eternal. Everything of earth grows dull and dim when seen by Cross light.

So was it with the world's *approval*. Paul would not ask the world to be pleased with him, since it knew not his Lord, or only knew Him to crucify Him. Can a Christian be ambitious to be written down as one of the world's foremost men when that world cast out his Lord? They crucified our Master; shall His servants court their love? Such approval would be all distained with blood. They crucified my Master, the Lord of Glory; do I want them to smile on me, and say to me, "Reverend Sir" and "Learned Doctor"? No, the friendship of the world is enmity with God, and therefore to be dreaded. Mouths that spit on Jesus shall give me no kisses. Those who hate the doctrine of the atonement hate my life and soul, and I desire not their esteem.

Paul also saw that the world's *wisdom* was absurd. That age talked of being wise and philosophical! Yes, and its philosophy brought it to crucify the Lord of Glory. It did not know perfection, nor perceive the beauty of pure unselfishness. To slay the Messiah was the outcome of the culture of the Pharisee; to put to death the greatest Teacher of all time was the ripe fruit of Sadducean thought. The cogitations of the present age have performed no greater feat than to deny the doctrine of satisfaction for sin. They have crucified our Lord afresh by their criticisms and their new theologies; and this is all the world's wisdom ever does. Its wisdom lies in scattering doubt, quenching hope, and denying certainty; and therefore the wisdom of the world to us is sheer folly. This century's philosophy will one day be spoken of as an evidence that softening of the brain was very usual among its scientific men. We count the thought of the present moment to be methodical madness, Bedlam-out-of-doors; and those who are furthest gone in it are credulous beyond imagination. God hath poured contempt upon the wise men of this world; their foolish heart is blinded, they grope at noonday.

And so it was with the world's *pursuits.* Some ran after honor, some toiled after learning, others labored for riches; but to Paul these were all trifles since he had seen Christ on the cross. He that has seen Jesus die will never go into the toy business; he puts away childish things. A child, a pipe, a litte soap, and many pretty bubbles: such is the world. The Cross alone can wean us from such play.

Paul concludes this epistle by saying, "From henceforth let no man trouble me: for I bear in my body the marks of the Lord Jesus." He was a slave, branded with his Master's name. That stamp could never be got out, for it was burned into his heart. Even thus, I trust, the doctrine of the atonement is our settled belief, and faith in it is part of our life. We are rooted and grounded in the unchanging verities. Do not try to convert me to your new views; I am past it. Give me over. You waste your breath. It is done: on this point the wax takes no further impress. I have taken up my standing, and will never quit it. A crucified Christ has taken such possession of my entire nature, spirit, soul, and body, that I am henceforth beyond the reach of opposing arguments. Brethren, sisters, will you enlist under the conquering banner of the Cross? Once rolled in the dust and stained in blood, it now leads on the armies of the Lord to victory! Oh that all ministers would preach the true doctrine of the Cross! Oh that all Christian people would live under the influence of it, and we should then see brighter days than these! Unto the Crucified be glory for ever and ever. Amen.

D.L. Moody
(1837—1899)

A Boston shoe salesman, won to Christ by his Sunday school teacher, became God's instrument for worldwide revival. Seventeen-year-old Dwight Lyman Moody's job in his uncle's shoestore depended on his promise to go to Sunday school. His teacher, Edward Kimball, one day went to the store and led young Moody to Jesus.

Born in Northfield, Massachusetts, February 5, 1837, Dwight was four when his father's death left the family in poverty. He worked hard on a farm until he went to Boston to work for his uncle.

Chicago became home to him in 1856, as he added salesmanship to his shoestore work. However, his Sunday school and mission work occupied so much time that he eventually entered full-time Christian service.

Every Sunday Chicago's North Market Hall was transformed into a fast-growing Sunday school for what today would be called "underprivileged" children. Moody also became president of the YMCA in Chicago and was extensively involved in programs and building projects. He began speaking to large audiences, gradually going into revival campaigns.

In 1870 an international YMCA convention brought Moody into contact with song leader Ira Sankey. The two began conducting campaigns all across the United States; thousands of people were saved. When the team went to England, Scotland, and Ireland the world witnessed what many felt was the greatest revival of the century. Moody traveled over one million miles and spoke to over 100 million people, all before the days of rapid transit and mass media communication. Hundreds of thousands of people were saved under his ministry.

He also established the Moody Bible Institute and what is now the Moody Memorial Church in Chicago.

Although frequently criticized for his lack of education, Moody had few equals in the power of persuasion. His biblical preaching abounded with illustration. He was called "the apostle of love," and his overwhelming purpose in life was to lead men to Christ. It was Moody who said, "The world has yet to see what God can do with a man who is completely yielded to Him." He set out to be that man and consequently became one of the most successful evangelists in American history.

What Think Ye of Christ?
By D.L. Moody

Saying, What think ye of Christ? Whose son is he? They say unto him, The son of David (Matthew 22:42).

I suppose there is no one here who has not thought, more or less, about Christ. You have heard about Him, and read about Him, and heard men preach about Him. For eighteen hundred years men have been talking about Him, and thinking about Him; and some have their minds made up about who He is, and doubtless some have not. And although all these years have rolled away, this question comes up, addressed to each of us, today, "What think ye of Christ?"

I do not know why it should not be thought a proper question for one man to put to another. If I were to ask you what you think of any of your prominent men, you would already have your mind made up about him. If I were to ask you what you think of your noble Queen, you would speak right out and tell me your opinion in a minute. If I were to ask about your prime minister, you would tell me freely what you had for or against him. And why should not people make up their minds about the Lord Jesus Christ, and take their stand for or against Him? If you think well of Him, why not speak well of Him and range yourselves on His side? And if you think ill of Him, and believe Him to be an impostor, and that He did not die to save the world, why not lift up your voice and say you are against Him? It would be a happy day for Christianity if men would just take sides—if we could know positively who was really for Him, and who was against Him.

It is of very little importance what the world thinks of anyone else. The Queen and the statesman, the peers and the princes, must soon be gone. Yes, it matters little, comparatively, what we think of them. Their lives can only interest a few, but every living soul on the face of the earth

90

is concerned with this Man. The question for the world is, "What think ye of Christ?" I do not ask you what you think of the Episcopal Church, or of the Presbyterians, or the Baptists, or the Roman Catholics; I do not ask you what you think of this minister or that, of this doctrine or that. But I want to ask you what you think of the living person of Christ?

I should like to ask, Was He really the Son of God—the great God-man? Did He leave heaven and come down to this world for a purpose? Was it really to seek and to save? I should like to begin with the manger, and follow Him up through the thirty-three years He was here upon earth. I should ask you what you think of His coming into this world and being born in a manger when it might have been a palace; why He left the grandeur and the glory of heaven, and the royal retinue of angels; why He passed by palaces and crowns and dominion, and came down here alone?

I should like to ask what you think of Him as a *teacher*. He spake as never man spake. I should like to take Him up as a preacher. I should like to bring you to that mountain side, that we might listen to the words as they fall from His gentle lips. Talk about the preachers of the present day! I would rather a thousand times be five minutes at the feet of Christ, than listen a lifetime to all the wise men in the world. He used just to hang truth upon anything. Yonder is a sower, a fox, a bird, and He just gathers the truth round them, so that you cannot see a fox, a sower, or a bird, without thinking what Jesus said. Yonder is a lily of the valley; you cannot see it without thinking of His words, "They toil not, neither do they spin." He makes the little sparrow chirping in the air preach to us. How fresh those wonderful sermons are, how they live today! How we love to tell them to our children; how the children love to hear! "Tell me a story about Jesus"—how often we hear it; how the little ones love His sermons! No storybook in the world will ever interest them like the stories that He told. And yet how profound He was; how He puzzled the wise men; how the scribes and the Pharisees could never fathom Him! Oh, do you not think He was a wonderful preacher?

I should like to ask you what you think of Him as a *physician*. A man would soon have a reputation as a doctor if he could cure as Christ did. No case was ever brought to Him but what He was a match for. He had but to speak the word, and disease fled before Him. Here comes a man covered with leprosy. "Lord, if thou wilt thou canst make me clean," he cries. "I will," says the Great Physician, and in an instant the leprosy is gone. The world has hospitals for incurable diseases; but there were no incurable diseases with Him.

Now see Him in the little home at Bethany, binding up the wounded hearts of Martha and Mary, and tell me what you think of Him as a *comforter*. He is a husband to the widow and a father to the fatherless. The weary may find a resting-place upon that breast, and the friendless may reckon Him their friend. He never varies, He never fails, He never dies. His sympathy is ever fresh, His love is ever free. O widow and orphans, O sorrowing and mourning, will you not thank God for Christ the comforter?

But these are not the points I wish to take up. Let us go to those who knew Christ and ask what they thought of Him. If you want to find out what a man is nowadays, you inquire about him from those who know him best. I do not wish to be partial; we will go to His enemies, and to His friends. We will ask them, What think ye of Christ? We will ask His friends and His enemies. If we only went to those who liked Him, you would say, "Oh, he is so blind; he thinks so much of the man that he can't see his faults. You can't get anything out of him, unless it be in his favor; it is a one-sided affair altogether." So we shall go in the first place to His enemies, to those who hated Him, persecuted Him, and cursed and slew Him. I shall put you in the jury box, and call upon them to tell us what they think of Him.

First, among the witnesses, let us call upon the Pharisees. We know how they hated Him. Let us put a few questions to them. Come, Pharisees, tell us what you have against the Son of God. What do *you* think of Christ? Hear what they say! *This man receiveth sinners.* What an argument to bring against Him! Why, it is the very thing that makes us love Him. It is the glory of the gospel. He receives sinners. If He had not, what would have become of us? Have you nothing more to bring against Him than *this?* Why, it is one of the greatest compliments that was ever paid Him. Once more, when He was hanging on the tree, you had this to say of Him, "He saved others, Himself He cannot save." And so He did save others, but He could not save Himself and save us too. So He laid down His own life for yours and mine. Yes, Pharisees, you have told the truth for once in your lives! *He saved others.* He died for others. He was a ransom for many; so it is quite true what you think of Him—*He saved others, Himself He cannot save.*

Now, let us call upon Caiaphas. Let him stand up here in his flowing robes; let us ask him for his evidence. "Caiaphas, you were chief priest when Christ was tried; you were president of the Sanhedrin; you were in the council-chamber when they found Him guilty; you yourself condemned Him. Tell us; what did the witnesses say? On what grounds did you judge Him? What testimony was brought against Him?"

"He hath spoken blasphemy," says Caiaphas. "He said, 'Hereafter shall ye see the Son of Man sitting on the right hand of power, and coming in the clouds of heaven.' When I heard that, I found Him guilty of blasphemy; I rent my mantle, and condemned Him to death." Yes, all that they had against Him was that He was the Son of God; and they slew Him for the promise of His coming for His bride.

Now, let us summon Pilate. Let him enter the witness box. Pilate, this Man was brought before you; you examined Him; you talked with Him face to face, *what think ye of Christ?* "I find no fault in him," says Pilate. "He said he was the King of the Jews" (just as he wrote it over the cross); "but I find no fault in him." Such is the testimony of the man who examined Him! And, as He stands there, the center of a Jewish mob, there comes along a man, elbowing his way, in haste. He rushes up to Pilate and, thrusting out his hand, gives him a message. He tears it open; his face turns pale as he reads—"Have thou nothing to do with this just man: for I have suffered many things this day in a dream because of Him." It is from Pilate's wife—her testimony to Christ. You want to know what His enemies thought of Him? You want to know what the heathen thought? Well, here it is, "no fault in Him;" and the wife of a heathen, "this just man!"

And now, look—in comes Judas. He ought to make a good witness. Let us address him. "Come, tell us, Judas, what think ye of Christ. You knew the Master well; you sold Him for thirty pieces of silver; you betrayed Him with a kiss; you saw Him perform those miracles; you were with Him in Jerusalem. In Bethany, when He summoned up Lazarus, you were there. What think ye of Him?" I can see him as he comes into the presence of the Chief priests; I can hear the money ring as he dashes it upon the table—"*I have betrayed innocent blood!*" Here is the man who betrayed Him, and this is what he thinks of Him! Yes, my friends, God has made every man who had anything to do with the death of His Son put their testimony on record that He was an innocent Man.

Let us take the Centurion, who was present at the execution. He had charge of the Roman soldiers. He had told them to make Him carry His cross; he had given orders for the nails to be driven into His feet and hands, for the spear to be thrust in His side. Let the Centurion come forward. "Centurion, you had charge of the executioners; you saw that the order for His death was carried out; you saw Him die; you heard Him speak upon the cross. *Tell us, what think you of Christ?*" Hark! Look at him; he is smiting his breast as he cries, "*Truly, this was the Son of God!*"

I might go to the thief upon the cross, and ask what he thought of Him. At first he railed upon Him and reviled Him. But then he thought better of it. "This man hath done nothing amiss," he says. I might go further. I might summon the very devils themselves and ask them for their testimony. Have they anything to say of Him? Why, the very devils called Him the Son of God! In Mark we have the unclean spirit crying, "Jesus thou Son of the most high God." Men say, "Oh, I believe Christ to be the Son of God, and because I believe it intellectually, I shall be saved." I tell you the devils did that. And they did more than that, *they trembled.*

Let us bring in His friends. We want you to hear their evidence. Let us call that prince of preachers. Let us hear the forerunner, the wilderness preacher, John. Save the Master Himself, none ever preached like this man—this man who drew all Jerusalem and all Judea into the wilderness to hear him; this man who burst upon the nations like the flash of a meteor. Let John the Baptist come with his leathern girdle and his hairy coat, and let him tell us what he thinks of Christ. His words, though they were echoed in the wilderness of Palestine, are written in the Book forever, "Behold the Lamb of God, which taketh away the sin of the world." This is what John the Baptist thought of Him. "I bare record that this is the Son of God." No wonder he drew all Jerusalem and Judea to him, because he preached Christ. And whenever men preach Christ, they are sure to have plenty of followers.

Let us bring in Peter, who was with Him on the mount of transfiguration, who was with Him the night He was betrayed. "Come, Peter, tell us what you think of Christ. Stand in the witness box and testify of Him. You denied Him once. You said, with a curse, you did not know Him. Was it true, Peter? Don't you know Him?" "Know Him!" I can imagine Peter saying; "It was a lie I told them. I *did* know Him." Afterwards I can hear him charging home their guilt upon these Jerusalem sinners. He calls Him "both Lord and Christ." Such was the testimony on the Day of Pentecost. "God hath made that same Jesus, both Lord and Christ." And tradition tells us that when they came to execute Peter, he felt he was not worthy to die in the way his Master died, and he requested to be crucified with his head downwards. So much did Peter think of Him!

Now let us hear from the beloved disciple John. He knew more about Christ than any other man. He had laid his head on his Savior's bosom. He had heard the throbbing of that loving heart. Look into his Gospel if you wish to know what he thought of Him.

Matthew writes of Him as the Royal King come from His throne. Mark writes of Him as the Servant, and Luke as the Son of Man. John takes up his pen, and with one stroke, forever settles the question of Unitarianism. He goes right back before the time of Adam. "In the beginning was the Word, and the Word was with God, and the Word was God." Look into Revelation. He calls Him "the bright and morning star." So John thought well of Him—because he knew Him well.

We might bring in Thomas, the doubting disciple. "You doubted Him, Thomas? You would not believe He had risen, and you put your fingers into the wound in His side. What do you think of Him?" "*My Lord and my God!*" says Thomas.

Then go over to Decapolis and you will find Christ has been there casting out devils. Let us call the men of that country and ask what they think of Him. *"He hath done all things well"* they say.

But we have other witnesses to bring in. Take the persecuting Saul, once one of the worst of His enemies. Breathing out threatenings, he meets Him. "Saul, Saul, why persecutest thou Me?" says Christ; and He might have added, "What have I done to you? Why do you treat Me thus, Saul?" And then Saul asks, "Who art Thou, Lord?" "I am Jesus of Nazareth, whom thou persecutest." You see, He was not ashamed of His name; although He had been in heaven, "I am *Jesus of Nazareth.*" What a change did that one interview make to Paul! A few years after we hear him say, "I have suffered the loss of all things, and do count them but dung, that I may win Christ." Such a testimony to the Savior!

But I shall go still further. I shall go away from earth into the other world. I shall summon the angels and ask what they think of Christ. They saw Him in the bosom of the Father before the world was. Before the dawn of creation; before the morning stars sang together, He was there. They saw Him leave the throne and come down to the manger. What a scene for them to witness! Ask these heavenly beings what they thought of Him then. For once they are permitted to speak; for once the silence of heaven is broken. Listen to their song on the plains of Bethlehem, "Behold, I bring you good tidings of great joy, which shall be to all people. For unto you is born this day in the city of David a Saviour, which is Christ the Lord." He leaves the throne to save the world. Is it a wonder the angels thought well of Him?

Then there are the redeemed saints—they that see Him face to face. Here on earth He was never known, no one seemed really to be acquainted with Him; but He was known in that world where He had been from the foundation. What do they think of Him there? If we could hear from heaven, we should hear a shout which would glorify and magnify His name. We are told that when John was in the Spirit on the Lord's day, and being caught up, he heard a shout around him, ten thousand times ten thousand, and thousands and thousands of voices, "Worthy is the Lamb that was slain to receive power, and riches, and wisdom, and strength, and honour, and glory, and blessing!" Yes, He is worthy of all this. Heaven cannot speak too well of Him. Oh, that earth would take up and join with heaven in singing, "WORTHY to receive power, and riches, and wisdom, and strength, and honour, and glory, and blessing"!

But there is yet another witness, a higher still. Some think that the God of the Old Testament is the Christ of the New. But when Jesus came out of Jordan, baptized by John, there came a voice from heaven. God the Father spoke. It was His testimony to Christ: "This is my beloved Son, in whom I am well pleased." Ah, yes! God the Father thinks well of the Son. And if God is well pleased with Him, so ought we. If the sinner and God are well pleased with Christ, then the sinner and God can meet. The moment you say as the Father said, "I am well pleased with Him," and accept Him, you are wedded to God. Will you not believe the testimony? Will you not believe this witness, this last of all, the Lord of hosts, the King of kings Himself? Once more He repeats it, so that all may know it. With Peter and James and John, on the mount of transfiguration, He cries again, "This is my beloved Son; hear him." And that voice went echoing and re-echoing through Palestine, through all the earth from sea to sea; yes, that voice is echoing still, *Hear Him! Hear Him.*"

My friend, will you hear Him today? Hark! what is He saying to you? "Come unto me, all ye that labour and are heavy laden, and I will give you rest. Take my yoke upon you, and learn of me; for I am meek and lowly in heart; and ye shall find rest unto your souls. For my yoke is easy, and my burden is light." Will you not think well of such a Savior? Will you not believe in Him? Will you not trust in Him with all your heart and mind? Will you not live for Him? If He laid down His life for us, is it not the least we can do to lay down ours for Him? If He bore the cross and died on it for me, ought I not to be willing to take it up for Him? Oh, have we not reason to think well of Him? Do you think it is right and noble to lift up your voice against such a Savior? Do you think it is just to cry, "Crucify Him! crucify Him!" Oh, may God help all of us to glorify the Father, by thinking well of His only begotten Son.

Joseph Parker
(1830—1902)

Joseph Parker, born in Northumberland, England, in 1830, was led to Christ at an early age. With little formal training, he studied the Scriptures extensively on his own. In 1852 he became associate pastor to John Campbell, who spent two years teaching Parker and helping him in his Christian life. He was called to pastor Banbury Congregational Church in Oxfordshire in 1853, where he stayed for five years. New buildings had to be erected to accommodate the crowds that came to hear him preach. Five years later he went to pastor in Manchester and there became friends with the great expositor Alexander Maclaren.

Parker went to London in 1869 to pastor what was at that time the Poultry Church. There he preached through the entire Bible and published the sermons in twenty-five volumes titled *The People's Bible,* which he considered to be his greatest accomplishment. During his thirty-three years in London, the church relocated and became known as the City Temple. Parker was so well known that his church became a stopping point for tourists in the city. Although a contemporary of such notables as Spurgeon and Maclaren, Parker never lacked attention and was acclaimed as a champion for truth in his day.

Parker possessed a strong, energetic personality and preached with vigor and enthusiasm; his sermons were simple yet highly original. He once said, "If I have not seen Him myself, I cannot preach Him." He preached faithfully with this thought before him until his death in 1902.

10

A Word to the Weary
By Joseph Parker

The Lord God hath given me the tongue of the learned, that I should know how to speak a word in season to him that is weary (Isa. 50:4).

The power of speaking to the weary is nothing less than a divine gift. As we see the divinity in our gifts shall we be careful of them, thankful for them: every gift seems to enshrine the giver, God. But how extraordinary that this power of speaking to the weary should not be taught in the schools. It is not within the ability of man to teach other men how to speak to the weary-hearted, the wounded in spirit, the sore in the innermost feelings of the being. But can we lay down directions about this and offer suggestions? Probably so, but we do not touch the core of the matter. There is an infinite difference between the scholar and the genius. The scholar is made, the genius is inspired. Information can be imparted, but the true sense, the sense that feels and sees God, is a gift direct from heaven.

It is a common notion that anybody can sing. Why can you sing? Why, because I have been taught. That is your mistake. You can sing mechanically, exactly, properly, with right time, right tune, but really and truly you cannot sing. Here is a man with his music and with the words; he sings every note, pronounces every word, goes through his lesson, finishes his task, and nobody wants to hear him anymore. Another man takes up the same music, the same words, and the same hearers exclaim, ''Oh, that he would go on forever!'' How is that?—the words exactly the same, the notes identical—how? Soul, fire, everburning, never consuming, making a bush like a planet. The great difficulty in all such cases is the difficulty of transferring to paper a proper or adequate conception of the power of the men who thus sway the human heart. There are some men whose biographies simply belie them, and yet every sentence in the biography is true in the letter. But the biography is little else than a travesty and a caricature, because the power was personal; it was in the face, in the voice, in the presence, in the gait, in the touch—an incommunicable power; the hem of the garment trembled under it, but no biographer could catch it in his scholarly ink.

Very few ministers can enter a sick chamber with any probability of doing real and lasting good. They can read the Bible, and they can pray, and yet, when they have gone, the room seems as if they had never been there. There is no sense of emptiness or desolation. Other men, probably not so much gifted in some other directions, will enter the sick room, and there will be a light upon the wall, summer will gleam upon the windowpane, and angels will rustle in the air, and it will be a scene of gladness and a vision of triumph. How is that? "The Lord God hath given me the tongue of the learned that I might know how—how to speak a word in season to him that is weary." The Lord God hath not only given me a word to say but hath given me learning to teach me how to speak it. Place the emphasis upon the how, and then you develop all the mystery, all the tender music, all the infinite capacity of manner.

We may say the right word in the wrong tone; we may preach the gospel as if it were a curse. The common notion is that anybody can go into the Sunday school and teach the young. We sometimes think that it would be well if a great many persons left the Sunday school all over the world. Teach the young—would God I had the great gift to break the bread for the children, and to be able to lure and captivate opening minds, and to enter into the spirit of the words—"Delightful task! to rear the tender thought, To teach the young idea how to shoot." It requires to be father and mother and sister and nurse and genius to speak to the young. They may hear you and not care for you. They may understand your words and be repelled by your spirit. You require the tongue of the learned to know how to speak, and that tongue of the learned is not to be had at school, college, university—it is not included in any curriculum of learning—it is a gift divine, breathing an afflatus, an inspiration—the direct and distinct creation of God, as is the star, the sun. The speaker, then, is Jesus Christ, the Son of God, the representative of the Father, the incarnate Deity—He it is who is charged with the subtle learning; He it is whose lips tremble with the pathos of this ineffable music.

Tho the gift itself is divine, we must remember that it is to be exercised seasonably. The test is, "that I should know how to speak a word in season." There is a time for everything. It is not enough to speak the right word, it must be spoken at the right moment. Who can know when that is! We cannot be taught. We must feel it, see it hours beyond: nay, must know when to be silent for the whole twenty-four hours and to say, "Tomorrow, at such and such a time, we will drop that sentence upon the listening ear." "The day after tomorrow, he will probably be in circumstances to admit of this communication being delivered with sympathy and effect." How few persons know the right time—the right time in conversation. Some people are never heard in conversation tho they are talking all the time. They talk so unseasonably; they talk when other people are talking; they cannot wait; they do not know how to come in along the fine line of silence. They do not understand the German expression "Now an angel has passed," and they do not quickly enough follow in his wake. Consequently, tho chattering much they are saying nothing—tho their words be multitudinous, the impression they make is a blank.

I have a ripe seed in my hand. As an agriculturist I am going to sow it. Any laborer in the field can tell me that I should be acting foolishly in sowing it just now. Why? "It is out of season," the man says. "There is a time for the doing of that action: I will tell you when the time returns—do it then, and you may expect a profitable result of your labor."

Then I will change the character and be a nurse, and I will attend to my patient (perhaps I will over attend to him—some patients are killed by over nursing), and I will give the patient this medicine—it is the right medicine. So it is, but you are going to give it at the wrong time, and if you give the medicine at the wrong time, tho itself be right, the hour being wrong you will bring suffering upon the patient, and you yourself will be involved in pains and penalties. Thus we touch that very subtle and sensitive line in human life, the line of refined discrimination. You may say "I am sure I told him." You are right—you did tell him and he did not hear you. You may reply, "I am perfectly confident I delivered the message,—I preached the exact words of the gospel." So you did, but you never got the hearing heart, your manner was so unsympathetic, so ungentle, so cruel (not meant to be—unconsciously so), that the man never understood it to be a gospel. You spoiled the music in the delivery, in the giving of the message. The Lord God giveth the tongue of the learned, that he to whom it is given may know how to speak—how to speak the right word—how to speak the right word at the right point of time. You want divine teaching in all things, in speech not least.

This is a curious word to find in the Bible. Does the Bible care about weary people? We have next to no sympathy with them. If a man be weary, we give him notice to quit. If he ask us to what place he can retire, we tell him that it is his business not ours. Now the tenderness of this Book is one of the most telling, convincing arguments on behalf of its inspiration, and its divine authority. This Book means to help us, wants to help us, it says, "I will try to help you, never hinder you. I will wait for you, I will soften the wind into a whisper, I will order the thunder to be silent, I will quiet the raging sea; I will wait upon you at home, in solitude, at midnight, anywhere—fix the place, the time, yourself, and when your heart most needs me I will be most to your heart." Any book found in den, in gutter, that wants to do this, should be received with respect. The purpose is good. If it fail, it fails in a noble object.

Everywhere in this Book of God we find a supreme wish to help man. When we most need help the words are sweeter than the honeycomb. When other books are dumb, this Book speaks most sweetly. It is like a star: it shines in the darkness, it waits the going down of the superficial sun of our transient prosperity, and then it breaks upon us as the shadows thicken. This is the real greatness of God: He will not break the bruised reed. Because the reed is bruised, therefore the rude man says he may break it. His argument in brief is this: "If the reed were strong, I should not touch it, but seeing that it is bruised what harm can there be in completing the wound under which it is already suffering? I will even snap it and throw the sundered parts away." That is the reasoning of the rude man—that is the vulgar view of the case. The idea of the healing is the idea of a creator. He who creates also heals. Herein we see God's estimate of human nature: if He cared only for the great, the splendid, the magnificent, the robust, and the everlasting, then He would indeed be too like ourselves. The greatness of God and the estimate which He places upon human nature are most seen in all these ministrations in reference to the weak and the weary and the young and the feeble and the sad. Made originally in the image of God, man is dear to his Maker, tho ever so broken. Oh, poor prodigal soul with the divinity nearly broken out of thee, smashed, bleeding, crushed, all but in hell—while there is a shadow of thee outside perdition, He would heal thee and save thee. Thou art a ruin, but a grand one—the majestic ruin of a majestic edifice, for knowest thou not that thou wast the temple of God?

When we are weary, even in weariness, God sees the possibility of greatness that may yet take place and be developed and supervene in immortality. How do we talk? Thus: "The survival of the fittest." It is amazing with what patience and magnanimity and majestic disregard of circumstances we allow people to die off. When we hear that thousands have perished, we write this epitaph on their white slate tombstones: "The survival of the fittest required the decay of the weakest and the poorest." We pick off the fruit which we think will not come to perfection. The gardener lays his finger and thumb upon the tree, and he says, "This will not come to much"—he wrenches the poor unpromising piece of fruit off the twig and throws it down as useless. In our march we leave the sick and wounded behind. That is the great little, the majestic insignificant, the human contradiction. We go in for things that are fittest, strongest, most promising, healthy, self-complete, and therein we think we are wise. God says, "Not a lamb must be left out—bring it up. Not a sick man must be omitted. Not a poor publican sobbing his 'God be merciful to me a sinner' must be omitted from the great host. Bring them all in, sick, weary, wounded, feeble, young, illiterate, poor, insignificant, without name, fame, station, force—all in. Gather up the fragments that nothing be lost." Let us go to that Shepherd—He will spare us and love us. When our poor strength gives out, He will not set His cruel heel upon us and kill us. He will gather us in His arms and make the whole flock stand still till He has saved the weakest one.

Did we but know the name for our pain we should call it Sin. What do we need, then, but Christ the Son of God, the Heart of God, the Love of God? He will in every deed give us rest. He will not add to the great weight which bows down our poor strength. He will give us grace, and in His power all our faintness shall be thought of no more. Some of us know how dark it is when the full shadow of our sin falls upon our life, and how all the help of earth and time and man does but mock the pain it cannot reach. Let no man say that Christ will not go so low down as to find one so base and vile as he. Christ is calling for thee; I heard His sweet voice lift itself up in the wild wind and ask whither thou hadst fled, that He might save thee from death and bring thee home. There is no wrath in His face or voice, no sword is swung by His hand as if in cruel joy, saying, "Now at last I have My chance with you." His eyes gleam with love: His voice melts in pity: His words are gospels, every one. Let Him but see thee sad for sin, full of grief because of the wrong thou hast done, and He will raise thee out of the deep pit and set thy feet upon the rock.

T. DeWitt Talmage
(1832—1902)

Thomas DeWitt Talmage started out to be a lawyer. Instead he became a pulpit orator and a prolific author and editor. He was born in 1832 near Bound Brook, New Jersey, to deeply religious parents. Three of his brothers became ministers. When Talmage began feeling a "leaning toward the ministry," he left the study of law and entered New Brunswick Theological Seminary. He graduated in 1856 and pastored his first church that same year. He later pastored in New York and Philadelphia and served as a Union Chaplain during the Civil War.

In 1869 Talmage accepted a call to pastor Central Presbyterian Church in Brooklyn, New York, with less than twenty members. The church grew rapidly under his vigorous leadership. Within a year the first Brooklyn Tabernacle was erected. (Three buildings of this congregation were destroyed by fire.) Soon his congregation numbered over 5,000. Additional millions read his sermons each week, for hundreds of newspapers around the world published them regularly. (Upon his death the *New York Times* stated, "The whole human race was his congregation.")

Blessed with unusual oratorical ability, Talmage was known for his descriptive word pictures and his humor. He attacked atheism and evolution and did not shun controversial issues. Talmage traveled throughout the world preaching to large crowds in messages that appealed to the common man. Some criticized his "showmanship and sensationalism," while others lauded his practical treatment of everyday problems. He retired from active ministry in 1899, with a reputation as one of the great pulpit orators of his time. He edited *Christian Herald* from 1890 until his death in 1902.

11

The A and the Z
By T. DeWitt Talmage

I am Alpha and Omega (Revelation 1:8).

Alpha is the first letter of the Greek alphabet, and Omega is the last; so that Christ in this text represents Himself as the A and the Z.

That is one reason why I like the Bible; its illustrations are so easy to understand. When it represents the gospel as a *hammer,* everybody knows it is to knock something to pieces; or as *salt,* everybody who has put down meat in barrels knows it is to keep things from spoiling; or as a *salve,* that it is to cure the old sores of the heart. The Bible illustrations go not on stilts, but in a plain way walk straight into the understanding. When a physician in the sickroom, or a philosopher in his conversation, or a minister in the pulpit begins to use big words, and to bother you with technicalities, you may make up your mind that he is trying to confound you with his learning. I do not want a man in ordinary conversation to call a dandelion a *Taraxacum dens leonis,* or a wart "an enlargement of the vascular papilla." A dandelion is a dandelion, and a wart is a wart.

A woman went to hear the great Dr. Alexander preach, and came home disappointed, saying, "I do not think he is such a great man after all, for I could understand every word he said."

When we learn to call things by their plain names, we will be getting back to the old Bible way of teaching. Anybody who knows the *a b c's* understands that the text means that Christ is the Beginning and the End of everything good.

1. He is the A and the Z of the physical universe. By Him were all things made that are made. He made Galilee as well as hushed it. He made the fig tree as well as blasted it. He made the rock as well as rent it. No wonder He could restore the blind man, for He first made the optic nerve and the retina. No wonder that He could give hearing to the deaf

man, for He first set the drum of the ear. No wonder He could cure the withered arm, for He made the bone and strung the muscle. He flung out of nothing the first material out of which the world was formed. He set spinning around the first axle, and drove the first pivot, and hung to the throne the first constellation. The eighteen millions of suns in the Milky Way are eighteen million coursers of fire, by Christ's hand held to their path as they fly up the steeps of heaven. The comet of 1811, that was one hundred and thirty-three million miles long, answered the bit of light, and by His hand was turned any whither. Jesus shepherds all the great flock of worlds. All these doves of light flew out of His bosom. Christ set one leg of the compass at the foot of the throne and swung the other around to mark the orbits of the worlds. Standing tonight in the observatory of Mount Zion, I take a telescope mightier than that of Herschel or of Ross—namely, the Word of God—and I see impressed on nearest and farthest star, I AM THE ALPHA!

It is exciting to see a ship launched. The people gather in a temporary gallery erected for their accommodation. The spectators are breathless, waiting for the impediments to be removed, when down the ship rushes with terrific velocity, the planks smoking, the water tossing, the flags flying, the people cheering, bands of music playing. But my Lord Jesus saw this ship of a world launched, with its furnaces of volcano, and flags of cloud, and masts of mountain, and walking-beams of thunderbolt, while the morning stars shouted, and the orchestras of heaven played, "Great and marvellous are thy works, Lord God Almighty!"

The same hand that put up this universe will pull it down. I think the time will come when the worlds will have done their work and must be removed, so that but two worlds will remain; the one a vast desert of suffering, swinging through immensity—the abode of the bad; the other a blooming paradise for all the good. For eternal ages will the two swing around in their orbits of light and darkness. We know not by what process any of the worlds will be taken down, save one: that will go by fire. Perhaps the most of the worlds will shatter in collision. Sirius and the North Star, Capella and Aldebaran, colliding into eternal ruin. The furnaces already on fire in the heart of the earth will burst their bounds, and the mountains kindle, and the great forests begin to crackle, and the wild beasts tumble off the crags in an avalanche of terror, and the metals melt, flowing in liquid down the gulches, and the ocean to steam and bubble, and finally to flame, and the round earth from all sides shoot out forked tongues of fire. All the universe will know who set on fire the one world, and who shattered the others, for Christ, my Lord, will stand amid the roar, and crackle, and thunder, and crash of that final undoing, proclaiming, I AM THE OMEGA!

2. Christ is the A and the Z of the Bible. Here is a long lane, over-shadowed by fine trees, leading up to a mansion. What is the use of the lane if there were no mansion at the end? There is no use in the Old Testament except as a grand avenue to lead us up to the Gospel Dispensation. You may go early to a concert. Before the curtain is hoisted, you hear the musicians tuning up the violins and getting ready all the instruments. After a while the curtain is hoisted and the concert begins. All the statements, parables, orations, and miracles of the Old Testament were merely *preparatory,* and when all was ready, in the time of Christ, the curtain hoists and there pours forth the Oratorio of the Messiah—all nations joining in the Hallelujah chorus.

Moses, in his account of the creation, shows the platform on which Christ was to act. Prophets and apostles took subordinate parts in the tragedy. The first act was a manger and a babe; the last a cross and its victim. The Bethlehem star in the first scenery shifted for the crimson upholstery of a crucifixion. Earth, and heaven, and hell the spectators. Angels applauding in the galleries; devils hissing in the pit.

Christ is the Beginning and the End of the Bible.

In Genesis, who was Isaac, bound amid the fagots? Type of Christ, the ALPHA. In Revelation, what was the water of life? Christ, the OMEGA. In Genesis, what was the ladder over Jacob's pillow? Christ, the ALPHA. In Revelation, who was the conqueror on the white horse? Christ, the OMEGA. In Exodus, what was the smitten rock? Christ the ALPHA. In Revelation, who was the Lamb before the throne? Christ, the OMEGA. Take Christ out of this Book, and there are other books I would rather have than the Bible. Take Him out, and you have the Louvre without the pictures; you have the Tower of London without the jewels. Take Him out, and man is a failure, and the world a carcass, and eternity a vast horror.

3. Christ is the A and the Z of the Christian ministry. A sermon that has no Christ in it is a dead failure. The minister who devotes his pulpit to anything but Christ is an impostor. Whatever great themes we may discuss, Christ must be the beginning and Christ the end. From His hand we get our commission at first, and to that same hand we at last surrender it. Though the colleges may give you a diploma, and Presbytery lay their hands on your head, if Christ send you not forth, you go on a fool's errand; and though the schools reject you as incompetent, if the Lord God tells you to preach, you have a right to go, and there is at least one pulpit in the land where your right to proclaim the gospel is acknowledged. A sermon devoted to metaphysics is a stack of dry cornstalks after the corn has been ripped out with the husking-peg. A sermon given up to sentimental and flowery speech is as a nosegay flung to a drowning sailor. A sermon devoted to moral essay is a basket of

chips to help on the great burning. What the world wants now is to be told in the most flat-footed way of Jesus Christ, who comes to save men from eternal damnation. Christ the Light, Christ the Sacrifice, Christ the Rock, Christ the Star, Christ the Balm, Christ the Guide. If a minister should live one thousand years, and preach ten sermons each day, those subjects would not be exhausted. Do you find men tempted? Tell them of Christ the Shield. Or troubled? Tell them of Christ the Comfort. Or guilty? Tell them of Christ the Pardon. Or dying? Tell them of Christ the Life.

Scores of ministers, yielding to the demands of the age for elegant rhetoric, and soft speech, and flattering apostrophe, have surrendered their pulpits to the Devil, "horse, foot, and dragoon." If these city exquisites won't take the old-fashioned gospel, then let them go on the downward road where they want to go, and we will give our time to the great masses who want to hear the plain gospel, and who are dying by the millions because they do not hear it. Be Christ the burden of our talk; Christ the inspiration of our prayers; Christ the theme of our songs; Christ now, and Christ forever. Oh for more consecration! After Luther was prepared to preach, he said to his professor, Dr. Staupitz, "I cannot preach. I should die in three months. Indeed, I cannot do it." "Well," said the professor, "if you must die, you must; but preach, man—preach, man—and then live or die, as it happens." In that stern hour when we feel that we shall never preach again, and we have ascended for the last time the pulpit, the gown will be nothing, the surplice will be nothing, philosophy nothing, Presbyteries nothing, Conferences nothing, General Assemblies nothing, But CHRIST EVERYTHING!

> *Let Zion's watchmen all awake,*
> *And take the alarm they give;*
> *Now let them, from the mouth of God,*
> *Their awful charge receive.*
> *May they that Jesus, whom they preach,*
> *Their own Redeemer see;*
> *And watch thou daily o'er their souls*
> *That they may watch for thee.*

4. Christ is the A and the Z in the world's rescue. When the world broke loose, the only hand swung out to catch it was that of Jesus. At Long Branch, on the beach, on a summer's day, hundreds of people are sporting; but suddenly someone cries, "Look there! A man is drowning." Out of hundreds, perhaps there is only one strong swimmer. He plunges in and brings the man safely ashore. On the beach of heaven, one day, there sat myriads of immortals, merry with a great gladness; but the voice of one of the immortals cried out, "See there! A world is drowning! To the rescue! Where are the wreckers? Launch the

lifeboats! Who will go?" Angels did not dare venture. Heaven itself stands helpless before the scene. It knows how to wave a palm or shout in a coronation, but not how to take out of the floods a drowning world. Jesus bounds from the throne and throws His robe on one side, His crown on the other. Swift as a roe on the mountains, He comes down over the hills. The shining ones stand back as He says, "Lo! I come." Amid the wrathful surges He beats His way out to the dying world; and while, out in the deep waters, with bloody agony He wrestled with it, and it seemed for a little while uncertain whether it would take Him down or He would lift it up, those on the beach trembled, and in an hour grew ages older; and when at last, in His great strength, He lifted it in His right hand and brought it back, there went up a hosanna from all the cloud of witnesses. He began the work and He shall complete it. Ring all the bells of earth and heaven today in honor of Christ the ALPHA and Christ the OMEGA!

5. Christ is the A and the Z in heaven. He is the most honored personage in all that land. He is known as a World-Liberator. The first one that a soul entering heaven looks for is Jesus. The great populations of heaven seek Him out, follow Him over the hills, and shout at His chariot-wheel. Passing along those streets, spirits blessed cry out to one another, "Look! that is Jesus." Methinks that if the hosts of heaven go forth in some other realm to fight, their battle-cry is "JESUS." Jesus on the banners. Jesus in the song. At His feet break the doxologies. Around His throne circle the chief glories. Where the white Lamb of heaven goes, there go all the flocks. The first tree in the heavenly paradise Jesus planted. The first fountain He struck from the rock. The first pillar of light He lifted. At heaven's beginning—CHRIST, THE ALPHA. Then travel far on down the years of eternity, and stop at the end of the remotest age, and see if the song has not taken up some other burden, and some other throne has not become the center of heaven's chief attractions. But no; you hear it thrummed on the harps, and poured from the trumpets, and shouted in universal acclaim, CHRIST, THE OMEGA!

Now, what is this glorious One to you, my hearer? Have you seen Him? Have you heard His voice? Have you walked this earth, and never seen in the bent grass where His feet had just been? Of all the stars in the midnight heavens, has not one pointed you to where He lay? Trudging on across this desert with thy burden of sins, have you ever made the camels kneel? Is this one, the First and the Last of heaven nothing to thee? Poor wanderer, without Christ, what of thy death hour? what of the judgment day? what of eternity? If it shall be found at the last that thou has rejected this thy only hope, in what dark hole of the universe wilt thou lay thyself down to suffer, and gnash thy teeth, and howl forever? You must have Christ or die. But one ladder out of the pit! But one lifeboat from the wreck! Get in it. Lay hold of the oars with both hands, and pull, if need be, until the blood starts. The world is after you. The Devil is after you. The avenger of blood is after you. But, more than all, Christ is after you, and His cry is, "O Israel, thou hast destroyed thyself; but in me is thine help"!

Sam Jones
(1847—1906)

Samuel Porter Jones was born in 1847 in Oak Bowrey, Alabama; his family moved to Cartersville, Georgia, when he was nine years old. Showing promise as a young man, Jones studied law after graduation and was admitted to the Georgia bar in 1868. However, he began to drink heavily and almost destroyed his career and his marriage. When his father pled with Sam on his deathbed to become a Christian, Jones quit drinking and was converted at the age of twenty-four.

Jones began preaching and was licensed by the Methodist Episcopal Church of Georgia in 1872. After serving as an itinerant preacher for eight years, Jones became a financial agent for an orphanage in Georgia. During this time he continued to preach and established himself as a prominent evangelist.

By 1884 Jones was so well known that he entered evangelistic work on a large scale. He was soon conducting meetings in the larger cities across America with astounding results. Jones held some eighteen crusades in Nashville, Tennessee; one of these was probably the greatest campaign of his ministry. He preached to 5,000 people three times daily and saw an estimated 10,000 conversions. A contemporary of D.L. Moody and Billy Sunday, Jones also preached a successful meeting in Brooklyn for T. DeWitt Talmage. Although he lacked the manpower and large organization of Sunday, Jones always preached to overflow crowds, until his death in 1906 on the eve of his ninety-fifth birthday.

12

Prepare for the Life to Come
By Sam Jones

Turn you to the strong hold, ye prisoners of hope: even today do I declare that I will render double unto thee (Zech. 9:12).

The all-absorbing theme with God and angels and good men is the salvation of the living. Not the salvation of men who lived fifty years ago, or a hundred years ago. They have had their opportunities and enjoyed their privileges, and they have met their destiny. Not the salvation of men who shall live a hundred years hence; they have yet to be born and yet to enjoy their privileges and opportunities. But the absorbing theme of God, and angels, and good men is the salvation of men and women who live and walk and talk upon the face of the earth tonight. And isn't it passing strange that this great question should so engage the heart and mind of God, and of angels, and of good men, and yet, perhaps you, and you, and you should be the only creatures in all God's vast universe that seem to be totally disinterested in this great question? And now we purpose tonight, not to draw upon our imagination or try in the least to impose upon your credulity, but we stand squarely on the Book, and we will talk about what we know.

There are some things that we all know in common. I know that I am twenty-four hours nearer the cemetery than when I assembled with you in this house last night. You know you have one day less to live than you had this morning when the sun arose upon this world. You know that these moments bear our life away and are carrying us into the great beyond. You know that in your youthful days your heart was softer, your conscience was more tender, and your will was more easily affected by truth, and by grace, than it is tonight. You know that you are not such a husband as you ought to be. You know you do not set such an example to your children as you ought to. You know your life and character tonight are not what they ought to be before God and man. I say that when we begin to talk about these things that we know, we are getting very close together, and there are some things that we know from the teachings of that Book. And now we come squarely to the text: "Turn you to the strong hold, ye prisoners of hope."

We stop at this point to say that there are three classes of prisoners with hope, and there are three classes of prisoners without hope. Now let us find our latitude and longitude on spiritual things. Now let us find where we are on this occasion. It is the privilege of every man to know his bearings tonight, to know just where he is, and to know whither he is tending.

The first class of prisoners without hope that the Book speaks of are the angels who kept not their first estate but sinned against God and were driven away and put in chains of everlasting darkness, to await the final judgment day. While you and I have had a chance of life, and while peace and pardon are for the fallen man, those angels who kept not their first estate are in that lone land of deep despair, without a ray of heavenly light or a spark of hope, forever and forever. As I look upon an immortal spirit whose chains confine it to hopeless and everlasting despair, my heart shudders as I look upon the picture. But I never saw an angel. I have never been brought into sympathy with angels by association. I know very little of them. Angels have not flesh and blood. They are not subjected to wrinkles and gray hairs and old age and death, like you and I, and perhaps they are separated from our sympathy.

But this Book speaks of another class of prisoners without hope. *That is that man and that woman who have walked the streets, enjoyed just such privileges as you and I enjoy, and then die without God and without hope in the world.* There may be some gospel truth in that old couplet:

While the lamp holds out to burn,

The vilest sinner may return.

But when fate snuffs the candle and it goes out in death, then all hope is gone forever. I ask you, mother, did you ever pray for your boy since he breathed his last breath? Wife, have you ever offered prayer for your husband since he bade you goodbye in death? Sister, have you wrestled with God at the mercy seat for the salvation of your brother since he passed out of the world? No, sir, the common convictions of humanity are all together on this proposition, that as the tree falleth, so it shall be forever, and that, instead of there being anything in death to reverse and to sanctify and to save, death is the opening of the door and the passing out of the soul into eternity.

I have preached the gospel in more than twenty states, perhaps, of this Union. I may preach the gospel in every state of this grand old Union. If God were to call me to China I would go to China and preach the gospel as willingly and as cheerfully as I bade wife and children good-bye to come to your city. But there's one place I never have preached the gospel, and there's one place I never shall preach the gospel of Jesus Christ, and that is out here in the cemetery. I shall never stand among the tombstones of earth and beg the bones of the cemetery to come to Christ. No, sir! Never! What you and I do with this question, we must do between this and the gate of the cemetery. What you and I do upon this question, we must do before the doctor lays his hand upon our pulse for the last time and bids our weeping wife or loved ones to prepare for the worst—that death shall come in an hour. What you and I do upon this question must be before that clock on the mantel-piece seems to click louder than ever before. What you and I do must be done before wife or loved ones shall bathe their handkerchiefs in their tears and weep over us as we pass out of time into eternity. If that Book teaches anything clearly, it teaches there is no knowledge or device or repentance in the grave, whither we are all tending. I tell you, my brother, that whatever we may be in life, or what preparations we may make and what character we form in this life, shall settle destiny for us when life shall bid us walk out of the body and go into the great beyond. And this man and this woman, who have lived and died in our midst, enjoyed the same privileges, en-joyed the same opportunities that you and I enjoy, and yet, in spite of all overtures of grace and the wagon-loads of sermons that have been wasted upon them, in spite of all, have come to death's hour without prepara-tion, and passed into eternity to be judged by the God of all the earth!

And perhaps 1,000 of this congregation at this moment, if you were to die in your pew before I am through preaching, would be prisoners without hope, forever. Your heart in your bosom is a muffled drum beating your funeral march to the tomb. And every step you and I take from this hour to our dying couch, shall be toward the cemetery, and yet we rush right upon the gates of the cemetery unprepared for death and unprepared for eternity.

I see men whiling away and throwing away hours of their lives. Many and many in this city will be like the millionaire of London who gave his life to making money, and when stricken suddenly with men-ingitis, his doctor hurried to him and said to him, "You have meningitis and you'll be dead in two hours."

And the wealthy, worldly man looked him in the face and said: "Doctor, if you'll keep me alive till tomorrow morning at 8 o'clock, I'll give you $500,000. I'll give it to you cheerfully."

The doctor looked at him and said: "I have prescriptions to give and I have remedies for disease, but, my friend, I have no time to sell. Time belongs to God."

Oh, poor, wayward, worldly man that whiled away all the precious hours of life, and now, forsooth, when death meets him, tells his physician, "I will give you half a million dollars if you will keep me alive for sixteen hours." Oh, poor humanity, throwing away hours and privileges that are worth all the world!

Oh, sir, if there is a fact in my history for which I am thankful and hope to praise God for in heaven forever, it is the fact that God did not let me die in my sins. It is the fact that in and through the abounding mercy and grace of God, I was brought to see myself and repent of my sins and make peace with God before I went hence and was no more among men.

I have often thought of the experience and incident of a young man, vigorous and healthy and strong, raised by pious parents, and on his dying couch he sent for his pastor. The pastor was a personal friend of his, and when he walked into the room and saw his sunken condition, the poor boy looked up in the preacher's face and said: "I have sent for you but not to pray for me. I have given all my life to sin and worldliness, and I have not courage now to turn over the poor dying man to God. I have not sent for you to pray, but I have sent for you that I might give you a message to my friends at my funeral service. I want you to tell my friends at my funeral that I am dying a lost man, and lost forever. But tell them that if any man had slapped me on the shoulder ten years ago and said: 'Tom, ten years from today you will be dying without religion,' I would have told him: 'No, sir. I had a good mother. I have respect for religion, and I intend to give my heart to God.' And," said he, "if any man had slapped me on the shoulder twelve months ago and said: 'Tom, twelve months from today you will be dying without religion,' I would have looked the man in the face and said: 'You don't know me; I will never die without religion; my purposes are fixed to seek and obtain religion before I die.' " Said he: "If a man had ten days ago said to me: 'Tom, ten days from now you will be dying without religion,' I would have said: 'No, sir; you don't know me;' and," said he—and I want you to listen to this, the saddest thing a dying man ever said—"at last, at last, after all my mother's prayers and all my good resolutions and all the means that have been brought to bear upon me, at last, at last, I am dying without religion." And that is the saddest thing mortal man ever said upon his dying couch. And if you die tonight, the world would sit around your corpse tomorrow and say: "At last! at last! After all his resolutions and all his purposes, he died without religion."

But there is another class of prisoners without hope. Thank God we are not among fallen angels! Thank God, we are not among the dead! There is another class of prisoners without hope, and that is the *men and women of this city that are just as certain to be damned as they walk the streets of this city today*. There are men in this city who have not heard a sermon for twenty years; there are men in this city who have settled it—"I never in tend to hear another.'' There are men in this city who have fenced, effectually fenced, their souls off from good and thrown around them bulwarks and doors that the grace and Spirit of God can never penetrate in this world. And when I walk out on the streets of our town and find a man as he walks the street, that has settled it—"I never intend to repent," I would as soon shake hands with a dead man as to shake hands with him. He is dead to all that could lift his soul to God, dead to all that could make him good and happy, dead to all that could save him in time, and dead to all that could save him in eternity.

In my short life as a preacher, I want to tell you tonight I have seen men reject and reject and reject the mercies of God until I have almost heard the gates of mercy close in their faces forever.

Just as certain as he breathes, he is a doomed man. He never will repent. The chances are all against us. The chances are all against us, now may be. Brother, will your heart ever be as tender as it has been in the past? Will you ever be worked up under gospel truth as you have been in the past? And if after all your tender years are gone and all the influences of your youthful days fail to reach you, are not the probabilities tonight that you never will repent, that you will die like you are, "a prisoner without hope?"

I wonder if there is a man here listening to me tonight that you could not move him with the gospel and the thunders of all the worlds. I wonder if there are men here tonight who are not just as disinterested in what I say as if they had no soul to save, and there was no immortal interest at stake. My brother, let others do just as they please, and let others throw away their time and their souls, but let's you and I make our peace with God and our calling and election sure, so that when we fail on earth we may secure a mansion in the skies.

But, I thank God, there is a different side to this question, and let us consider it but a moment. *There are three classes of prisoners with hope. The first class we mentioned are the faithful men and women of the church of God, striving, struggling, day after day, to keep the commandments of God, and love and serve Him with all their hearts.* They are prisoners, but, thank God prisoners of hope—prisoners of hope. Every good man that walks the face of the earth is a prisoner of hope.

My mother was once a prisoner of hope, but when death cut the ligaments that bound her to earth, she went home to God, and for thirty years she has been walking the golden streets, one of God's free men, forever. My precious father was a prisoner, but, thank God, a prisoner of hope! And when at last he, upon his dying couch, pushed the doctors back from his bed, he overleaped the circle of loved ones about his dying couch, and above star and moon he went until he overvaulted the very throne of God itself, and tonight he walks the golden streets, a child of

God and a free man forever. Thank God these chains will not last always. Thank God these temptations are not forever. Thank God these environments will not last further than the grave! Bless the Lord, O, my soul! There is a world

Where the wicked cease from troubling,

And the weary are at rest.

We, I say, are bent upon that gracious home up beyond the skies.

I never see a wife grow pale and suffer that I don't bless my God there is a country where no wife shall ever pale, and where no sickness shall ever come. I never see my precious children suffer and swing like the pendulum of the clock between life and death that I don't thank God there is a country where health blossoms forever upon the cheek and the light of life shall ever sparkle from the eyes of our children. Oh, thank God, there is a world of freedom! And these faithful Christians are on their way to the world where freedom shall be enjoyed in its most blessed and its most glorious sense. Brother, you are a prisoner of hope, and as long as that star of hope shines over my pathway, here is one man that is ready to deny himself and take up his cross and follow Christ. As long as that star shines over my pathway, like St. Paul I will throw aside everything and count it nothing, and neither will I count my life dear unto myself, but that I may run with patience the race to that city of God where sickness and sorrow and pain and death are felt and feared no more.

Blessed be God! There is an assurance in every man's heart that inspires him by day and by night. St. Paul said: That blessed hope! That blessed hope!

Well, thank God, there is another class of prisoners with hope. *That man out there that does not belong to any church, but he stood up here yesterday afternoon and said, "I run the white flag up; I surrender to God; I want to be a Christian."* Brother hear me tonight: God loves the meanest man, just like God loves the best man. Brother, yonder is a father that loves a son with all his heart, and that son is headed to a drunkard's grave. Does that father's love save that boy from the drunkard's grave? There is a mother with all her affections wrapped around her boy, and yet he drinks, and drinks, and drinks, until at last he leaps out from the presence of his mother into a drunkard's eternity, and that mother will go to his grave twice a week and carry flowers and plant them on the mound above him, and bathe the dust that covers his body in her precious tears; but did that mother's love save that boy from the drunkard's grave? Neither can God's love save his son—you and me—unless we bring ourselves in the compass of grace and let Him save us.

That man who has in his heart the burning desire to be a Christian is a prisoner of hope, and I tell you, my brother, the man who says tonight:

"I surrender to God; I give my life to him; I seek the cross," that man is a prisoner of hope. And you will never be damned if you will follow the inspiration and the desire—"God help me to be a Christian."

Friend, let's you and I look after our hearts tonight. Is there down in our souls an intense, burning desire to be a Christian? If there is, let us surrender to that desire tonight and say: "I will make my peace with God."

And then, there is another class of prisoners with hope, and that is *those men and women who have not made up their minds at all, but they are thinking on this question.* Oh, brother, there is a chance there that you may be saved, and I wish every poor man here tonight with the desire in his heart to be a Christian, I wish you would, like Garfield— President Garfield—when they probed his wounds he looked at the doctors and he said: "Doctors, is there any chance for my life?"

The doctors answered back: "Yes, there is a chance."

And Mr. Garfield said: "Well, I will take that chance." And he did. He wrestled and grappled with death for three long months as no hero in America, perhaps, ever did; and if that man and that woman will take the chance—a chance that you have tonight—and grapple with it with all your ransomed powers as grandly and nobly as Garfield did with life, then I say to you it will issue into a bright, happy, joyous experience here, and heaven in the end.

"Turn you to the strong hold, ye prisoners of hope: even today do I declare that I will render double unto thee."

Now a word on this part. A great many people think, "Well, after all, I am not ready yet to seek religion. If I were to seek religion now, I would have to give up everything, and just live a poor, sad, groping pauper the balance of my life." Well, you never made a bigger mistake in your life. Listen:

"Even today do I declare that I will render double unto thee."

"Double." I never read that passage that I do not think of the incident a church brother told me once. He said there was a young man in a revival meeting he was carrying on who was seeking religion earnestly for two or three days. One day he walked out of the church after the young man and said to him, "You are in earnest; you are in earnest. I cannot see why you are not blessed and saved."

"Oh," said the young man, "I think I know the trouble. Every time I go the altar and seek God on my knees, this fact comes up before my eyes. I clerk in a grocery store that retails liquor by the quart and pint, but not by the drink, and every time I kneel down and pray, the fact that I am clerking and selling liquor by the quart and pint comes up before me and stops my prayers."

"Well," said the preacher, "I would give up my clerkship."

"If I do," replied the young man, "it looks as if my mother and sisters will starve. My mother is a widow, and my sisters are orphans; and every bite they eat comes from what I earn. I would surrender it in a moment if it were not for that."

"Well," said the preacher, "trust God and do the thing you ought to do, my brother."

He told me the young man went on down to the store and told his employer: "Sir, I have been seeking religion earnestly, and I cannot be pardoned; I cannot pray as long as I clerk for you and sell whiskey in this house."

That boy told his employers, "I cannot stay any longer with you."

They said, "Well, we are sorry to give you up. You have been a good boy since you have been with us." And they paid him off. They were paying him $50 a month. That boy went back to the services and surrendered his heart to God. And he went home and lifted up his heart to God.

The next morning, just after breakfast, he received a note from his old employers. He went down to their store, and they said, "Walk into the liquor-room that was." He walked in and he saw that every barrel had been rolled out; and they said to him, "We have closed out that part of the business, and if you will come back and clerk for us again we will give you $100 a month."

"Today do I declare that I will render double unto thee."

No man ever lost anything by surrendering a wrong and giving his life to God. No, sir. Well, some man in the house may say, "I do not believe your anecdote." But I can tell you one a heap bigger than that. Fourteen years ago—my brethren of the ministry, hear me—fourteen years ago I gave my life and heart and all to God and entered into His service, and I read in that Book—and I thought it was a big statement—

"If you will forsake houses and lands and all to follow me, I will give you a hundredfold more in this life and everlasting life in the world to come."

Well, I took God at His word. When I started out to follow God, I left our little home in Cartersville, but, blessed be God, he has given me a hundred homes wherever I have gone—just as good as a home could be. And I left one mother—a gracious stepmother she was to me—I left her to follow Christ, and bless His holy name, He has given me a thousand mothers wherever I have gone, who have been as good to me as my own precious mother. I left a few friends in my own home to follow Christ, but, blessed be God, He has given me a thousand friends for every one I have left. And, blessed be God, I have now a thousandfold more in this life and bright hope of everlasting life in the world to come. God help every man here tonight to say, I will turn to the strong hold! I will be a Christian! I will give myself to God!

Alexander Maclaren
(1826—1910)

Alexander Maclaren grew up in Glasgow, Scotland, where he was born in 1826. His Christian father encouraged him to become a minister, and at age sixteen he entered Stepney College, a Baptist school. Three years later he graduated from London University. He began pastoring a church in Southampton when he was twenty (in 1846) and remained there twelve years. In 1858 he was called to pastor Union Chapel in Manchester, England, where he served until his death in 1910.

Thousands came to hear his deep, thorough Bible expositions. He was honored during those years with Doctor of Divinity degrees from the Universities of Glasgow and Edinburgh. He twice served as president of the Baptist World Congregation.

Maclaren's life was consumed with the preparation and delivery of sermons. He was a profound Bible scholar and a prolific writer. His Bible commentaries are read and studied throughout the English-speaking world. Maclaren possessed an excellent English style and has probably been read more than any other preacher except Charles Spurgeon. He spent long hours in study, often devoting two hours daily to studying the Bible in the original languages. Although he spent many hours in preparation, he always spoke without notes and became one of the most outstanding orators of his day.

13

The Pattern of Service
By Alexander Maclaren

And he took him aside from the multitude, and put his fingers into his ears, and he spit, and touched his tongue; and looking up to heaven, he sighed, and saith unto him, Ephphatha, that is, Be opened (Mark 7:33,34).

For what reason was there this unwonted slowness in Christ's healing works? For what reason was there this unusual emotion ere He spoke the word which cleansed?

As to the former question, a partial answer may perhaps be that our Lord is here on half-heathen ground, where aids to faith were much needed, and His power had to be veiled that it might be beheld. Hence the miracle is a process rather than an act; and, advancing as it does by distinct stages, is conformed in appearance to men's works of mercy, which have to adapt means to ends, and creep to their goal by persevering toil. As to the latter, we know not why the sight of this one poor sufferer should have struck so strongly on the ever-tremulous chords of Christ's pitying heart; but we do know that it was the vision brought before His spirit by this single instance of the world's griefs and sicknesses, in which mass, however, the special case before Him was by no means lost, that raised His eyes to heaven in mute appeal, and forced the groan from His breast.

The missionary spirit is but one aspect of the Christian spirit. We shall only strengthen the former as we invigorate the latter. Harm has been done, both to ourselves and to this great cause, by seeking to stimulate compassion and efforts for heathen lands by the use of other excitements, which have tended to vitiate even the emotions they have aroused, and are apt to fail us when we need them most. It may therefore be profitable if we turn to Christ's own manner of working, and His own emotions in His merciful deeds, set forth in this remarkable narrative, as containing lessons for us in our missionary and evangelistic work. I must necessarily omit more than a passing reference to the slow process of healing which this miracle exhibits. But that, too, has its teaching for us, who are so often tempted to think ourselves badly used, unless the fruit of our toil grows up, like Jonah's gourd, before our eyes. If our Lord was content to reach His end of blessing step by step, we may well accept patient continuance in well-doing, as the condition indispensable to reaping in due season.

But there are other thoughts still more needful which suggest themselves. Those minute details which this evangelist ever delights to give of our Lord's gestures, words, looks, and emotions, not only add graphic force to the narrative, but are precious glimpses of the very heart of Christ. That fixed gaze into heaven, that groan which neither the glories seen above nor the conscious power to heal could stifle, that most gentle touch, as if removing material obstacles from the deaf ears, and moistening the stiff tongue that it might move more freely in the parched mouth, that word of authority which could not be wanting even when His working seemed likest a servant's, do surely carry large lessons for us. The condition of all service, the cost of feeling at which our work must be done, the need that the helpers should identify themselves with the sufferers, and the victorious power of Christ's Word over all deaf ears—these are the thoughts which I desire to connect with our text, and to commend to your meditation today.

We have here set forth the foundation and condition of all true work for God in the Lord's heavenward look.

The profound questions which are involved in the fact that, as man, Christ held communion with God in the exercise of faith and aspiration, the same in kind as ours, do not concern us here. I speak to those who believe that Jesus is for us the perfect example of complete manhood, and who therefore believe that He is "the leader of faith," the head of the long procession of those who in every age have trusted in God and been lightened. But, perhaps, though that conviction holds its place in our creeds, it has not been as completely incorporated with our thoughts as it should have been. There has, no doubt, been a tendency, operating in much of our evangelical teaching, and in the common stream of orthodox opinion, to except, half unconsciously, the exercises of the religious life from the sphere of Christ's example, and we need to be reminded that Scripture presents His vow, "I will put my trust in Him," as the crowning proof of His brotherhood, and that the prints of His kneeling limbs have left their impressions where we kneel before the throne. True, the relation of the Son to the Father involves more than communion—namely, unity. But if we follow the teaching of the Bible, we shall not presume that the latter excludes the former, but understand that the unity is the foundation of perfect communion, and the communion the manifestation, so far as it can be manifested, of the unspeakable unity. The solemn words which shine like stars—starlike in that their height above shrinks their magnitude and dims their brightness, and in that they are points of radiance partially disclosing, and separated by, abysses of unlightened infinitude—tell us that in the order of eternity, before creatures were, there was communion, for "the Word was with God," and there was unity, for "the Word was God." And in the records of the life manifested on earth the consciousness of unity loftily utters itself in the unfathomable declaration, "I and my Father are one"; whilst the consciousness of communion, dependent like ours on harmony of will and true obedience, breathes peacefully in the witness which He leaves to Himself: "The Father hath not left me alone; for I do always those things that please him."

We are fully warranted in supposing that that wistful gaze to heaven means, and may be taken to symbolize, our Lord's conscious direction of thought and spirit to God as He wrought His work of mercy. There are two distinctions to be noted between His communion with God and ours before we can apply the lesson to ourselves. His heavenward look was not the renewal of interrupted fellowship, but rather, as a man standing firmly on firm rock may yet lift his foot to plant it again where it was before and settle himself in his attitude before he strikes with all his might; so we may say Christ fixes Himself where He always stood, and grasps anew the hand that He always held, before He does the deed of power. The communion that had never been broken was renewed; how much more the need that in our work for God the renewal of the—alas! too sadly sundered—fellowship should ever precede and always accompany our efforts! And again, Christ's fellowship was with the Father. Ours must be with the Father through the Son. The communion to which we are called is with Jesus Christ, in whom we find God.

Christ is truth for the understanding, authority for the will, love for the heart, certainty for the hope, fruition for all the desires, and for the conscience at once cleansing and law. Fellowship with Him is no indolent passiveness, nor the luxurious exercise of certain emotions, but the contact of the whole nature with its sole adequate object and rightful Lord.

Such intercourse, brethren, lies at the foundation of all work for God. It is the condition of all our power. It is the measure of all our success. Without it we may seem to realize the externals of prosperity, but it will be all illusion. With it we may perchance seem to spend our strength for naught; but heaven has its surprises; and those who toiled, nor left their hold of their Lord in all their work, will have to say at last with wonder, as they see the results of their poor efforts, "Who hath begotten me these? Behold, I was left alone; these, where had they been?"

Consider in few words the manifold ways in which the indispensable prerequisite of all right effort for Christ may be shown to be communion with Christ.

The heavenward look is the renewal of our own vision of the calm verities in which we trust, the recourse for ourselves to the realities which we desire that others should see. And what is equal in persuasive power to the simple utterance of your own intense conviction? He only will infuse his own religion into other minds, whose religion is not a set of hard dogmas, but is fused by the heat of personal experience into a river of living fire. It will flow then, not otherwise. The only claim which the hearts of men will listen to, in those who would win them to spiritual beliefs, is that ancient one: "That which we have seen with our eyes, which we have looked upon, declare we unto you." Mightier than all arguments, than all "proofs of the truth of the Christian religion," and penetrating into a sphere deeper than that of the understanding, is the simple proclamation, "We have found the Messias." If we would give sight to the blind, we must ourselves be gazing into heaven. Only when we testify of that which we see, as one might who, standing in a beleaguered city, discerned on the horizon the filmy dust-cloud through which the spearheads of the deliverers flashed at intervals, shall we win any to gaze with us till they too behold and know themselves set free.

Christ has set us the example. Let our prayers ascend as His did, and in our measure the answers which came to Him will not fail us. For us, too, "praying, the heavens" shall be "opened," and the peace-bringing Spirit fall dove-like on our meek hearts. For us, too, when the shadow of our cross lies black and gaunt upon our paths, and our souls are troubled, communion with heaven will bring the assurance, audible to our ears at least, that God will glorify Himself even in us. If, after many a weary day, we seek to hold fellowship with God as He sought it on the Mount of Olives, or among the solitudes of the midnight hills, or out in the morning freshness of the silent wilderness, like Him we shall have men gathering around us to hear us speak when we come forth from the secret place of the Most High. If our prayer, like His, goes before our mighty deeds, the voice that first pierced the skies will penetrate the tomb, and make the dead stir in the their grave-clothes. If our longing, trustful look is turned to the heavens, we shall not speak in vain on earth when we say, "Be opened."

We have here pity for the evils we would remove set forth by the Lord's sigh.

What was it that drew that sigh from the heart of Jesus? One poor

man stood before Him, by no means the most sorely afflicted of the
many wretched ones whom He healed. But He saw in him more than a
solitary instance of physical infirmities. Did there not roll darkly before
His thoughts that whole weltering sea of sorrow that moans round the
world, of which here is but one drop that He could dry up? Did there not
rise black and solid against the clear blue, to which He had been looking,
the mass of man's sin, of which these bodily infirmities were but a poor
symbol as well as consequence? He saw as none but He could bear to
see, the miserable realities of human life. His knowledge of all that man
might be, of all that the most of men were becoming, His power of con-
templating in one awful aggregate the entire sum of sorrows and sins,
laid upon His heart a burden which none but He has ever endured. His
communion with heaven deepened the dark shadow on earth, and the
eyes that looked up to God and saw Him could not but see foulness
where others suspected none, and murderous messengers of hell walking
in darkness unpenetrated by mortal sight. And all that pain of clearer
knowledge of the sorrowfulness of sorrow, and the sinfulness of sin, was
laid upon a heart in which was no selfishness to blunt the sharp edge of
the pain nor any sin to stagnate the pity that flowed from the wound. To
Jesus Christ, life was a daily martyrdom before death had "made the
sacrifice complete," and He bore our griefs, and carried our sorrows
through many a weary hour before He "bare them in his own body on
the tree." Therefore, "Bear ye one another's burdens, and so fulfil the
law" which Christ obeyed, becomes a command for all who would draw
men to Him. And true sorrow, a sharp and real sense of pain, becomes
indispensable as preparation for, and accompaniment to, our work.

Mark how in us, as in our Lord, the sigh of compassion is connected
with the look to heaven. It follows upon that gaze. The evils are more
real, more terrible, by their startling contrast with the unshadowed light
which lives above cloudracks and mists. It is a sharp shock to turn from
the free sweep of the heavens, starry and radiant, to the sights that meet
us in "this dim spot which men call earth." Thus habitual communion
with God is the root of the truest and purest compassion. It does not
withdraw us from our fellow feeling with our brethren, it cultivates no
isolation for undisturbed beholding of God. It at once supplies a standard
by which to measure the greatness of man's godlessness, and therefore of
his gloom, and a motive for laying the pain of these upon our hearts, as if
they were our own. He has looked into the heavens to little purpose who
has not learned how bad and how sad the world now is, and how God
bends over it in pitying love.

And that same fellowship, which will clear our eyes and soften our
hearts, is also the one consolation which we have when our sense of all
the ills that flesh is heir to becomes deep, near to despair. When one

thinks of the real facts of human life, and tries to conceive of the frightful meanness and passion and hate and wretchedness, that has been howling and shrieking and gibbering and groaning through dreary millenniums, one's brain reels, and hope seems to be absurdity, and joy a sin against our fellows, as a feast would be in a house next door to where was a funeral. I do not wonder at settled sorrow falling upon men of vivid imagination, keen moral sense, and ordinary sensitiveness, when they brood long on the world as it is. But I do wonder at the superficial optimism which goes on with its little prophecies about human progress, and its rose-colored pictures of human life, and sees nothing to strike it dumb forever in men's writhing miseries, blank failures, and hopeless end. Ah! brethren, if it were not for the heavenward look, how could we bear the sight of earth! But there is more within our view than earth; "we see Jesus"; we look to the heaven, and as we behold the true Man, we see more than ever, indeed, how far from that pattern we all are; but we can bear the thought of what men as yet have been, when we see that perfect example of what men shall be. The root and the consolation of our sorrow for man's evils is communion with God.

We have here loving contact with those whom we would help, set forth in the Lord's touch.

The reasons for the variety observable in Christ's method of communicating supernatural blessing were, probably, too closely connected with unrecorded differences in the spiritual conditions of the recipients to be distinctly traceable by us. But tho we cannot tell why a particular method was employed in a given case, why now a word, and now a symbolic action, now the touch of His hand, and now the hem of His garment, appeared to be the vehicles of His power, we can discern the significance of these divers ways, and learn great lessons from them all.

His touch was sometimes obviously the result of what one may venture to call instinctive tenderness, as when He lifted the little children in His arms and laid His hands upon their heads. It was, I suppose, always the spontaneous expression of love and compassion, even when it was something more.

The touch of His hand on the ghastly glossiness of the leper's skin was, no doubt, His assertion of priestly functions, and of elevation above all laws of defilement; but what was it to the poor outcast, who for years had never felt the warm contact of flesh and blood? It always indicated that He Himself was the source of healing and life. It always expressed His identification of Himself with sorrow and sickness. So that it is in principle analogous to, and may be taken as illustrative of, that transcendent act whereby He became flesh, and dwelt among us. Indeed, the very word by which our Lord's taking the blind man by the hand is described in the chapter following our text is that employed in the Epistle to the Hebrews when, dealing with the true brotherhood of Jesus, the writer says, "For verily he took not on him the nature of angels; but he took on him the seed of Abraham." Christ's touch is His willing contact with man's infirmities and sins, that He may strengthen and hallow.

And the lesson is one of universal application. Wherever men would help their fellows, this is a prime requisite, that the would-be helper should come down to the level of those whom he desires to aid. If we wish to teach, we must stoop to think the scholar's thoughts. The master who has forgotten his boyhood will have poor success. If we would lead to purer emotions, we must try to enter into the lower feelings which we labor to elevate. It is of no use to stand at the mouth of the alleys we wish to cleanse, with our skirts daintily gathered about us, and smelling-bottle in hand, to preach homilies on the virtue of cleanliness. We must go in among the filth, and handle it, if we want to have it cleared away. The degraded must feel that we do not shrink from them, or we shall do them no good. The leper, shunned by all, and ashamed of himself because everybody loathes him, hungers in his hovel for the grasp of a hand that does not care for defilement, if it can bring cleansing. Even in regard to common material helps the principle holds good. We are too apt to cast our doles to the poor like the bones to a dog, and then to wonder at what we are pleased to think men's ingratitude. A benefit may be so conferred as to hurt more than a blow; and we cannot be surprised if so-called charity which is given with contempt and a sense of superiority, should be received with a scowl, and chafe a man's spirit like a fetter. Such gifts bless neither him who gives nor him who takes. We must put our hearts into them, if we would win hearts by them. We must be ready, like our Master, to take blind beggars by the hand, if we would bless or help them. The despair and opprobrium of our modern civilization, the gulf growing wider and deeper between Dives and Lazarus, between Belgravia and Whitechapel, the mournful failure of legalized help, and of delegated efforts to bridge it over, the darkening ignorance, the animal sensuousness, the utter heathenism that lives in every town of England, within a stone's throw of Christian houses, and near enough to hear the sound of public worship, will yield to nothing but that sadly forgotten law which enjoins personal contact with the sinful and the suffering, as one chief condition of raising them from the black mire in which they welter.

The same principle might be further applied to our Christian work, as affecting the form in which we should present the truth. The sympathetic identification of ourselves with those to whom we try to carry the gospel will certainly make us wise to know how to shape our message. Seeing with their eyes, we shall be able to graduate the light. Thinking their thoughts, and having in some measure succeeded, by force of sheer community of feeling, in having as it were got inside their minds, we shall unconsciously, and without effort, be led to such aspects of Christ's all-comprehensive truth as they most need. There will be no shooting over people's heads, if we love them well enough to understand them. There will be no toothless generalities, when our interest in men keeps their actual condition and temptations clear before us. There will be no flinging fossil doctrines at them from a height, as if Christ's blest gospel were, in another than the literal sense, "a stone of offense," if we have taken our place on their level. And without such sympathy, these and a thousand other weaknesses and faults will certainly vitiate much of our Christian effort.

We have here the true healing power and the consciousness of wielding it set forth in the Lord's authoritative word.

All the rest of His action was either the spontaneous expression of His true participation in human sorrow, or a merciful veiling of His glory that sense-bound eyes might see it the better. But the word was the utterance of His will, and that was omnipotent. The hand laid on the sick, the blind, or the deaf was not even the channel of His power. The bare putting forth of His energy was all-sufficient. In these we see the loving, pitying Man. In this blazes forth, yet more loving, yet more compassionate, the effulgence of manifest God. Therefore so often do we read the very syllables with which His "voice then shook the earth," vibrating through all the framework of the material universe. Therefore do the Gospels bid us listen when He rebukes the fever, and it departs; when He says to the demons, "Go," and they go; when one word louder in its human articulation than the howling wind hushes the surges; when "Talitha cumi" brings back the fair young spirit from dreary wanderings among the shades of death. Therefore was it a height of faith not found in Israel when the Gentile soldier, whose training had taught him the power of absolute authority, as heathenism had driven him to long for a man who would speak with the imperial sway of a God, recognized in His voice an all-commanding power. From of old, the very signature of divinity has been declared to be "He spake, and it was done"; and He, the breath of whose lips could set in motion material changes, is that eternal Word, by whom all things were made.

What unlimited consciousness of sovereign dominion sounds in that imperative from His autocratic lips! It is spoken in deaf ears, but He knows that it will be heard. He speaks as the fontal source, not as the recipient channel of healing. He anticipates no delay, no resistance. There is neither effort nor uncertainty in the curt command. He is sure that He has power, and He is sure that the power is His own.

There is no analogy here between us and Him. Alone, fronting the whole race of man, He stands—utterer of a word which none can say after Him, possessor of unshared might, and of His fulness do we all receive. But even from that divine authority and solitary sovereign consciousness we may gather lessons not altogether aside from the purpose of our meeting here today. Of His fulness we have received, and the power of the Word on His lips may teach us that of His word, even on ours, as the victorious certainty with which He spake His will of healing may remind us of the confidence with which it becomes us to proclaim His name.

His will was almighty then. Is it less mighty or less loving now? Does it not gather all the world in the sweep of its mighty purpose of mercy? His voice pierced then into the dull cold ear of death, and has it become weaker since? His word spoken by Him was enough to banish the foul spirits that run riot, swine-like, in the garden of God in man's soul trampling down and eating up its flowers and fruitage; is the Word spoken of Him less potent to cast them out? Were not all the mighty deeds which He wrought by the breath of His lips on men's bodies prophecies of the yet mightier which His Will of love, and the utterance of that Will by stammering lips, may work on men's souls? Let us not in our faint-heartedness number up our failures, the deaf that will not hear, the dumb that will not speak His praise; nor unbelievingly say Christ's own word was mighty, but the word concerning Christ is weak on our lips. Not so; our lips are unclean, and our words are weak, but His Word—the utterance of His loving will that men should be saved—is what it always was and always will be. We have it, brethren, to proclaim. Did our Master countenance the faithless contrast between the living force of His word when He dwelt on earth, and the feebleness of it as He speaks through His servant? If He did, what did He mean when He said, "He that believeth on me, the works that I do shall he do also; and greater works than these shall he do; because I go unto my Father"?

B.H. Carroll
(1843—1914)

Benajah Harvey Carroll was born in 1843 in Carrollton, Mississippi. His family moved to Arkansas when he was young, and later to Texas, where he graduated from Baylor University at the age of eighteen. Carroll served four years in the Confederate Army during the Civil War; strangely enough, he remained an infidel during this time and was not converted until he was twenty-two years old. One year later he was ordained and entered the ministry.

Carroll pastored several churches in Texas, and in 1871 he became pastor of the First Baptist Church of Waco, where he served for thirty years. He became head of the department of Bible at Baylor University in 1901 and later worked with George W. Truett in raising the funds to retire the school's massive indebtedness. However, his most notable work occurred when he founded the Southwestern Baptist Theological Seminary; he was the school's first president, from 1908 to 1914.

B.H. Carroll was a great defender of the faith in an age of denominational debates. He possessed extraordinary argumentative abilities and was a powerful pulpit orator. His intellectual skills and eloquence held people spellbound as he preached, often for more than an hour at a time. Carroll was also an avid reader and is said to have read 250 pages per day for over forty-eight years. Many feel that he had a photographic memory due to his accuracy in recalling details of information he had read years earlier. In breadth of learning and depth of research, Carroll ranks with the profound scholars of his day. He left behind a treasury of biblical knowledge in his notable work, *An Interpretation of the English Bible.* He died in 1914, respected everywhere for his commitment to the authority of the Word of God.

14

Sermon to Preachers
By B.H. Carroll

I magnify mine office (Rom. 11:13).

However far, and by whatever license a minister may depart from the primary meaning of a text in its immediate connection, it is always obligatory that he should first give the primary and contextual import and then explain how the general principle contained in it may be safely applied to all his deductions from it. In the present case the connection is this: The apostle seems to anticipate an objection in the minds of the Gentiles whom he addresses, that he, their apostle, should manifest such concern for the salvation of the Jews. He justifies his solicitude for the redemption of his Jewish brethren, though he is an apostle to the Gentiles, and even magnifies his office as their apostle that by their glorious success in the gospel the Jews may be excited to emulation and thereby some of them be saved. He argues, that if the Gentiles derived benefit from the fall of the Jews, they would derive yet more by their recovery. Nor does he content himself with the salvation of only ''some of them.'' He looks to the salvation of the whole Jewish nation and to this end he speaks in the text and its connections: ''For I speak to you Gentiles...I magnify mine office: if by any means I may provoke to emulation them which are my flesh.''

But while this is the primary meaning of the text, in its connections it embodies a great principle of wider application. It is this great principle which burns in my heart and which I feel impelled to discuss before this convention. The fairness and safety of this wider application may be gathered from Eph. 4:11-16, in which it is alleged that God gave apostles, pastors, teachers, and evangelists for the same glorious purpose. Therefore if the office of one is to be magnified, so the office of the others to the same end. Hence the

THEME: *The office of a minister must be magnified—glorified always, everywhere, and by all incumbents.*

In discussing this theme, it is purposed to emphasize three thoughts: The office itself, why it should be magnified, how to magnify it.

I. The office. First impress on your minds the fact that the work of the ministry is official. It is an office in the true and common acceptation of that term. Let us define.

Webster's International Dictionary says: "Office—A special duty, trust, charge, or position, conferred by authority for a public purpose; a position of trust or authority; as, an executive or judicial office; a municipal office. A charge or trust of sacred nature, conferred by God himself; as, the office of a priest under the old dispensation, and that of the apostles in the new," quoting our text as an example. Mark the essential elements of an office. The duty, trust, or charge is special. It is conferred by authority. It is for a public purpose. In the case of a religious office, the trust is sacred and God Himself confers it. While in civil affairs it is the duty of every citizen to do all in his power toward the enforcement of law and the preservation of order, certain functions devolve exclusively on officers appointed for the purpose. A private citizen cannot perform the official duties of the sheriff, judge, governor, or president. So in the church and kingdom of Christ. While it is the privilege of every Christian to tell the story of the Cross and to otherwise aid in the dissemination of the gospel, yet in magnifying individual duties and privileges let it never be forgotten that God has called out a special class of men and set them apart officially and committed to them certain official duties. "This is a true saying, If a man desire the office of a bishop, he desireth a good work." The truth of the proposition just set forth is more recognized than realized. Let us impress ourselves with it by carefully reconsidering some things well known to all of us.

1. The terms by which God designates His ministers not only indicate office but suggest the nature of the office and its duties. In many places the minister is called a shepherd. A shepherd performs special duties committed to him alone. He must watch over the flock, feed them when hungry, heal them when sick, guard them in peril, keep them from worries and alarms, and shelter them in the fold.

He is called a bishop, which means an overseer. The overseer has special duty and authority. He directs the labors of those he oversees.

2. The form or ceremony by which the minister is set apart to his work indicates an office. He is separated to this work by prayer and laying on of the hands of the presbytery (Acts 13:2,3; 1 Tim. 4:14).

3. The special provision made for his support indicates an office (1 Cor. 9:1-14). As there is a salary for the governor of a state, or the sheriff of a county, or a soldier in the army, so the Lord hath ordained

that they who preach the gospel should live of the gospel. Now it is evident that all Christians cannot live of the gospel—cannot be put on a salary, out of the common fund. The fact, therefore, that special provision is made for the financial and material support of a certain class who devote their time and labor to a solemn trust for the public benefit is a demonstration that such class are in office. There is no escape from this alternative: Either the preacher is an object of charity in receiving pecuniary aid from his congregation, or he receives it in compensation for official duties.

4. Ministerial responsibility is proof of office. I mean to say that there is a responsibility laid on every preacher that does not rest on any private member of the church, and that in the great day of account he must answer to God for the manner in which he has discharged his official duties.

Now, by these four facts—the terms employed to designate his work, the form by which he is set apart to that work, the provision made for his support while engaged in it, and his responsibility for its performance, it is demonstrable that he fills an office in the ordinary sense of that word and the duties of such office are in contradistinction to the duties of private members of the church. These private members are not called shepherds, bishops, ambassadors, or even stewards in the sense that he is a steward. They are not ordained. They rely upon their secular business for a support. They have not his responsibility.

II. Why the office should be magnified.

1. Because of him who appoints. The dignity of every office is measured largely by the dignity of the appointing power. The servant is not above his master. When one holds an official position under the commission of a king, that royal signature ennobles every official action performed under its authority and confers on it the royal sanction, however paltry it may seem in itself. But what earthly potentate can be compared in majesty with the King of kings and Lord of lords, who as the eternal God, Himself specially calls every man, appoints every man, and sends forth under His supreme authority every man who lawfully enters the ministry? How does such a commission, handed down from the supreme court of heaven, infinitely transcend in majesty and dignity any commission issued by any lower court, so finite in time and power!

2. This office should be magnified because of the work involved in it. What is the minister to do? For what service is he commissioned? Even those in high authority sometimes necessarily commission their servants to perform trifling and unimportant services. But is such your work, my brethren? Let us re-read our commission tonight. The Scriptures which introduced this service tell their own story. They were earnestly and solemnly read—were they reverently heard? By them our work is di-

vided into two distinct parts—reconciliation and edification—the reconciliation of sinners to God and the upbuilding of the reconciled in their most holy faith. How awful the responsibility, how solemn the obligation, how important the service of carrying to the lost the word and hope of eternal life! Salvation! Salvation! How much it means. Life! Eternal life!

And what service does the minister render to them? He brings sight for blindness; light for darkness; forgiveness for guilt; hope for despair; a heavenly inheritance for spiritual bankruptcy; fatherhood for orphanage; and thrusts back the triumphant devil from off the prostrate victim and stands him up unshackled before God, "redeemed, regenerated, and disenthralled."

And how like it, in importance, is the other part? "Take heed therefore unto yourselves, and to all the flock, over the which the Holy Ghost hath made you overseers, to feed the church of God, which he hath purchased with his own blood" (Acts 20:28). "Feed my lambs. Feed my sheep" (John 21:15,16). "And he gave some, apostles; and some, prophets; and some, evangelists; and some, pastors and teachers; for the perfecting of the saints, for the work of the ministry, for the edifying of the body of Christ: till we all come in the unity of the faith, and of the knowledge of the Son of God, unto a perfect man, unto the measure of the stature of the fullness of Christ: that we henceforth be no more children, tossed to and fro, and carried about with every wind of doctrine, by the sleight of men, and cunning craftiness, whereby they lie in wait to deceive; but speaking the truth in love, may grow up into him in all things, which is the head, even Christ: from whom the whole body fitly joined together and compacted by that which every joint supplieth, according to the effectual working in the measure of every part, maketh increase of the body unto the edifying of itself in love" (Eph. 4:11-16).

Ministers of God, have you studied these Scriptures? Have you gauged these responsibilities? Have you measured these duties? My brethren, let our bare hearts be the target of the fiery arrows of interrogation: Are any sheep of our flock hungry? Is any lamb astray? Are wolves howling around the fold committed to our care? Are any laborers idle under our oversight? Are the "babes in Christ" in our charge growing? Have you heard any of them crying for the "sincere milk of the word," while you crammed them with solid food they were unable to digest? Are our people unified in the faith? Are any of the young converts tossed to and fro, and carried about with every wind of doctrine? Are they at the mercy of every theological tramp, who for revenue, seeks to sidetrack them from their straight road of service? Are they a prey to religious cranks, who poison them with patent nostrums and quack medicines? Is the body over which you preside fitly joined together? Does every joint

supply compactness? Does every part work effectually? Does the body increase? Is it edified? O watchman, have you blown the trumpet at the
coming of the sword? My brethren in the ministry, was this Scripture
written for our sakes: "Woe be to the shepherds of Israel that do feed
themselves! Should not the shepherds feed the flocks? Ye eat the fat, and
ye clothe you with the wool, ye kill them that are fed: but ye feed not the
flock. The diseased have ye not strengthened, neither have ye healed that
which was sick, neither have ye bound that which was broken, neither
have ye brought again that which was driven away, neither have ye
sought that which was lost; but with force and with cruelty have ye ruled
them. And they were scattered, because there is no shepherd: and they
became meat to all the beasts of the field when they were scattered"
(Ezek. 34:2-5).

Have we stood cowardly silent while some "have thrust with side and
with shoulder, and pushed all the diseased with their horns, till they have
scattered them abroad"? Oh, "when the chief Shepherd shall appear,"
shall we "receive a crown of glory that fadeth not away"? Brethren, I
press this question: Are not reconciliation and edification work enough?
And should we not magnify our office because of the work?

3. This office is to be magnified because of the extraordinary means
appointed for the accomplishing of the work of reconciliation and edification. I waste no words on the Koran nor the Book of Mormon. I mention no vagaries of human speculation, nor hallucinations of earthly
philosophy. I hold up no glow-worm light of science. I speak not of the
Constitution of the United States nor of any statutes evolved from it. But
I do speak of the inspired Word of God as the instrument appointed for
reconciliation and edification. When we consider this inspired volume,
as the means of glorifying his office placed in the preacher's hands, we
would not dare mention in comparison the office of the Supreme Court
of the United States, which expounds only the principles of earthly
jurisprudence. Let them quote Blackstone and Kent. Let them cite the
decisions of their defunct predecessors. Let them painfully and laborious-
ly gather up the doubtful opinions of dead men—that is their business.
But the man of God takes a Word inviolable and infallible—which was
breathed on those who wrote it; this must he expound and illustrate. It is
the Word which God at sundry times and in divers manners, spake in
time past unto the fathers by the prophets and in these last days by his
Son. This word "is quick, and powerful, and sharper than any twoedged
sword, piercing even to the dividing asunder of soul and spirit, and of the
joints and marrow, and is a discerner of the thoughts and intents of the
heart." This "word of the Lord endureth forever." It is brighter and
more potent than the light of all the heavenly bodies (Ps. 19). It is more
credible than a visitor from the dead (Luke 16:28-31). It is surer than the

evidences of the senses (2 Peter 1:13-19). Therefore the preacher is "charged" i.e., put on his oath, "before God, and the Lord Jesus Christ, who shall judge the quick and the dead at his appearing and his kingdom, [to] preach the word" (2 Tim. 4:1,2). Such extraordinary and potential means would not have been provided for an office that men could refuse to magnify.

4. The office should be magnified because of him who accompanies the official and gives efficacy to his words. I speak of the Holy Spirit, whose presence and power constitute the only guarantee of ministerial success. Paul may plant and Apollos water, but God alone gives the increase. To what earthly office, however great, are such presence and power attached? The minister is a "laborer together with God." No reverent mind can think of this presence and power, and depreciate the office which they sanctify and energize.

5. The office is to be magnified on account of the extraordinary qualifications required of the officer. Qualifications mental, moral, and spiritual. I maintain that there is no other office known among men that calls for the kind and degree of qualifications which God's Word requires for ministerial office. He must have gifts, graces, and character such as no human law requires for any earthly office. While the measure of his knowledge and scholarly education is not prescribed, he must be apt to teach. Without this aptness he never can be a preacher.

He must wrap himself in a mantle of personal purity whiter than the ermine of a judge. This mantle no minister can smirch with impunity. He must be unspotted before the world and must preserve a good report of them that are without. He may as well resign when the world seriously questions his sincerity or his morals. In an age of mammon, while the world bows before its golden calf, he must not be covetous. "Not for filthy lucre" must he take charge of any flock. While other men hate and fight, he must be no "striker or brawler." His spiritual qualifications are yet higher. He must be full of the Holy Spirit. He is the instrument of the Spirit. He must ever yield to the motion of the Spirit.

Therefore, because of his extraordinary appointment, because of his extraordinary work, because of the extraordinary means furnished him, because of the extraordinary presence, and because of the extraordinary qualifications required, it is demonstrable that this office should be magnified above every other office. We now come to the main question:

III. How shall the office be magnified? Brethren, I feel pressed in spirit tonight when I look out over this audience—among whom are so many ministers, so many older than myself, so many of longer service in the ministry. And I speak with great diffidence, but I do desire to express very earnestly and without the slightest reservation my own deep and abiding convictions concerning the truth of God as I understand it, in answering the question how all ministers may magnify their office.

1. By a profound realization of its importance. Pardon a personal reference, for men only theorize when they go beyond their personal experience. In delivering addresses on other subjects I have been singularly free from embarrassment, but I never stand up to preach without trembling. It is not stage fright, for perhaps I esteem too slightly the judgment of men and women, whether expressed in praise or censure. But there is something about preaching which affects me even more than the approach of death. I was not driven into the ministry. I never fled from God's message, like Jonah. I never hid behind modest apologies, but I never in my life stood up to preach except once,—which exception I profoundly regret,—without first isolating myself from all human company, even the dearest, and prostrating myself in the spirit before the dread and awful God, imploring him, in deepest humility, to bless me that one time. Perhaps I am wrong. I would not judge harshly, but I cannot rid myself of the conviction that a man who can lightly, who can arrogantly, who can with seeming effrontery of manner, get up in the pulpit, get up unstaggered with the weight of responsibility resting on him, get up as an ambassador for God, as if God was his ambassador, is disqualified for this holy office. Just think of it seriously. Eternal interests hinge on every sermon. Every sentence may be freighted with eternal weal or woe. Every word may be the savor of life unto life or of death unto death. Would any one of deep moral sense deliver idly or lightly even a political oration if every word uttered might be a winged bullet of death, or a message of reprieve from a death sentence? What must be this moral character, what the turpitude of his nature, if he was more concerned to display his wit or logic or eloquence than to measure the effect of his speech on human suffering or joy! But can such trifling, however selfish, compare with his, who, standing up for God in matters which cost the life of Christ and engaged the attention of the three worlds,—men, angels, and devils—who stands up as heaven's agent to dispense terms of life and conditions of pardon, or to denounce eternal judgments, and there poses as a wit or attitudinizes as a rhetorician, or plays the actor, as if the whole service were a theatrical display and heaven and hell were but scenic paintings to accentuate his dramatic talent!

Therefore the impression never leaves me that no irreverent man should ever dare preach. I do not care how much he knows, nor how well he can declaim, nor how many his admirers. I shudder—cold chills of apprehension creep over me when I hear him. Is it the office of a mountebank? Is it the vocation of a circus clown? It is the lifework of a privileged jester? Oh, the agony of Paul's question: "Who is sufficient for these things?" Oh, the richness of his experience: "I was with you in weakness, and in fear, and in much trembling. And my speech and my preaching was not with enticing words of man's wisdom, but in demonstration of the Spirit and of power." If one of you were commissioned to give directions of safety to a crowd of men, women, and children standing on a quivering sandbank—encircled by an ever rising flood, which moment by moment encroached on the narrow space where they stood, and your word meant life or death to every strong man, to every loving woman, to every clinging child, would you, could you— how could you, standing on a safe shore, speak those words in the carefully practiced declamation of a rhetorician?

2. Profound and abiding gratitude to God for putting you in the ministry will help you to magnify your office. Your heart must gratefully appreciate that you, a worm as other men; that you, not on account of your own merit; you, from among thousands naturally as good—and perhaps better by grace—you were selected by the Divine Master for this distinguished honor; as much higher above the crowns of earth as the stars in heaven are above their reflection in a well. How can I ever forget the impression made on my heart, or get beyond its influence on my life, when I heard Dr. Broadus at Jefferson, Texas, in the Southern Baptist Convention, preach from the text: "I thank Christ Jesus, my Lord, for that he hath enabled me, putting me into this ministry." Let thy call to preach unseal a ceaselessly flowing fountain of gratitude. Rejoice in the honor conferred on you. You who desire to magnify your office, let me pass the question around and press its point on every heart: Are you glad you are a preacher? Are you? Are you grateful? Do you thank Him? Do you appreciate it as a priceless treasure?

3. You can magnify your office by "studying," i.e., being diligent, "To show thyself approved unto God, a workman that needeth not to be ashamed, rightly dividing the word of truth."

This diligence applies to every department of ministerial work and therefore includes a profound acquaintance with all the revealed will of God in its proper order and relation. This knowledge and the use made of it must be "unto the approval of God," and not of man. But how can a man magnify his office who is too lazy to study that Word which it is his business to preach? Who lives year after year in ignorance of the very rudiments of Bible-teaching? Who has not studied that sacred library, book by book, and chapter by chapter? I refer not so much to mere mental study as to heart study. I mean such study as places the heart against every Bible doctrine, and prays: "Lord God, filtrate into my heart the very essence of this doctrine—let me receive into my soul experimentally just what is the mind of the Spirit; let me so assimilate it as food that it will be a part of my being; let me not only know it, but be nourished by it."

My brother, if you would magnify your office, make the Word of God your life study. Let down your buckets into the wells of salvation; lengthen your cords and let them down deep, and draw up the water fresh and sparkling every day, and give it out freely to your thirsty congregations. Burn all your written sermons that you carry around in your valise. Don't you know that when you keep on gnawing the same sermons they become like what a wolf leaves of a once juicy antelope—dry bones? An unchanged sermon never suits two congregations. Conditions vary. Be fresh. Be flexible. Learn proper adjustments. Study the needs of the people before you, and preach from a full heart that within that very hour has sought the Spirit's guidance as to the theme, and the Spirit's power as to utterance.

4. You can magnify your office by giving yourself wholly to it. No man should give himself wholly to a work that is too scant in character and too small in volume to call out and employ all his reserve force, and to develop to their full capacity every faculty of his being. But in the ministry God has committed to a man an office as high as heaven, as deep as hell, as broad as space. There is a broad margin for all his powers. There is room enough for all possible development in all directions. Let me again refer to myself. When I was converted I was making $2,500 a year, more than I have ever received since. I was ambitious of distinction and promotion. I had luxurious tastes and a wonderful appreciation of conveniences. Now, to abandon all this pride, ambition, and prospect of luxury, to come down to a few hundreds a year, grudgingly given, was very grinding to my sensitiveness. But the crisis was one for solution. I determined never to be burdened with its solution but once. Without a dollar in my pocket or in sight; with a wife, baby, and feather bed as the sum total of earthly possessions, I settled that question once for all.

I made a solemn covenant with God, that while I lived I would never have any other business or profession or calling than to preach the gospel—to give myself wholly to that, "sink or swim, live or die, survive or perish," to turn back to any other never, NEVER, NEVER, FOREVER. I learned to see that it was a small matter if I die. I remembered the Master's words: "He that findeth his life shall lose it: and he that loseth his life for my sake shall find it." Indeed, it might be the best for me to die. It might be the best that I should starve to death. I didn't know. Who can tell? But I was certain that whether I starved or fattened it was my duty to preach the gospel.

My brother, take home to thyself the charge of Paul to Timothy: "Give attendance to reading, to exhortation, to doctrine. Neglect not the gift that is in thee, which was given thee by prophecy, with the laying on of the hands of the presbytery. Meditate on these things; give thyself wholly to them." How is it you can undertake so many lifeworks? I call upon you to interpret this Scripture: "No man that warreth entangleth himself with the affairs of this life." Is it not directly in connection with the charge to Timothy to "commit thou to faithful men, who shall be able to teach others also" the things which he had heard and learned? You cannot deny it. Does it not fairly apply to preachers of today? You cannot deny it. Then will you answer candidly to your own heart and to God: Are you so entangled? Does the entanglement help you as a preacher? Are you content to remain so?

5. You can magnify this office by regarding God's interests, solemnly committed to you, as transcendently above place and congregation and world. This is a hard saying. I know it by experience. How seductive the temptation to a preacher to yield to selfish considerations as to where he shall preach and what he shall preach!

And how most shameful of all the weakness when he gets in front of the Cross and hides it from the people to show off himself! Some years ago I invited a minister to preach for me the following Sunday. He came with a valise full of written sermons on various sensational topics. He read over to me about a dozen of them—who can doubt my patience in view of it?—and asked me, the pastor of the flock, which one would make the most favorable impression for him on my congregation. I turned on him in scorn, and said: "That matter is one of supreme indifference to my people. I wanted you to so preach from an humble, full, and loving heart of our Divine Redeemer as to make a favorable impression for Him, but as no man can preach Jesus when self fills his vision, I withdraw my invitation for you to occupy my pulpit." He did not preach for me then, nor has he since. And I am glad he is out of Texas and out of the Baptist church.

The temptation sometimes comes in another form, wafted on the seductive breath of flattery. People "with itching ears," who cannot endure sound doctrine and holy living, will come with honeyed words about his "broadness and liberality." "He is no mossback," "no straight-jacket." "He belongs to higher culture and criticism." Ah, me! if the preacher drinks once of this intoxicating champagne, you may count the days till he hearts the gospel as a squirrel hearts an acorn, leaving only a shattered shell, without even a germ of life. It sometimes comes in the growls of his congregation. "He presses some things too much." "He is crazy on the subject of missions. He urges too many collections." "He has too much zeal." Woe to him and to his people if he heed the growling.

Finally, you may magnify your office by continually renewing your consecration. When you enter this office, and so long as you are in it, over how much of you do you consent that God should write His name and put the obligation of exclusive service? Do you say: "Lord Jesus, Thou has put me into Thy ministry. I am but a little child. I know not how to go out or to come in. I am unworthy of so great honor. I shall surely fail if Thou art not with me. What I am to do, how I am to do it, and where I go, do Thou choose for me; only be Thou with me. It seems, Good Master, that every part of me has been washed whiter than snow in Thy cleansing blood, every part of me subject of divine grace, every part of me redeemed by thy power and love and dying groans. But Lord Jesus, if Thou canst find any part of me that the blood has not touched, then write not Thy name on that lost part. But over every part the blood has touched, there write Thy name, whether brain, or eye, or ear, or hand, or heart, or mouth, or foot, over all, all over all, write Thy name of authority and ownership forever. Let me be Thy faithful servant in time, and Thy welcome servant in eternity."

To illustrate this consecration: At the examination of a candidate for ordination I once heard a deacon ask this question: "In going into this work, have you burned the bridges behind you or only taken up the planks with a view to relaying them in case you should want to cross back to secular affairs?" I thought it a wonderfully pertinent question that went to the heart of the matter. It is better for the preacher never to even look backward toward the place where the bridge once stood. And never let him seek to please himself as to where he shall preach. Let the Lord of the harvest determine the where as well as the what and how. Turn not a longing eye to big churches and fat salaries. Let the Master say where, whether under burning skies in Africa's malarial jungles, or where "wolves are howling on lone Onalaska's shore." This consecration involves that you fully trust Him for material support and spiritual power. Be not faithless. The Master points you to the lilies and the sparrows. You are more valuable than they. He tells you that "verily you shall be clothed and you shall be fed." Not a hair of your head shall perish. He will care for your wife and children if you trustingly serve him. I do not say trust the brethren. That is a broken reed. But to deny that Jesus will keep His promise to you is to deny the veracity of God. Trust Him for your power. Even today I had a talk with a young brother staggering under the responsibility of presenting a great work tomorrow. His eyes were full of tears, as he said: "I have no strength at all for this great service." I laid my hand on him and said: "Let Jesus be your power. Lash yourself with God's promises to the throne of His onmipotence, and your weakness will become strength." I have promised to spend much of the night with him praying that the power of God and not of man may rest upon him.

Indeed, "we have this treasure in earthen yessels." Oh, how earthen! When I first read of the quarrel between Paul and Barnabas, I said: "Earthen vessels." And when preachers now quarrel, the bleeding church cries out: "Earthen! earthen!" I could get down on my knees before God in your presence to make one yearning plea; that you make this convention one of peace, power, and brotherly love. Put relentless hands down into your hearts, and tear out by the roots everything that will not advance the interests of the Redeemer's kingdom here in this meeting. Tear it out. It depends on you. Let every watchman blow his trumpet at the coming of the sword. Let every sentinel cry out on his post: "To arms! They come! The foe—the foe!" Let every leader leap to the front of his battalion and stay to the front in every good word and work, lest there be a retreat while the mournful bugles sound a recall and the dirge of defeat be the music to which we march.

I magnify my office, oh, my God, as I get nearer home. I can say more truthfully every year, "I thank God that He put me in this office"; I thank Him that He would not let me have any other; that He shut me up to this glorious work; and when I get home among the blessed on the bank of everlasting deliverance and look back toward time and all of its clouds, and sorrows, and pains, and privations, I expect to stand up and shout for joy that down there in the fog and mists, down there in the dust and in the struggle, God let me be a preacher. I magnify my office in life; I magnify it in death; I magnify it in heaven; I magnify it, whether poor or rich, whether sick or well, whether strong or weak, anywhere, everywhere, among all people, in any crowd. Lord God, I am glad that I am a preacher, that I am a preacher of the glorious gospel of Jesus Christ.

J. Wilbur Chapman
(1859—1918)

Once called by D.L. Moody the "greatest evangelist in the country," John Wilbur Chapman was born in Richmond, Indiana, in 1859, of godly parents. A Sunday school teacher led him to Christ while he was still a child, but it was under Moody's personal counsel that he received assurance of salvation. When he decided to enter the ministry, Chapman attended Oberlin College (founded by Charles Finney) but later graduated from Lake Forest University. He also graduated from Lane Theological Seminary in 1882 and received his LLD degree from Heidelberg University.

Chapman successfully pastored several churches, the most significant of which was Bethany Presbyterian in Philadelphia. The church experienced unprecedented growth under his leadership, and Chapman was in constant demand to conduct revival meetings; he therefore resigned the church in 1893 to enter full-time evangelistic work. (He returned to Bethany as pastor in 1895 briefly, and church attendance soared to over 12,000.)

Chapman became secretary of the Presbyterian Committee on Evangelism in 1902, a position he held until his death in 1918. During this time he conducted successful revival meetings in various parts of the world, with thousands converted. One campaign in Boston was reported to have had a nightly attendance of 20,000 and over 7,000 people converted.

J. Wilbur Chapman became the first director of the Winona Lake Bible Conference, which served as a center for evangelistic activity in the United States for years to come. Billy Sunday worked on his staff for a time and received valuable training under his ministry. Chapman also helped establish other Christian conference grounds.

Chapman's great organizational skill had a lasting effect on urban evangelism technique. He planned the cooperation of dozens of ministers, utilized advertising and other forms of publicity, held many prayer meetings, and saw hundreds of churches grow and benefit as a result. His message focused upon the atoning work of Christ, and the salvation of souls was his chief objective. A combination pastor-evangelist, this man of God also wrote the words to "One Day!" That famous gospel hymn is still being sung in churches throughout the world.

An Old-Fashioned Home
By J. Wilbur Chapman

What have they seen in thy house? (2 Kings 20:15).

If you will tell me what is in your own house by your own choice I will tell you the story of your home life and will be able to inform you whether yours is a home in which there is harmony and peace or confusion and despair. Let me read the names of the guests in your guest book, allow me to study the titles of the books in your library in which you have special delight, permit me to scan your magazines which you particularly like, allow me to listen to your conversation when you do not know that you are being overheard, give me the privilege of talking but for a moment to your servants, and make it possible for me to visit with your friends in whom you have particular delight—and I will write a true story of what you have been, of what you are, and of what you will be but for the grace of God, even though I may not know you personally at all. In other words, whatever may be seen in your home determines what your home is.

I was a man grown before I visited Washington, the capital of the nation. I was the guest of a member of the President's Cabinet. Riding with him the first evening, when the moon was shining, we suddenly came upon the National Capitol, and I said to my host, "What in the world is that?" He said, with a smile, as if he pitied me, "That is the Capitol building, and that is the home of the nation." I am sure he was right in a sense, because the building is magnificent, and is in every way the worthy home of such a nation as ours; but I think I take issue with him, after careful thought, in his statement that the Capitol building is the home of the nation. I can recall a visit made to a home which was not in any sense palatial, where the old-fashioned father every morning and evening read his Bible, knelt in prayer with his household about him, commended to God his children each by name, presented the servants at the throne of grace, and then sang with them all one of the sweet hymns of the church; and from the morning prayer they went forth to the day of victory, while from the evening prayer they went to sleep the undisturbed sleep of the just, with the angels of heaven keeping watch over them.

I recall another home in the state of Ohio where the father and mother were scarcely known outside of their own county. The size of their farm was ten acres, but they reared two boys and two girls whose mission has been worldwide and whose names are known wherever the church of Christ is known and wherever the English language is spoken. These, in the truest sense, are the homes of the nation, and such homes give us men and women as true as steel.

Napoleon once was asked, "What is the greatest need of the French nation?" He hesitated a moment and then said, with marked emphasis, "The greatest need of the French nation is mothers." If you will ask me the greatest need in America I could wish in my reply that I might speak with the power of a Napoleon and that my words might live as long, for I would say, the greatest need of the American nation today is homes, not palatial buildings, but homes where Christ is honored, where God is loved, and where the Bible is studied.

Hezekiah had been sick unto death. The word of the Lord by the mouth of the Prophet came to him, saying, "Set thy house in order, for thou shalt die." Then he recovered for a season. The King of Babylon sent messengers to him and when the messengers had gone Isaiah asked him the question of the text, "What have they seen in thy house?"

The dearest and most sacred spot upon the earth is home. Around it are the most sacred associations, about it cluster the sweetest memories. The buildings are not always palatial, the furnishings are not always of the best, but when the home is worthy of the name, ladders are let down from heaven to those below, the angels of God come down, bringing heaven's blessing and ascend, taking earth's crosses. Such a home is the dearest spot on earth, because there your father worked and your mother loved. There is no love which surpasses this.

I have a friend, George R. Stuart, who says that when God Himself would start a nation He made home life the deciding question. He selected Abraham as the head of the home, and in Genesis, the eighteenth chapter and the nineteenth verse, he gives the reason for this in these words: "For I know him, that he will command his children and his household after him."

There are two great principles which must prevail in every home:
First: *Authority,* suggested by the word "command."
Second: *Example,* suggested by the expression, "He will command

his children and his household after him.''

In order that one may rightly command he must himself be controlled or be able to obey an authority higher than his own. It is absolutely impossible for one to be the father he ought to be and not be a Christian, or to be worthy of the name of mother and not yield allegiance to Jesus Christ. If we are to set before those about us a right example, we cannot begin too soon. Your children are a reproduction of yourself, weakness in them is weakness in yourself, strength in them is but the reproduction of your own virtue.

A convention of mothers met some years ago in the city of Cincinnati and was discussing the question as to when one ought properly to begin to train the child for Christ. One mother said, ''I begin at six''; another suggested seven as the proper age; another said ''I begin when my child takes his first step, and thus point him to Christ, or when he speaks his first word I teach him the name of Jesus.'' Finally an old saint arose and said, ''You are all of you wrong; the time to begin to train the child is the generation before the child is born,'' and this we all know to be true.

Example counts for everything in a home. If there is any blessing in my own life or others, if there has been any helpfulness in my ministry to others, I owe it all to my mother, who lived before me a consistent Christian life and died giving me her blessing; and to my father, who with his arms about me one day said, ''My son, if you go wrong it will kill me.'' I was at one time under the influence of a boy older than myself and cursed with too much money. I had taken my first questionable step at least, and was on my way one night to a place which was at least questionable if not sinful. I had turned the street corner and ahead of me was the very gate to hell. Suddenly, as I turned, the face of my father came before me and his words rang in my very soul. If my father had been anything but a consistent Christian man I myself, I am sure, would have been far from the pulpit, and might have been in the lost world.

The real purpose of every home is to shape character for time and eternity. The home may be one of poverty, the cross of self-sacrifice may be required, suffering may sometimes be necessary, but wherever a home fulfills this purpose it is overflowing with joy. One of my friends has drawn the following picture which he says is fanciful, but which I think is absolutely true to life:

Back in the country there is a boy who wants to go to a college and get an education. They call him a bookworm. Wherever they find him—in the barn or in the house—he is reading a book. ''What a pity it is,'' they say, ''that Ed cannot get an education!'' His father, work as hard as he will, can no more than support the family by the products of the farm. One night Ed has retired to his room and there is a family conference about him. The sisters say, ''Father, I wish you would send Ed to college; if you will we will work harder than we ever did, and we will make our old dresses do." The mother says, "Yes, I will get along without any hired help; although I am not as strong as I used to be, I think I can get along without any hired help." The father says, "Well, I think by husking corn nights in the barn I can get along without any assistance." Sugar is banished from the table, butter is banished from the plate. That family is put down on rigid, yea, suffering, economy that the boy may go to college. Time passes on. Commencement day has come and the professors walk in on the stage in their long gowns and their classic but absurd hats. The interest of the occasion is passing on, and after a while it comes to a climax of interest as the valedictorian is introduced. Ed has studied so hard and worked so well that he has had the honor conferred upon him. There are rounds of applause, sometimes breaking into vociferation. It is a great day for Ed. But away back in the galleries are his sisters in their old plain hats and faded clothes, and the old-fashioned father and mother; dear me, she has not had a new hat for six years; he has not had a new coat for a longer time. They rise and look over on the platform, then they laugh and they cry, and as they sit down, their faces grow pale, and then are very flushed. Ed gets the garlands and the old-fashioned group in the gallery have their full share of the triumph. They have made that scene possible, and in the day that God shall more fully reward self-sacrifice made for others, He will give grand and glorious recognition. "As his part is that goeth down to battle, so shall his part be that tarrieth by the stuff."

This experience describes a home in the truest sense of the word better than all the palaces the world has ever known where love is lacking and the spirit of God is gone.

There are two great forces in every home.

I speak of the father and the mother, not but that the children have their part in either making or breaking a household, but these two are the mightiest of agencies.

The mother stands first. There are certain things which must be true of every mother. She must be a Christian. The father may fail if he must, but let the mother fail and God pity the children. She must be consistent. The children may forget the inconsistencies of the father but when the mother fails the impression is lasting as time and almost as lasting as eternity. She must be prayerful. I do not know of anything that lifts so many burdens or puts upon the face such a look of beauty as the spirit of prayer. And she must study her Bible. When we pray we talk with God, but when we read the Bible God talks with us and every mother needs His counsel.

A poor young man stood before a judge in a great court to be sentenced to death. When asked if he had anything to say, he bowed his head, and said, "Oh, your honor, if I had only had a mother!"

Her love always stimulates love. It lasts when everything else fails. A man cannot wander so far from God as to forget his mother, or go so deep in sin as to be unmindful of her sweet influence.

The following is a sketch, full of touching interest, of a little ragged newsboy who had lost his mother. In the tenderness of his affection for her he was determined that he would raise a stone to her memory.

His mother and he had kept house together and they had been all to each other, but now she was taken, and the little fellow's loss was irreparable. Getting a stone was no easy task, for his earnings were small; but love is strong. Going to a cutter's yard and finding that even the cheaper class of stones was far too expensive for him, he at length fixed upon a broken shaft of marble, part of the remains of an accident in the yard, and which the proprietor kindly named at such a low figure that it came within his means. There was much yet to be done, but the brave little chap was equal to it.

The next day he conveyed the stone away on a little four-wheeled cart, and managed to have it put in position. The narrator, curious to know the last of the stone, visited the cemetery one afternoon, and he thus describes what he saw and learned:

"Here it is," said the man in charge, and, sure enough, there was our monument, at the head of one of the newer graves. I knew it at once. Just as it was when it left our yard, I was going to say, until I got a little nearer to it and saw what the little chap had done. I tell you, boys, when I saw it there was something blurred my eyes, so's I couldn't read it at first. The little man had tried to keep the lines straight, and evidently thought that capitals would make it look better and bigger, for nearly every letter was a capital. I copied it, and here it is; but you want to see it on the stone to appreciate it:

MY MOTHER
SHEE DIED LAST WEAK
SHEE WAS ALL I HAD. SHEE
SED SHEAD BEE WAITING FUR—

and here the boy's lettering stopped. After awhile I went back to the man in charge and asked him what further he knew of the little fellow who brought the stone. "Not much," he said: "Not much. Didn't you notice a fresh little grave near the one with the stone? Well, that's where he is. He came here every afternoon for some time working away at that stone, and one day I missed him, and then for several days. Then the man came out from the church that had buried the mother and ordered the grave dug by her side. I asked if it was for the little chap. He said it was. The boy had sold all his papers one day, and was hurrying along the street out this way. There was a runaway team just above the crossing, and—well—he was run over, and lived but a day or two.'' He had in his hand when he was picked up an old file sharpened down to a point, that he did all the lettering with. They said he seemed to be thinking only of that until he died, for he kept saying, ''I didn't get it done, but she'll know I meant to finish it, won't she? I'll tell her so, for she'll be waiting for me,'' and he died with those words on his lips. When the men in the cutter's yard heard the story of the boy the next day, they clubbed together, got a good stone, inscribed upon it the name of the newsboy, which they succeeded in getting from the superintendent of the Sunday school which the little fellow attended, and underneath it the touching words: ''He loved his mother.''

God pity the mother with such an influence as this if she is leading in the wrong direction!

It is necessary also to say just a word about the father. There are many pictures of fathers in the Bible. Jacob gives us one when he cries, ''Me ye have bereaved of my children.''

David gives another when he cries, ''O Absalom, my son.'' The father of the Prodigal adds a new touch of beauty to the picture when he calls for the best robe to be put upon his boy. I allow no one to go beyond me in paying tribute to a mother's love, but I desire in some special way to pay tribute to the devotion and consistency of a father.

There are special requisites which must be made without which no father can maintain his God-given position. He must be a Christian. I rode along a country road with my little boy some time ago. I found that he was speaking to my friends just as I spoke to them. One man called my attention to it and said, ''It is amusing, isn't it?'' To me it was anything but amusing. If my boy is to speak as I speak, walk as I walk, then God help me to walk as a Christian.

He must be a man of prayer. No man can bear the burdens of life or meet its responsibilities properly if he is a stranger to prayer.

He must be a man of Bible study. One of the most priceless treasures I have is a Bible my father studied, the pages of which he turned over and over, and which I never used to read without a great heart throb.

I con its pages o'er and o'er;
Its interlinings mark a score
Of promises most potent, sweet,
In verses many of each sheet;
Albeit the gilding dull of age,
And yellow-hued its every page,
No book more precious e'er may be
Than father's Bible is to me.

''Its tear-stained trace fresh stirs my heart
The corresponding tear to start;

Of trials, troubles herein brought,
For comfort never vainly sought,
For help in sorest hour of need,
For love to crown the daily deed,
No book more precious e'er may be
Than father's Bible is to me.

He must also erect in his house a family altar. I know that many businessmen will say this is impossible, but it is not impossible. If your business prevents your praying with your children, then there must be something wrong with your business. If your life prevents it, then you ought to see to it that your life is made right and that quickly.

My friend, George R. Stuart, one of the truest men I know, gave me the following picture of a Christian home. He said: "When I was preaching in Nashville, at the conclusion of my sermon a Methodist preacher came up and laid his hand upon my shoulder and said, 'Brother Stuart, how your sermon today carried me back to my home! My father was a local preacher, and the best man I ever saw. He is gone to heaven now. We have a large family; mother is still at home, and I should like to see all the children together once more and have you come and dedicate our home to God before precious old mother leaves. If you will come with me, I will gather all the family together next Friday for that purpose.' I consented to go. The old home was a short distance from the city of Nashville. There were a large number of brothers and sisters. One was a farmer; one was a doctor; one was a real estate man; one was a bookkeeper; one was a preacher; and so on, so that they represented many professions of life. The preacher brother took me out to the old home, where all the children had gathered. As we drove up to the gate I saw the brothers standing in little groups about the yard, whittling and talking. Did you ever stand in the yard of the old home after an absence of many years, and entertain memories brought up by every beaten path and tree and gate and building about the old place? I was introduced to these noble-looking men who, as the preacher brother told me, were all members of churches, living consistent Christian lives, save the younger boy, who had wandered away a little, and the real object of this visit was to bring him back to God.

"The old mother was indescribably happy. There was a smile lingering in the wrinkles of her dear old face. We all gathered in the large, old-fashioned family room in the old-fashioned semicircle, with mother in her natural place in the corner. The preacher brother laid the large family Bible in my lap and said, 'Now, Brother Stuart, you are in the home of a Methodist preacher; do what you think best.'

"I replied, 'As I sit today in the family of a Methodist preacher, let us begin our service with an old-fashioned experience meeting. I want each child, in the order of your ages, to tell your experience.' The oldest arose and pointed his finger at the oil portrait of his father, hanging on the wall, and said in substance about as follows: 'Brother Stuart, there is the picture of the best father God ever gave a family. Many a time he has taken me to his secret place of prayer, put his hand on my head, and prayed for his boy. And at every turn of my life, since he has left me, I have felt the pressure of his hand on my head, and have seen the tears upon his face, and have heard the prayers from his trembling lips. I have not been as a good man since his death as I ought to have been, but I stand up here today to tell you and my brothers and sisters and my dear old mother that I am going to live a better life from this hour until I die.' Overcome with emotion, he took his seat, and the children in order spoke on the same line. Each one referred to the place of secret prayer and the father's hand upon the head. At last we came to the youngest boy, who, with his face buried in his hands, was sobbing and refused to speak. The preacher brother very pathetically said, 'Buddy, say a word; there is no one here but the family, and it will help you.'

"He arose, holding the back of his chair, and looked up at me and said, 'Brother Stuart, they tell me that you have come to dedicate this home to God; but my old mother here has never let it get an inch from God. They tell you that this meeting is called that my brothers and sisters may dedicate their lives to God, but they are good. I know them. I am the only black sheep in this flock. Every step I have wandered away from God and the life of my precious father, I have felt his hand upon my head and heard his blessed words of prayer. Today I come back to God, back to my father's life, and so help me God, I will never wander away again.'

"Following his talk came a burst of sobbing and shouting, and I started that old hymn, 'Amazing grace (how sweet the sound!) that saved a wretch like me!' etc., and we had an old-fashioned Methodist class-meeting, winding up with a shout. As I walked away from that old homestead I said in my heart, 'It is the salt of a good life that saves the children.' A boy never gets over the fact that he had a good father.''

"What have they seen in thy house?" If we are to help our children for time and eternity, our homes must be better, our lives must be truer, our ambition to do God's will must be supreme. When these conditions are met it will be possible for us to answer the question of the text.

R.A. Torrey
(1856—1928)

Born into a wealthy religious family in Hoboken, New Jersey, in 1856, Ruben Archer Torrey had no "apron-string religion." Instead of heeding his mother's plea to become a preacher, he entered Yale at age fifteen to study law. A desperate struggle against God almost resulted in his suicide. He was saved and called of God that fateful night.

At Yale University Torrey came under the influence of D.L. Moody, who told him, "You'd better get to work for the Lord." After attending Yale Divinity School, Torrey pastored for four years in Ohio and then pursued further education in Germany. He came out of a struggle with skepticism determined to "follow the Bible wherever it leads me." He returned to America and began pastoring a church in Minneapolis. In 1889 Moody asked him to come to Chicago and head what is now the Moody Bible Institute, and Torrey accepted the challenge.

Torrey's first year in Chicago saw the implementation of evangelistic outreaches for the students in which over 2,000 people were converted. After Moody's death in 1899, Torrey remained as president until 1908. He also pastored Moody Memorial Church for twelve years. It is difficult to overstate his positive influence over both institutions.

From 1902 to 1906 he also conducted evangelistic crusades worldwide, which resulted in a reported 200,000 conversions. In 1908 he resigned the institute and church to pursue evangelism, but in 1912 he became the dean of the Bible Institute of Los Angeles. He pastored the Church of the Open Door in Los Angeles for ten years. In 1924 he resigned to enter a Bible conference ministry and fulfilled speaking engagements until his death in 1928.

Torrey was not only a great preacher and educator but also the author of some forty books. His great scholarship enriched people's understanding of the Bible. His zeal for personal soulwinning and the fullness of the Holy Spirit greatly influenced men such as John R. Rice. R.A. Torrey holds an honored place among the world's spiritual leaders.

16

Ten Reasons Why I Believe the Bible Is the Word of God
By R.A. Torrey

Thy word is a lamp unto my feet, and a light unto my path (Ps. 119:105).

When a student at Yale Theological Seminary, I was first confronted seriously with the question: Why do you believe the Bible is the Word of God? It was the one all-absorbing thought that engaged my mind by day and by night. I sought help from God and from books, and after much painful study and thought I came out of the darkness of skepticism into the broad daylight of faith and certainty that the Bible from beginning to end is God's Word. This address is the outcome of that experience. My subject is, "Why I Believe the Bible Is the Word of God."

First, from the testimony of Jesus Christ. Many people accept the authority of Christ who do not accept that of the Bible as a whole. We all must accept His authority. But if we accept the authority of Christ we must accept the authority of the Bible as a whole. He testifies definitely and specifically to the divine authorship of the whole Bible.

We find His testimony as to the Old Testament in Mark 7:13. Here He calls the law of Moses the "Word of God." That of course covers only the first five books of the Old Testament, but in Luke 24:27 we read, "And beginning at Moses and all the prophets, he expounded unto them in all the scriptures the things concerning himself," and in the forty-fourth verse He says, "All things must be fulfilled, which were written in the law of Moses, and in the prophets, and in the psalms." More specifically still, in Matthew 5:18, Jesus says, "One jot or one tittle shall in no wise pass from the law, till all be fulfilled." So if we accept the authority of Christ we must accept the divine authority of the entire Old Testament.

Now, as to the New Testament. We find Christ's endorsement of it in John 14:26, "the Holy Ghost, whom the Father will send in my name, he shall teach you all things and bring all things to your remembrance, whatsoever I have said unto you." Here we see that not only was the teaching of the apostles to be fully inspired, but also their recollection of what Christ Himself taught. In the gospel we have, not the apostles' recollection of what He said, but the Holy Ghost's recollection, and the Spirit of God never forgets. In John 16:13,14, Christ said that the Holy Ghost should guide the apostles "into all truth." Therefore in the New Testament teaching we have the whole sphere of God's truth.

Second, from its fulfilled prophecies. There are two classes of prophecies in the Bible: first, the explicit, verbal prophecies; second, those of the types. In the first we have the definite prophecies concerning the Jews, the heathen nations, and the Messiah. Taking the prophecies regarding the Messiah as an illustration, look at Isaiah 53, Micah 5:2, Daniel 9:25-27. In these prophecies, written hundreds of years before the Messiah came, we have the most explicit statement as to the manner and place of His birth, His reception by men, how His life would end, His Resurrection, and His victory following His death. When made, these prophecies were exceedingly improbable, and seemingly impossible of fulfillment, but they were fulfilled to the very minutest detail of manner and place and time. How are we to account for it? Man could not have foreseen these improbable events—they lay hundreds of years ahead—but God could, and it is God who speaks through these men.

But the prophecies of the types are more remarkable still. Everything in the Old Testament—history, institutions, ceremonies—is prophetic. The high priesthood, the ordinary priesthood, the Levites, the prophets, priests, and kings, are all prophecies. In all these things, as we study them minutely and soberly in the light of the history of Jesus Christ and the church, we see, wrapped up in the ancient institutions ordained of God to meet an immediate purpose, prophecies of the death, atonement, and Resurrection of Christ, the day of Pentecost, and the entire history of the church. We see the profoundest Christian doctrines of the New Testament clearly foreshadowed in these institutions of the Old Testament. There is only one scientific way to account for them, namely, He who knows and prepares for the end from the beginning is the Author of that Book.

Third, from the unity of the Book. This is an old argument, but a very satisfactory one. The Bible consists, as you know, of sixty-six books, written by more than thirty different men; extending, in the period of its composition, over more than 1,500 years; written in four different languages, in many different countries, and by men on every plane of social life—from the herdman and fisherman and cheap politician, to the king on his throne—written under all sorts of circumstances. Yet in all this wonderful conglomeration we find an absolute unity of thought.

Suppose a vast building had been erected, the stones for which were brought from the quarries in Rutland, Vermont; Berea, Ohio; Kasota, Minnesota; and Middletown, Connecticut. Each stone was hewn into shape in the quarry from which it was brought. These stones were of all varieties of shape and size, cubical, rectangular, cylindrical, and so forth, but when they were brought together every stone fitted in its place, and when put together there rose before you a temple absolutely perfect. How would you account for it? You would say that back of these individual workers in the quarries was the mastermind of the architect who planned it all. So in this marvelous temple of God's truth which we call the Bible, we are forced to say that back of the human hands that wrought was the Mastermind that thought.

Fourth, from the immeasurable superiority of the teachings of the Bible to those of any other and all other books. It was very fashionable five or ten years ago to compare the teachings of the Bible with the teachings of Zoroaster, and Buddha, and Confucius...and a number of other heathen authors. The difference between the teachings of the Bible and those of these men is found in three points—first, the Bible has in it nothing but truth, while all the others have truth mixed with error. It is true Socrates taught how a philosopher ought to die; he also taught how a woman of the town ought to conduct her business. Second, the Bible contains all truth. There is no truth to be found anywhere on moral or spiritual subjects that you cannot find, in substance, within the covers of that Old Book. I have often, when speaking on this subject, asked anyone to bring me a single truth on moral or spiritual subjects which, on reflection, I could not find within the covers of this Book, and no one has ever been able to do it.

The third point of superiority is this: that the Bible contains more truth than all other books together. Get together from all literature of ancient and modern times all the beautiful thought you can...into one book, and even then you will not have a book that will take the place of this one Book. This is not a large book...and yet in this one little Book there is more truth than in all the books which man has produced in all the ages of his history. This is not man's book but God's Book.

Fifth, from the history of the Book, from its victory over attack. This Book has always been hated. No sooner was this Book given to the world than it met the hatred of men, and they tried to stamp it out. Celsus tried it by the brilliancy of his genius, Porphyry by the depth of his philosophy, but they failed. For eighteen centuries every engine of destruction that human science, philosophy, wit, reasoning, or brutality could bring to bear upon a book has been brought to bear upon that Book to stamp it out of the world; but it has a mightier hold on the world today than ever before. If that were man's book it would have been annihilated and forgotten hundreds of years ago.

Sixth, from the character of those who accept and those who reject the Book. Two things speak for the divinity of the Bible—the character of those who accept it, and equally, the character of those who reject it. I do not mean by that that every man who professes to believe the Book is better than every man who does not, but show me a man living an unselfish, devoted life, who, without reservation, has surrendered himself to do the will of God, and I will show you a man who believes the Bible to be God's Word. On the other hand, show me a man who rejects the divine authority of that Book, and I will show you a man living a life of greed, or lust, or spiritual pride, or self-will. Now, the people best acquainted with God say the Bible is His Book; those who are least acquainted with God say it is not. Which will you believe? The nearer men live to God, the more confident they are that the Bible is God's Word; the farther they get away from Him, the more confident they are that it is not. If a man should walk into a saloon and lay a Bible down on the bar, and order a drink, we should think there was a strange incongruity in his actions, but if he should lay a work on Colonel Ingersoll, or any infidel writing, on the bar, and order a drink, we would not feel that there was any incongruity.

Seventh, from the influence of the Book. There is more power in that little Book to save men, and purify, gladden, and beautify their lives, than in all other literature put together—more power to lift men up to God. I have in mind as I speak, a man who was the most complete victim of strong drink I ever knew . . . who had been stupefied and brutalized and demonized by the power of sin, and he was an infidel. At last, the light of God shone into his darkened heart, and by the power of that Book he has been transformed into one of the humblest, sweetest, noblest men I know today. What other book would have done that? What other book has the power to elevate not only individuals but communities and nations that this Book has?

Eighth, from the inexhaustible depth of the Book. Nothing has been added to it in 1,800 years, yet a man like Bunsen, or Neander, cannot exhaust it by the study of a lifetime. George Muller has read it through more than 100 times and says it is fresher every time he reads it. Could that be true of any other book? A book that man produces, man can exhaust, but all men together have not been able to get to the bottom of this Book. How are you going to account for it? Only in this way—that in this Book are hidden the infinite and inexhaustible treasures of the wisdom and knowledge of God.

Ninth, from the fact that as we grow in knowledge and holiness we grow toward the Bible. Every thoughtful person has, when he started out to study the Bible, found many things with which he did not agree, but as he went on studying and growing in likeness to God, the nearer he got to God, the

nearer he got to the Bible. The nearer and nearer we get to God's standpoint, the less and less becomes the disagreement between us and the
Bible. What is the inevitable mathematical conclusion? When we get
where God is, we and the Bible will meet. In other words, the Bible was
written from God's standpoint. Like almost all other young men, my
confidence became shaken, and I came to the fork in the road more than
forty times and followed my own reason, and in the outcome found
myself wrong and the Bible right every time. I trust that from this time
on I shall have sense enough to follow the teachings of the Bible,
whatever my own judgment may say.

Tenth, from the direct testimony of the Holy Spirit. We started with God
and shall end with God. We started with the testimony of the second Person of the Trinity and will close with that of the third Person of the Trinity. The Holy Spirit sets His seal in the soul of every believer to the divine
authority of the Bible. It is possible to get to a place where we need no
argument to prove that the Bible is God's Word. Christ says, "My sheep
know my voice," and God's children know His voice, and I know that
voice that speaks to me from the pages of that Book is the voice of my
Father.

You will sometimes meet a pious old lady who will tell you that she
knows that the Bible is God's Word, and when you ask her for a reason
for believing that it is God's Word she can give you none. She simply
says she knows it is God's Word. You say that is mere superstition. Not
at all. She is one of Christ's sheep and distinguishes her Shepherd's voice
from every other voice. John 7:17 tells you "If any man will to do his
will, he shall know of the doctrine, whether it be of God." Just surrender
your will to the will of God, and you will put yourself in such an attitude
toward God that when you read this Book you will recognize that the
voice that speaks to you from it is the voice of God.

Some time ago, when I was speaking, there was in the audience a
graduate of Oxford University who came to me and said, "I don't wish
to be discourteous, sir, but my experience contradicts everything you
have said." Stepping into another room, I had a pledge written out, running somewhat as follows:

> I believe there is an absolute difference between right and
> wrong, and I hereby take my stand upon the right, to follow it
> wherever it carries me. I promise to earnestly endeavor to find
> out what the truth is, and if I ever find that Jesus Christ is the
> Son of God, I promise to accept Him as my Saviour and confess
> Him before the world.

I handed the paper to the gentleman and asked him if he was willing
to sign it. He answered, "Certainly," and did sign it. I said to him,
"You don't know there is not a God, and you don't know that God

doesn't answer prayer. I know He does, but my knowledge cannot avail for you. Now you have promised to search earnestly for the truth. I want you to offer a prayer like this: "God, if there be any God and Thou dost answer prayer, show me whether Jesus Christ is the Son, and if He is I will accept Him as my Saviour and confess Him before the world." This he agreed to do. I further requested that he would take the Gospel of John and read in it every day, reading only a few verses at a time, every time asking God before he read to give him light. This he also agreed to do. A short time ago I met this gentleman again, and he said to me that he could not understand how he had ever listened to the reasoning which he had, that it seemed to him utterly foolish now. I replied that the Bible would explain it to him, that "the natural man receiveth not the things of the Spirit of God," but that now that he had put himself in the right attitude toward God and His truth everything had been made plain. That man, by putting himself into the right attitude toward God, got to a place where he received the direct testimony of the Holy Ghost that this Bible is God's Word. And anyone else can do the same.

F.B. Meyer
(1847—1929)

One of the greatly loved preachers of his day, Frederick Brotherton Meyer was a pastor, author, Bible teacher, and evangelist. He was born in London in 1847 and grew up in a Christian home. After attending Brighton College, he graduated from London University in 1869.

Meyer began pastoring in 1870, and in 1872 he went to Priory Street Baptist Chapel as pastor. There he met D.L. Moody, who made a lasting impression upon his life and taught him valuable spiritual lessons.

Nine years later, F.B. Meyer began pastoring what was to become a church at Melbourne Hall, where he preached weekly to overflow crowds. He went to Christ Church in Lambeth in 1895, with only 100 attending. Within two years he was preaching regularly to over 2,000. He remained there for fifteen years and then traveled to South Africa and the Far East on mission endeavors. He returned to England to pastor for several years before he died in 1929.

A distinct feature of F.B. Meyer's ministry was his outcry against the social evils of his day. Not only was he effective in the temperance movement, but he was also responsible for the closing of over 500 houses of prostitution. He also formed a prison aid society.

Meyer was (and continues to be) deeply respected and loved for his devotional approach in his preaching. He had great influence upon such giants of the faith as J. Wilbur Chapman and Charles H. Spurgeon. It was Spurgeon who said, "Meyer preaches as a man who has seen God face to face."

17

God Is Near
By F.B. Meyer

In the year that king Uzziah died I saw also the Lord sitting upon a throne, high and lifted up, and his train filled the temple. Above it stood the seraphims: each one had six wings; with twain he covered his face, and with twain he covered his feet, and with twain he did fly. And one cried unto another, and said, Holy, holy, holy, is the Lord of hosts: the whole earth is full of his glory. And the posts of the door moved at the voice of him that cried, and the house was filled with smoke. Then said I, Woe is me! for I am undone; because I am a man of unclean lips, and I dwell in the midst of a people of unclean lips: for mine eyes have seen the King, the Lord of hosts. Then flew one of the seraphims unto me, having a live coal in his hand, which he had taken with the tongs from off the altar: and he laid it upon my mouth, and said, Lo, this hath touched thy lips; and thine iniquity is taken away, and thy sin purged (Isa. 6:1-8).

One afternoon about four o'clock, Isaiah, who was then in early middle life, found himself one of a great crowd of worshipers slowly ascending the temple's steps. Together with them he passed the lower platform and still climbed until at last he stood at the summit, at the Beautiful Gate of the temple. Standing there, he little realized that that afternoon was to be the epochal moment of his life; but that afternoon was to introduce an altogether new element into his life work.

Standing there upon that highest step, in the direct line of vision lay, first, the altar upon which the afternoon sacrifice was to be made; beyond it a laver where the priests washed their feet; and beyond that the tall cedar doors that opened upon the Holy Place, which indeed would have unfolded presently, as to Zachariah in after days when he went to offer incense while the people stood without in prayer.

On either side stood probably two hundred and fifty Levites, with the instruments of David in their hands, prepared to sing the psalms which were so famous, and about which their Babylonian captors in after days said: "Sing us one of the songs of Zion."

As Isaiah stood there wrapped in thought, those who were nearest him had no idea what was transpiring; but he was swept away from all those sights and sounds, from the sun in mid sky, from the glistening marble of the temple, from the music of the Levite band, from all the crowds that pressed him on every side, and he beheld the sapphire throne of the King Himself. He heard the prayer or chant of the seraphim, and for a moment his whole soul was steeped in the rapture of that vision. But a moment after he was plunged in the profoundest contrition of soul as he contrasted himself with those who served God with sinless lips, and he cried: "Woe is me! for I am undone; because I am a man of unclean lips."

Now why was this? Partly because after the golden years of Uzziah's reign, in which money and splendor were corrupting the hearts of the people, it was necessary that the leaders at least, or many like Isaiah who stood in the forefront, should be lifted to a higher level. You must understand from the previous chapters of his book how the dwellers of Zion, the men and women of Jerusalem, and, indeed, all the people, were being corrupted by the sin, the fashion, the worldliness, and the money making of their time, and how needful it was, therefore, that God should raise a new standard amongst them by the hand of Isaiah, who stood closest to Him.

It may be that in this country at this time, the very prosperity of your land, the years of peace, the great influx of populations, and the increase of wealth have been subtly undermining the religious life of your people, so that some of your holy customs are being broken down. Perhaps family worship is no longer maintained as it was. The children are no longer trained, as once, in the habits of godliness. The high morale of your people, derived from your noble ancestry, may have been disintegrating while you devoted your energies in other directions than in wholehearted devotion to God. At such times it is God's habit to call around Himself His Isaiahs, His servants, those who stand nearest to Him, the members of His Church, and to lift them up to a new level of Christian living, that from that moment they may be the pivot on which a lever may work to lift the entire nation.

As I have traveled through your great country, in city after city, I have met with crowds of your fellow countrymen, especially your ministers, and I have been struck with the hunger which exists on every hand for deeper and intenser spiritual life. It appears to me as if God were calling upon the people of His own Church in the United States to stand up before Jesus Christ as their King, to learn from Him some deeper and mightier power than that which has been vibrating lately amongst them. Let us confidently look to Him for it.

But before you and I can become what we want to be, there must first be a humbling process. We must be laid low in the dust before God. Just in proportion as we are prepared to descend, will we ascend. Let us get down in the dust before Jesus Christ our Lord, and let each one of us become convicted, and cry: "Woe is me! for I am undone; because I am a man of unclean lips."

There is here a threefold conviction of personal unworthiness, of the nearness of God, and of the one method by which the heart of man can be pacified.

There is, first, the conviction of unworthiness: "Woe is me! for I am undone."

The sixth chapter, of course, follows the fifth. If you read the latter you will understand how earnestly Isaiah had been pursuing his prophetic work. This man, who of all Israel seemed to be the purest and sweetest, is the man that bows the lowest and is most convinced of sin. God's children need to learn that lesson too. He had done good work, but God saw that he could do better, and so convicted him of the comparative unworthiness of his past ministry. Thus it befell that the man by whom God had spoken through five chapters was a man who confessed to having unclean lips.

Now you may have a good record lying behind you. It may be that for five chapters of your life you have been ministering to people, to children, to the waifs and strays of your city, and you have been greatly owned. But God wants to teach you a better lesson, to make you more mightily powerful, to baptize you more with the Holy Ghost and with fire. Therefore He takes even you, true-hearted as you are, and brings you down into the place where the Holy Spirit will hold up your past life, and bid you review it until you, who have been looked up to by everyone as an example, and quoted as the most devoted and earnest of men, and idolized by many who have been moved by your eloquence, as you come beneath the light that shall fall upon you from the face of Jesus Christ, shall cry: "I am an undone man."

You will notice that this conviction was wrought through the vision of Jesus, and indeed that is the only vision that will really convince us of sin. We need to stand beneath the light that falls from His face. He is amongst us at this moment. He is passing through this assembly and looking down deep into your hearts; and as you look up into His face, do you not realize that there is a look of grief and sorrow there, because in your work there has been so much of yourself and so little of His love? Does He not reveal to you the poverty of your motive, the lowness of your aim, your greater thought of what men might consider of you than of what He might say? Let the light of the living Christ fall upon you now, the light of the coming Christ, the silvery light of the Second Advent, the light of the judgment-seat of Christ, the light of the Great White Throne; and as this falls upon your heart today, and you see what He wants you to be and what you are, you shall say: "I am undone."

There is another thought. Isaiah saw the worship of the blessed ones: "One cried to another."

I like to think of that. It was as if one of them cried, "Your strains are not lifted high enough; higher, brothers, higher!" And he cried across the intervening space to the seraphim opposite, and bade them rise to a higher note, till the chorus swelled and rose and broke. I have heard a bird in the spring morning cry to all the songsters of the glade till the whole woodland has rung again. Sometimes in our prayer meeting an earnest man has shaken the very gates of heaven and has stirred the whole meeting. That is what we want. And as I tell you of a richer, fuller life, a life more abundant than many of you know, may you be convicted of the need of a new anointing, of a fresh application to the Son of God for the touch of fire. May ours be the seraph's reverence, with the veiled face; ours his modesty, with the veiled form; ours his balance of one-third obedience to two-thirds of contemplation. Then perhaps our cry may awaken similar results to his, and we shall cry, "Undone."

Next, the conviction that God is near. It is said the whole earth is full of God's glory. You and I would be prepared to admit that the glory of God shines in the spray above Niagara, or where the morning that is seen upon the Matterhorn and the evening glow upon the Jungfrau, or where the sun rises and sets upon the broad bosom of the Atlantic, or where the wake of the ships stirs the phosphorescence of the Mediterranean at night. But to be told that the whole earth is full of the glory of God, that startles us.

I know a place in London where a woman in a drunken frenzy put her child upon a hot iron bar; where a man beat to death his little crippled boy whose agonizing cries were heard at night. I should not have thought that the glory of God was there. But the seraphim say the whole earth is full of the glory of God. We are reminded of what Elizabeth Barrett Browning says:

Earth's crammed with Heaven,
And every common bush aflame with God,
But only he that sees takes off his shoes.

One day in London I was sitting in a dark omnibus. A man came in to examine our tickets, and I thought to myself, You will never be able to tell whether they have been punctured aright. As I watched, curious to notice, he touched a little spring on his breast, and in a tiny globe of glass a beautiful glow of electric light shone out. Manifestly the man could see anywhere, because he carried the light with which he saw. So we must understand that when the heart is full of God, you will find God anywhere and everywhere, as the miner carries the candle in his cap through the dark cavity of the earth, and lights his steps.

Oh, men and women, that is what we may rely on here! It is not that I can do anything, but God, heaven, eternity are near. It is not my words that shall achieve the result, but the Spirit of God, who is as much in this assembly as He was in the upper room upon the day of Pentecost. In the gentle movement of the trees of the forest, can you not hear the stepping of God's feet? And can you not detect the movement of God's Spirit at this moment upon your hearts? Does not this quiet hush, this eagerness, indicate the presence of the skirts of the Eternal as they fall upon us? The whole earth is full of God—all time, all space—and it is because God is here, because there is as much of the Holy Ghost in this place as ever there was in the upper room on the day of Pentecost, because the forces of God are unexhausted, because the mighty river of God which is full of water is flowing through this place, that you and I are certain of blessing.

I believe that if some people had been in that very upper room itself when the Holy Ghost descended, being purblind, blinded by prejudice and passion and worldliness, they would have heard only a noise, they would have perceived no flame. If they had been with John on Patmos, they might have heard the break of the waves upon the rocks, but they never would have heard the harping of the angels. On the other hand, if Peter or John were sitting where you are now, their faces would be lighted up with supernatural light, and they would say: "Did you not see? Did you not hear? God is here. The great God has come down from the heavens to bless these people. They have asked for it. They have claimed it. God has promised, and He has come."

"Where two or three are met, I am." The Spirit of God is here and is working amongst us also, as He hath done in other times and places. He first convicts us of a cold heart, of our deep need, and of our utter undoneness, and then He comes Himself and says: "I am here."

The last conviction is the one need of a penitent sinner. We read that when Isaiah cried, one of the seraphim immediately went for the live coal.

Now, mark this: the angel was not told to go, but he knew just what to do. The fact is, the angels have gone so often for the live coal that whenever they hear a sinner crying that he is undone, they go for it; they do not need to be told. It is as if a druggist's boy were so in the habit of getting the same medicine for the same symptoms that when the patient comes to the door, he knows just what medicine to seek, without going to the doctor to get advice.

The seraph took the live coal from off the altar, and that stood for blood and fire, the two things we want today. We want blood and fire.

Blood! Can you not hear the hiss of the blood of the lamb as it flows gurgling around that coal? As he takes it up with his tongs of gold and bears it to the prophet's lips, it takes the atoning blood with it. We want that first. I call upon all of you to claim that first—the blood! Nothing else will do. "This is he that came by water and blood; not by water only, but by water and blood." You and I need blood first. Let us then betake ourselves to our compassionate Lord, and seek from Him that forgiveness which He purchased on the cross. Do you want it? Are you quite satisfied? Do you look upon your past with perfect complacency? Is there nothing to regret? Are there no sins to put away?

It is natural to respond that you are undone. Then let us begin by opening our whole nature to Christ, and believe that His blood now cleanseth from all sin. Let us dare to believe that directly we turn to that blood, and claim the forgiveness which is based on it, the whole of our past sin is gone, blotted out, lost to view; and if we remind God about it, He will say: "My child, you need not tell me about it. I have forgotten it. It is as though it had never been."

Next we need the fire, the live coal.

Christmas Evans tells us in his diary that one Sunday afternoon he was traveling a very lonely road to attend an appointment in a village the other side of the slope, and he was convicted of a cold heart. He says: "I tethered my horse and went to a sequestered spot, where I walked to and fro in an agony as I reviewed my life. I waited three hours before God, broken with sorrow, until there stole over me a sweet sense of His forgiving love. I received from God a new baptism of the Holy Ghost. As the sun was westering, I went back to the road, found my horse, mounted it, and went to my appointment. On the following day I preached with such new power to a vast concourse of people gathered on the hillside that a revival broke out that day and spread through the whole principality."

Let us close with that. Convicted of a cold heart! Convicted of a worldly life! Convicted of self-seeking and pride! Convicted of having come short of God's glory! Then forgiveness. Then the baptism of fire and power.

God grant that the live coal, which has never lost its glow since the Day of Pentecost, may come to every heart, to every mouth, to every life; and that this day a fire shall begin to burn in every mission, in every Sunday school, in every church.

Billy Sunday
(1862—1935)

William Ashley (Billy) Sunday was converted from pro baseball to Christ at twenty-three but carried his athletic ability into the pulpit. Born in Ames, Iowa, in 1862, he lost his father to the Civil War and lived with his grandparents until age nine when he was taken to live in an orphanage. A life of hard work paid off in athletic prowess that brought him a contract with the Chicago White Stockings in 1883. His early success in baseball was diluted by strong drink; however, a few years later (1886) he was converted at the Pacific Garden Mission in Chicago and became actively involved in Christian work.

Sunday turned down a baseball contract in 1891, to join the staff of the YMCA. Two years later he became assistant to Evangelist J. Wilbur Chapman, invaluable preparation for what God had in store. When Chapman began pastoring, Sunday started his own evangelistic work and in his first campaign 200 people were saved in one week. World War I saw Billy Sunday winning hundreds of men in army camps. Thereafter he held meetings in every state, preaching over 75 times a month and 20,000 sermons before his death in 1935.

Billy Sunday was one of the most unusual evangelists of his day. He walked, ran, or jumped across the platform as he preached, sometimes breaking chairs. His controversial style brought criticism but won the admiration of millions. He attacked public evils, particularly the liquor industry and was considered the most influential person in bringing about the prohibition legislation after World War I. The following sermon was his most famous and is a scathing indictment of the liquor traffic. Sunday preached this sermon weekly for twenty years. It is estimated that over one million people were converted under his ministry.

18

Get on the Water Wagon
By Billy Sunday

Who hath woe? Who hath sorrow? Who hath contentions? Who hath babbling? Who hath wounds without cause? Who hath redness of eyes? They that tarry long at the wine; they that go to seek mixed wine. Look not thou upon the wine when it is red, when it giveth his colour in the cup, when it moveth itself aright. At the last it biteth like a serpent, and stingeth like an adder (Prov. 23:29-32).

I am the sworn, eternal, uncompromising enemy of the liquor traffic. I ask no quarter and I give none. I have drawn the sword in defense of God, home, wife, children, and native land, and I will never sheathe it until the undertaker pumps me full of embalming fluid; and if my wife is alive, I think I shall call her to my bedside and say, "Nell, when I am dead, send for the butcher and skin me, and have my hide tanned and made into drum heads and hire men to go up and down the land and beat the drums and say, 'My husband, "Bill" Sunday, still lives and gives the whiskey gang a run for its money.' "

Archbishop Ireland said, "I find social crime and ask what caused it? They say, 'Drink!' I find poverty. What caused it? 'Drink!' I find families broken up and ask what caused it; they tell me, 'Drink!' I find men behind prison bars and ask, 'What put you here?' They say, 'Drink!' I stand by the scaffold and ask, 'What made you a murderer?' They cry, 'Drink!' 'Drink!'

"If God would place in my hand a wand with which to dispel the evils of intemperance, I would strike at the door of every brewery, and every distillery, and every saloon until the accursed traffic was driven from the land."

The saloon is the sum of all villainies. It is worse than war, worse than pestilence, worse than famine. It is the crime of crimes. It is the mother of sins. It is the appalling source of misery, pauperism, and crime. It is the source of three-fourths of all the crime; thus it is the source of three-fourths of all the taxation necessary to prosecute the criminals and care for them after they are in prison. To license such an incarnate fiend of hell is one of the blackest spots on the American government.

What is this traffic in rum? "The Devil in solution," said Sir Wilfred Lawson, and he was right. "Distilled damnation," said Robert Hall, and he was right. "An artist in human slaughter," said Lord Chesterfield, and he was right. "Prisoners' General driving men to Hell," said Wesley, and he was right. "More destructive than war, pestilence, and famine," said Gladstone, and he was right. "A cancer in human society, eating out its vitals and threatening its destruction," said Abraham Lincoln; he was right.

"The most ruinous and degrading of all human pursuits," said William McKinley; he was right. "The most criminal and artistic method of assassination ever invented by the bravos of any age or nation," said Ruskin; he was right. "The most prolific hotbeds of anarchy, vile politics, profane ribaldry, and unspeakable sensuality," said Charles Parkhurst; he was right. "A public, permanent agency of degradation," said Cardinal Manning; he was right.

"A business that tends to lawlessness on the part of those who conduct it and criminality on the part of those that patronize it," said Theodore Roosevelt; he was right. "A business that tends to produce idleness, disease, pauperism, and crime," said the United States Supreme Court, and it was right.

Lord Chief Justice Alverstone, at the International Congress on Alcoholism, said, "After forty years at the bar and ten years as a judge, I have no hesitancy in saying that 90 percent of the crime is caused by strong drink."

Who foots the bills? The landlord who loses his rent; the baker, butcher, grocer, coal man, dry goods merchant, whose goods the drunkard needs for himself and family, but cannot buy; the charitable people, who pity the children of drunkards, and go down in their pockets to keep them from starving; the taxpayers who are taxed to support the jails, penitentiaries, hospitals, alms houses, reformatories, that this cursed business keeps filled.

Who makes the money? The brewers, distillers, saloon-keepers, who are privileged to fill the land with poverty, wretchedness, madness, crime, disease, damnation, and death, authorized by the sovereign right of the people, who vote for this infamous business.

I could build 1,570,250 houses for the working people and pay $2,000 for each house with the money we spend for booze in one year. If made into $20 gold pieces and piled one on top of the other, they would make a column 136 miles high. If made into silver dollars and laid side by side, they would reach 3,615 miles. If made into dimes it would be long enough to wrap a silver belt ten times around the world. In ten years I could build a silver automobile road to the moon.

When cities get out boom editions, how many call attention to the fact that it is saloon dominated? There is no place outside the brothel where the atmosphere is so saturated; there is no place where you can meet the filthiest characters. It is the stem around which clusters most of the infamies. The saloon unfits its owners, bartenders, and patrons for the duties of citizenship. It is usually found in political alliance with keepers and supporters of gambling dives. Gambling houses and houses of prostitution are usually so closely allied with the saloon, that when the saloon is driven out, they go.

The saloon is usually found in partnership with the foes of good government. It supports the boodle alderman, the corrupt lawmaker, the political boss and machine. It asks only to be let alone in its law-nullifying, vice, and crime-producing work. I have never known of a movement for good government that was not opposed by the saloon. If you believe in better civic conditions, if you believe in a great and better city, if you believe in men going home sober, if you believe in men going to heaven instead of hell, then down with the saloon.

People are fit for liberty. The wrath of an outraged public will never be quenched until the putrid corpse of the saloon is hanging from the gibbet of shame; "praise God from whom all blessings flow."

"But," says the whiskey man, "if we haven't saloons, we will lose the trade of the farmers; they will not come to town to trade, if there are no saloons." I say you lie, and by that statement you insult one of the best classes of men on earth.

The argument is often used that if you close the saloons, you thereby close breweries and distilleries and that will bring on a panic, for it will cut off the farmer's market for his corn, and that the brewer, who furnishes him a market for his corn, is his benefactor. Let us see.

A farmer brings to the brewer a bushel of corn. He finds a market for it. He gets fifty cents and goes his way, with the statement of the brewer ringing in his ears that the brewer is the benefactor. But you haven't gotten all the factors in the problem, Mr. Brewer, and you cannot get a correct solution of a problem without all the factors of a problem. You take the farmer's bushel of corn, brewer or distiller, and you brew and distill from it four and one-half gallons of spirits—thirty-six pints. I am not going to trace the thirty-six. It would take too long. But I want to trace three of them, and I will give you no imaginary stories plucked from the brain of an excited orator. I will take instances from the judicial pages of the Supreme Court and the circuit court judges' reports in Indiana and in Illinois to make my case.

A few years ago in the city of Chicago, a young man of good parents and good character, one Sunday crossed the street and entered a saloon, open against the law. He found there boon companions. There was laughter, song and jest, and much drinking. After awhile, drunk, insanely drunk, his money gone, he was kicked into the street. He found his way across to his mother's home. He importuned her for money to buy more drink. She refused him. He seized from the sideboard a revolver and ran out into the street with the expressed determination of entering the saloon and getting more drink, money or no money. His fond mother followed him into the street. She put her hand upon him in loving restraint. He struck it from him in anger and then his sister came and added her entreaty in vain. And then a neighbor, whom he knew, trusted, and respected, came and put his hand on him in gentleness and friendly kindness; but in an insanity of drunken rage, the young man raised the revolver and shot his friend dead in his own blood upon the street. There was a trial; he was found guilty of murder. He was sentenced to life imprisonment, and when the mother heard the verdict, she threw up her hands and fell in a swoon. In three hours she was dead.

In the streets of Freeport, Illinois, a young man of good family became involved in a controversy with a lewd woman of the town. He went in a drunken frenzy to his father's home, armed himself with a deadly weapon, and set forth in the city in search of the woman with whom he had quarreled. The first person he met in the public square in the city was one of the most refined and cultured women of Freeport. She carried in her arms her babe, but this young man in his drunken insanity mistook her for the woman he sought and shot her dead on the streets with her babe in her arms. He was tried and Judge Ferand, in sentencing him to life imprisonment, said: "You are the seventh man in two years to be sentenced for murder while intoxicated."

In the city of Anderson, you remember the tragedy in the Blake home. A young man came home intoxicated, demanding money of his mother. She refused it. He seized from the wood box a hatchet and killed his mother, and then robbed her. You remember he fled. The officers of the law pursued him, brought him back. An indictment was read to him, charging him with the murder of the mother who had gone down into the valley of the shadow of death to give him life, of her who had looked down into his blue eyes and thanked God for his life. And he said, "I am guilty, I did it all." And Judge McClure sentenced him to life imprisonment.

Now I have followed probably three of the thirty-six pints of the farmer's product of a bushel of corn and the three of them have struck down seven lives—the three boys who committed the murders, the three persons who were killed, and the little mother who died of a broken heart.

And now, I want to know, my farmer friend, if this has been a good commercial transaction for you. You sold a bushel of corn; you found a market; you got fifty cents; but a fraction of this product struck down seven lives, all of whom would have been consumers of your products for their life expectancy. And do you mean to say that is a good economic transaction to you? That disposes of the market question until it is answered; let no man argue further.

If ever there was a jubilee in hell it was when lager beer was invented.

I tell you, gentlemen, the American home is the dearest heritage of the people, for the people, and by the people, and when a man can go from home in the morning with the kisses of wife and children on his lips, and come back at night to a happy home, that man is a better man. Whatever takes away the comforts of home, whatever degrades that man or woman, whatever invades the sanctity of the home, is the deadliest foe to the home, to church, to state, and school—and the saloon is the deadliest foe to the home, the church, and the state on top of God Almighty's dirt. And if all the combined forces of hell should assemble in conclave, and with them all the men on earth that hate and despise God, and purity and virtue—if all the scum of the earth could mingle with the denizens of hell to try to think of the deadliest institutions to home, to church, and state, I tell you, sir, the combined hellish intelligence could not conceive of or bring forth an institution that could touch the hem of the garment of the open licensed saloon to damn the home and manhood and womanhood and business, and every other good thing on God's earth.

There is no law, divine or human, that the saloon respects. Lincoln said, "If slavery is not wrong, nothing is wrong." I say if the saloon, with its train of disease, crime, and misery is not wrong, then nothing on earth is wrong. If the fight is to be won we need men—men that will fight—the church, Catholic and Protestant, must fight it or run away, and thank God she will not run away, but fight to the last ditch.

The saloon comes as near being a rathole for a wage earner to dump his wages in as anything you can find. The only interest it pays is red eyes, foul breath, and the loss of your health. You go in with money, and you come out with empty pockets. You go in with character, and you come out ruined. You go in with a good position, and you lose it. You lose your position in the bank, or in the cab of the locomotive. And the saloon pays nothing back but disease and damnation and gives an extra dividend in delirium tremens and a free pass to hell. And then it will let your wife be buried in the potter's field, and your children go to the asylum. And yet you walk out and say that the saloon is a good institution, when it is the dirtiest thing on earth. It hasn't one leg to stand on and has nothing to commend it to a decent man or woman.

It is an infidel. It has no faith in God; has no religion. It would close every church in the land. It would hang its beer signs on the abandoned altars. It respects the thief and it esteems the blasphemer. It fills the prisons and the penitentiaries. It despises heaven, hates love, scorns virtue. It tempts the passions. Its music is the song of a siren. Its sermons are a collection of lewd, vile stories. It wraps a mantle about the hope of this world and that to come. Its tables are full of the vilest literature. It is the moral clearing house for rot and damnation and poverty and insanity.

The saloon is a liar. It promises good cheer and sends sorrow. It promises health and causes disease. It promises prosperity and sends adversity. It promises happiness and sends misery. Yes, it sends the husband home with a lie on his lips to his wife; and the boy home with a lie on his lips to his mother; and it causes the employee to lie to his employer. It degrades. It is God's worst enemy and the Devil's best friend. Seventy-five percent of impurity comes from the grogshop. It spares neither youth nor old age. It is waiting with a dirty blanket for the baby to crawl into this world. It lies in wait for the unborn.

One hears a good deal about what is called "personal liberty." These are fine, large, mouth-filling words and they certainly do sound first-rate; but when you get right down and analyze them they mean just about this: "Personal liberty" is for the man who, if he has the inclination and the price, can stand up to a bar and fill his hide so full of red liquor that he is transformed for the time into an irresponsible, dangerous, evil-smelling brute. But "personal liberty" is not for his patient, long-suffering wife who has to endure with what fortitude she may his blows and curses; nor is it for his children who, if they escape his insane rage, are yet robbed of every known joy and privilege of childhood, and too often grow up neglected, uncared for, and vicious as the result of their surroundings and the example before them. "Personal liberty" is not for the sober, industrious citizen who, from the proceeds of honest toil and orderly living, has to pay, willingly or not, the tax bills which pile up as the direct result of drunkenness, disorder, and poverty, the items of which are written in the records of every police court and poorhouse in the land; nor is "personal liberty" for the good woman who goes abroad in the town only at the risk of being shot down by some drink-crazed creature. This rant about "personal liberty" as an argument has no leg to stand upon.

Listen! Here is an extract from the *Saturday Evening Post,* taken from a paper read by a brewer. You will say that a man didn't say it: "It ap-

pears from these facts that the success of our business lies in the creation
of appetite among the boys. Men who have formed the habit scarcely
ever reform, but they, like others, will die, and unless there are recruits
made to take their places, our coffers will be empty, and I recommend to
you that money spent in the creation of appetite will return in dollars to
your tills after the habit is formed."

I feel like an old fellow in Tennessee who made his living by catching
rattlesnakes. He caught one with fourteen rattles and put it in a box with
a glass top. One day when he was sawing wood his little five-year-old boy,
Jim, took the lid off and the rattler wriggled out and struck him in the
cheek. He ran to his father and said, "The rattler has bit me." The
father ran and chopped the rattler to pieces, and with his jackknife he cut
a chunk from the boy's cheek and then sucked and sucked at the wound
to draw out the poison. He looked at little Jim, watched the pupils of his
eyes dilate and watched him swell to three times his normal size, watched
his lips become parched and cracked, and his eyes roll, and little Jim
gasped and died.

The father took him in his arms, carried him over by the side of the
rattler, got on his knees and said, "Oh, God, I would not give little Jim
for all the rattlers that ever crawled over the Blue Ridge Mountains."

And I would not give one boy for all the money you get from the hell-
soaked liquor business or from every brewery and distillery this side of
hell.

Listen! In a northwest city a preacher sat at his breakfast table one
Sunday morning. The doorbell rang. He answered it, and there stood a
little boy twelve years of age. He was on crutches, right leg off at the
knee, shivering, and he said, "Please sir, will you come up to the jail and
talk and pray with Papa. He murdered mamma. Papa was good and
kind, but whiskey did it and I have to support my three little sisters. I sell
newspapers and black boots. Will you go up and talk and pray with
Papa? And will you come home and be with us when they bring him
back? The Governor says we can have his body after they hang him."

The preacher hurried to the jail and talked and prayed with the man.
The man had no knowledge of what he had done. He said, "I don't
blame the law, but it breaks my heart to think that my children must be
left in a cold and heartless world. Oh, sir, whiskey, whiskey did it."

The preacher was at the little hut when up drove the undertaker's
wagon and they carried out the pine coffin. They led the little boy up to
the coffin; he leaned over and kissed his father and sobbed, and he said to
his sisters, "Come on, sisters, kiss Papa's cheeks before they grow cold."
And the little, hungry, ragged, whiskey orphans hurried to the coffin,
shrieking in agony. Police, whose hearts were adamant, buried their
faces in their hands and rushed from the house, and the preacher fell on

his knees and lifted his clenched fist and tear-stained face and took an oath before God, and before the whiskey orphans, that he would fight the cussed business until the undertaker carried him out in his coffin.

You men now have a chance to show your manhood. In the name of your pure mother, in the name of your manhood, in the name of your wife and the pure, innocent children that climb up in your lap and put their arms around your neck, in the name of all that is good and noble, fight the curse.

J. Gresham Machen
(1881—1937)

This great defender of the faith was born July 28, 1881, to godly parents in Baltimore, Maryland. Displaying outstanding intellectual skills as a young man, Machen entered Johns Hopkins University in 1898 and graduated first in his class. After completing graduate study at Princeton in 1905, he went to Germany and attended the Universities of Marburg and Goettingen.

In 1906 he returned to Princeton to teach. He was ordained as a Presbyterian minister in 1914 and served as professor of New Testament literature and exegesis at Princeton Theological Seminary until 1929.

During his tenure at Princeton Machen grew concerned over increasing modernism and compromise at the school. He became a staunch defender of conservative theology and wrote a brilliant treatise in 1923 entitled *Christianity and Liberalism.* When the situation at Princeton worsened, and was finally seen to be a hopeless battle, Machen withdrew from the school. With the help of men such as Robert Dick Wilson and O.T. Allis, he founded Westminster Theological Seminary in 1929. He later formed the Independent Board for Presbyterian Foreign Missions in June 1933.

When Machen's license was revoked by the Presbyterian Church in the USA, he and several others founded the Orthodox Presbyterian Church. Six months later, in 1937, Machen died of pneumonia while on a preaching engagement in North Dakota.

J. Gresham Machen is remembered as an outstanding conservative theologian and apologist. He took a militant stand for sound doctrine in such books as *The Christian Faith in the Modern World* and *The Virgin Birth of Christ.* He was also a profound Greek scholar; his *New Testament Greek for Beginners* is still widely used in seminaries throughout the country. The following sermon by Machen was his last address at Princeton before he left to begin Westminster Theological Seminary.

19

The Good Fight of Faith
By J. Gresham Machen

And the peace of God, which passeth all understanding, shall keep your hearts and minds through Christ Jesus (Phil. 4:7).
Fight the good fight of faith (1 Tim. 6:12a).

The Apostle Paul was a great fighter. His fighting was partly against external enemies—against hardships of all kinds. Five times he was scourged by the Jews, three times by the Romans; he suffered shipwreck four times; he was in perils of waters, in perils of robbers, in perils by his own countrymen, in perils by the heathen, in perils in the city, in perils in the wilderness, in perils in the sea, in perils among false brethren. And finally he came to the logical end of such a life, by the headsman's axe. It was hardly a peaceful life but was rather a life of wild adventure. Lindbergh, I suppose, got a thrill when he hopped off to Paris, and people are in search of thrills today; but if you wanted a really unbroken succession of thrills, I think you could hardly do better than to try knocking around the Roman Empire of the first century with the apostle Paul, engaged in the unpopular business of turning the world upside down.

But these physical hardships were not the chief battle in which Paul was engaged. Far more trying was the battle he fought against enemies in his own camp. Everywhere his rear was threatened by an all-engulfing paganism or by a perverted Judaism that had missed the real purpose of the Old Testament law. Read the Epistles with care and you see Paul always in conflict. At one time he fights paganism in life, the notion that all kinds of conduct are lawful to the Christian man, a philosophy that makes Christian liberty a mere aid to pagan license. At another time, he fights the effort of human pride to substitute man's merit as the means of salvation for divine grace; he fights the subtle propaganda of the

188

Judaizers with its misleading appeal to the Word of God. Everywhere we see the great apostle in conflict for the preservation of the church. It is as though a mighty flood were seeking to engulf the church's life; dam the break at one point in the levee, and another break appears somewhere else. Everywhere paganism was seeping through; not for one moment did Paul have peace; always he was called upon to fight.

Fortunately, he was a true fighter; and by God's grace he not only fought, but he won. At first sight, indeed, he might have seemed to have lost. The lofty doctrine of divine grace, the center and core of the gospel that Paul preached, did not always dominate the mind and heart of the subsequent church. The Epistles which Paul struck forth in conflict with the opponents in his own day remained in the New Testament as a perennial source of life for the people of God. Augustine, on the basis of the Epistles, set forth the Pauline doctrine of sin and grace; and then, after centuries of compromise with the natural man, the Reformation rediscovered the great liberating Pauline doctrine of justification by faith. So it has always been with Paul. Just when he seems to be defeated, his greatest triumphs, by God's grace, are in store.

The human instruments, however, which God uses in those triumphs are no pacifists—but great fighters like Paul himself. Little affinity for the great apostle has the whole tribe of the considerers of consequences, the whole tribe of the compromisers ancient and modern. The real companions of Paul are the great heroes of the faith. But who are those heroes? Are they not true fighters, one and all? Tertullian fought a mighty battle against Marcion; Athanasius fought against the Arians; Augustine fought against Pelagius; and as for Luther, he fought a brave battle against kings and princes and popes for the liberty of the people of God. Luther was a great fighter; and we love him for it. So was Calvin; so were John Knox and all the rest. It is impossible to be a true soldier of Jesus Christ and not fight.

God grant that you—students in this seminary—may be fighters, too! Probably you have your battles even now: you have to contend against sins gross or sins refined; you have, many of you, I know very well, a mighty battle on your hands against doubt and despair. Do not think it strange if you fall thus into diverse temptations. The Christian life is a warfare after all. John Bunyan rightly set it forth under the allegory of a Holy War; and when he set it forth, in his greater book, under the figure of a pilgrimage, the pilgrimage, too, was full of battles. There are, indeed, places of refreshment on the Christian way; the House Beautiful was provided by the King at the top of the Hill Difficulty, for the entertainment of pilgrims, and from the Delectable Mountains could sometimes be discerned the shining towers of the City of God. But just after the descent from the House Beautiful, there was the battle with Apollyon and the Valley of Humiliation, and later came the Valley of the Shadow of Death. Yes, the Christian faces a mighty conflict in this world. Pray God that in the conflict you may be true men, good soldiers of Jesus Christ, not willing to compromise with your great enemy, not easily cast down, and seeking ever the renewing of your strength in the Word and sacraments and prayer!

You will have a battle, too, when you go forth as ministers into the church. The church is now in a period of deadly conflict. The redemptive religion known as Christianity is contending, in our own church and in all the larger churches of the world, against a totally alien type of religion. As always, the enemy conceals his most dangerous assaults under pious phrases and half truths. Increasingly it is becoming necessary for a man to decide whether he is going to stand or not to stand for the Lord Jesus Christ as He is presented to us in the Word of God.

If you decide to stand for Christ, you will not have an easy life in the ministry. Of course, you may try to evade the conflict. All men will speak well of you if, after preaching no matter how unpopular a gospel on Sunday, you will only vote against that gospel in the councils of the church the next day; you will graciously be permitted to believe in supernatural Christianity all you please if you will only act as though you did not believe in it, if you will only make common cause with its opponents. Such is the program that will win the favor of the church. A man may believe what he pleases, provided he does not believe anything strongly enough to risk his life on it and fight for it. "Tolerance" is the great word. Always the gospel would have been received with favor by the world if it had been presented merely as one way of salvation; the offense came because it was presented as the only way, and because it made relentless war upon all other ways. God save us, then, from this "tolerance" of which we hear so much. God deliver us from the sin of making common cause with those who deny or ignore the blessed gospel of Jesus Christ! God save us from the deadly guilt of consenting to the presence as our representatives in the church of those who lead Christ's little ones astray; God make us, whatever else we are, just faithful messengers, who present, without fear or favor, not our word, but the Word of God.

But if you are such messengers, you will have the opposition, not only of the world, but increasingly, I fear, of the church. I cannot tell you that your sacrifice will be light. No doubt it would be noble to care nothing whatever about the judgment of our fellowmen. But to such nobility I confess that I for my part have not quite attained, and I cannot expect you to have attained to it. I confess that academic preferments, easy access to great libraries, the society of cultured people, and in general the thousand advantages that come from being regarded as respectable people in a respectable world—I confess that these things seem to me to be in themselves good and desirable things. Yet the servant of Jesus Christ, to an increasing extent, is being obliged to give them up. Certainly, in making that sacrifice we do not complain; for we have something with which all that we have lost is not worthy to be compared. Still, it can hardly be said that any unworthy motives of self-interest can lead us to adopt a course which brings us nothing but reproach. Where, then, shall we find a sufficient motive for such a course as that; where shall we find courage to stand against the whole current of the age; where shall we find courage for this fight of faith? I do not think that we shall obtain courage by any mere lust of conflict. In this Christian conflict I do not think we can be good fighters simply by being resolved to fight. For this battle is a battle of love; and nothing ruins a man's service in it so much as a spirit of hate.

No, if we want to learn the secret of this warfare, we shall have to look deeper; and we can hardly do better than turn again to that great fighter, the apostle Paul. What was the secret of his power in the mighty conflict; how did he learn to fight?

The answer is paradoxical; but it is very simple. Paul was a great fighter because he was at peace. He who said, "Fight the good fight of faith," spoke also of "the peace of God which passeth all understanding"; and in that peace the sinews of his war were found. He fought against the enemies that were without because he was at peace within; there was an inner sanctuary in his life that no enemy could disturb. There, my friends, is the great central truth. You cannot fight successfully with beasts, as Paul did at Ephesus; you cannot fight successfully against evil men, or against the Devil and his spiritual powers of wickedness in high places, unless when you fight against those enemies there is One with whom you are at peace.

But if you are at peace with that One, then you can care little what men may do. You can say with the apostles, "We must obey God rather than men"; you can say with Luther: "Here I stand, I cannot do otherwise, God help me. Amen"; you can say with Elisha, "they that be with us are more than they that be with them"; you can say with Paul: "It is God that justifieth, who is he that condemneth?" Without that peace of God in your hearts, you will strike little terror into the enemies of the gospel of Christ. You may amass mighty resources for the conflict; you may be great masters of ecclesiastical strategy; you may be very clever, and very zealous too; but I fear that it will be of little avail. There may be a tremendous din; but when the din is over, the Lord's enemies will be in possession of the field. No, there is no other way to be a really good fighter. You cannot fight God's battle against God's enemies unless you are at peace with Him.

But how shall you be at peace with Him? Many ways have been tried. How pathetic is the age-long effort of sinful man to become right with God: sacrifice, lacerations, almsgiving, morality, penance, confession! But alas, it is all of no avail. Still there is that same awful gulf. The real trouble remains; the burden is still on the back. How then shall peace be obtained?

My friends, it cannot be attained by anything in us. Oh, that that truth could be written in the hearts of every one of you! Oh, that it could be written in letters of flame for all the world to read! Peace with God cannot be attained by any act or any mere experience of man; it cannot be attained by good works, neither can it be attained by confession of sin, neither can it be attained by any psychological results of an act of faith. We can never be at peace with God unless God first be at peace with us. Peace cannot be attained for man by the great modern method of dragging God down to man's level; peace cannot be attained by denying that right is right and wrong is wrong; peace can nowhere be attained if the awful justice of God stand not forever sure.

How then can we sinners stand before that throne? How can there be peace for us in the presence of the justice of God? How can He be just and yet justify the ungodly? There is one answer to these questions. It is not our answer. Our wisdom could never have discovered it. It is God's answer. It is found in the story of the Cross. We deserved eternal death because of sin; the eternal Son of God, because He loved us, and because He was sent by the Father who loved us too, died in our stead, for our sins, upon the cross. That message is despised today; upon it the visible church as well as the world pours out the vials of its scorn, or else does it even less honor by paying it lip-service and then passing it by. The Cross remains foolishness to the world, men turn coldly away, and our preaching seems but vain. And then comes the wonder of wonders! The hour comes for some poor soul, even through the simplest and poorest preaching; the message is honored, not the messenger; there comes a flash of light into the soul, and all is as clear as day. "He loved me and gave himself for me," says the sinner at last, as he contemplates the Savior upon the cross. The burden of sin falls from the back, and a soul enters into the peace of God.

Have you yourselves that peace, my friends? If you have, you will not be deceived by the propaganda of any disloyal church. If you have the peace of God in your hearts, you will never shrink from controversy; you will never be afraid to contend earnestly for the faith. Talk of peace in the present deadly peril of the church, and you show, unless you be strangely ignorant of the conditions that exist, that you have little inkling of the true peace of God. Those who have been at the foot of the Cross will not be afraid to go forth under the banner of the Cross.

I know that it is hard to live on the heights of Christian experience. We have had flashes of the true meaning of the Cross of Christ; but then come long dull days. What shall we do in those dull times? Shall we cease to witness for Christ; shall we make common cause, in those dull days, with those who would destroy the corporate witness of the church? Perhaps we may be tempted to do so. When there are such enemies in our own souls, we may be tempted to say, what time have we for the opponents without? Such reasoning is plausible. But all the same it is false. We are not saved by keeping ourselves constantly in the proper frame of mind, but we were saved by Christ once for all when we were born again by God's Spirit and were enabled by Him to put our trust in the Savior. And the gospel message does not cease to be true because we for the moment have lost sight of the full glory of it. Sad will it be for those to whom we minister if we let our changing moods be determinative of the message that at any moment we proclaim, or if we let our changing moods determine the question whether we shall or shall not stand against the rampant forces of unbelief in the church. We ought to look not within, but without, for the content of what we are to preach, and for the determination of our witness-bearing; not to our changing feelings and experiences, but to the Bible as the Word of God. Then, and then only, shall we preach, not ourselves, but Christ Jesus the Lord.

There are many hopes that I cherish for you men, with whom I am united by such ties of affection. I hope that you may be gifted preachers; I hope that you may have happy lives; I hope that you may have adequate support for yourselves and for your families; I hope that you may have good churches. But I hope something for you far more than all that. I hope above all that, wherever you are and however your preaching may be received, you may be true witnesses for the Lord Jesus Christ; I hope that there may never be any doubt where *you* stand, but that always you may stand squarely for Jesus Christ, as He is offered to us, not in the experiences of men, but in the blessed written Word of God.

I do not mean that the great issue of the day must be polemically presented in every sermon that you preach. No doubt that would be exceedingly unwise. You should always endeavor to build the people up by simple and positive instruction in the Word. But never will such simple and positive instruction in the Word have the full blessing of God, if when the occasion does arise to take a stand, you shrink back. God hardly honors the ministry of those who in the hour of decision are ashamed of the gospel of Christ. God grant, instead, that in all humility, but also in all boldness, in reliance upon God, you may fight the good fight of faith. Peace is indeed yours, the peace of God which passeth all understanding. But that peace is given you, not that you may be onlookers or neutrals in love's battle, but good soldiers of Jesus Christ.

George W. Truett
(1867—1944)

Born in 1867 in Hayesville, North Carolina, George Washington Truett grew up on a farm in a Christian home. Books were a large part of his family's life and he became an avid reader. By the time he was eighteen years old, Truett was educated well enough to begin teaching. He later founded a high school of which he was principal for three years.

When the Truett family moved to Texas in 1889, George entered a junior college to begin the study of law. However, he later changed his mind and entered the ministry, pastoring East Waco Baptist Church while attending Baylor University, where he graduated in 1897.

After graduation, George W. Truett was called to be pastor of First Baptist Church in Dallas, Texas. The church had less than 800 members and was deeply in debt, but it experienced phenomenal growth under his leadership. He pastored there for over forty years, seeing thousands converted and over 7,000 added to the church. It was not uncommon to have hundreds of people turned away from the church due to overflow crowds who loved to hear him preach. In addition to pastoring one of the world's largest churches, Truett was three times elected president of the Southern Baptist Convention, and from 1934 to 1939 he was president of the Baptist World Alliance.

One of the leading religious figures in the nation during his lifetime, George Truett was first and foremost a great preacher. Possessing a powerful voice and a superb delivery, his central emphasis in the pulpit was evangelism. Truett preached extemporaneously, was skilled in the art of illustration, and had a charming eloquence that made an impact upon his hearers for more than four decades. He died in 1944 at age seventy-seven.

The Conquest of Fear
By George W. Truett

Fear not; I am the first and the last: I am he that liveth, and was dead; and, behold, I am alive for evermore, Amen; and have the keys of hell and of death (Rev. 1:17-18).

In this hour of worship, let us think together on Jesus' greatest saying concerning the conquest of fear. It is given in these words in the first chapter of the last book of the New Testament.

It is both the mission and the message of Jesus to deliver mankind from servile, enervating, down-dragging fear. And certainly the problem of fear is a problem to be reckoned with in many lives. One of the most outstanding and surprising disclosures of our stressful, nervous, modern civilization, is the fact that many people are in the thralldom of fear. This fact obtains with all classes of people—the high and the low, the rich and the poor, the educated and ignorant, the old and the young, with all ages and classes. They have fears of all kinds—fear of themselves, of others, of the past, present and future, of sickness, of death, of poverty, and on and on.

A little while ago, it was my privilege to preach twice daily for a week to one of our most influential American colleges. Its student body is large, and widely influential, and more mature in years than is the student body of most of our colleges. Before my arrival there, the president of the college sent a questionnaire to every student, asking that the students indicate any subjects upon which they would have the visiting minister speak. When the answers were tabulated, the president and faculty of the college, together with the visiting minister and others, were amazed by the fact that the majority of that large and mature student body had made this request: "Let the visiting minister tell us how we may conquer fear.''

The Bible is the one Book which answers that very question. There are two words which stand out in the Bible, like mountain peaks—the words, *Fear not!* With those words, God comforted Abraham: ''Fear not, Abram; I am thy shield, and thy exceeding great reward.'' With those same words He comforted Isaac at his lonely task of digging wells in the wilderness. With the same words He comforted Jacob, when his little Joseph was lost somewhere down in Egypt. So comforted He the Israelites at the Red Sea: ''And Moses said unto the people, Fear ye not, stand still, and see the salvation of the Lord, which he will shew you to-day.'' These two words, *Fear not!* standing out here and there in the Bible, are a part of our great inheritance as Christians. We shall do well to note them very carefully, wherever they occur in the Bible, and to note their contextual relations.

The three supreme matters which concern mankind are life, death, and eternity. Jesus here gives us an all-comprehensive statement concerning these three vast matters. He bids us to be unafraid of life, of death, and of eternity. It is Jesus' greatest saying concerning the conquest of fear. It was spoken to John, who was banished to Patmos because of his fealty to Christ. Let us now earnestly summon ourselves to think on this vast message of Jesus.

1. First, Jesus bids us to be unafraid of life. He reminds us that He is ''the first and the last: I am he that liveth.'' Is the fear of life real? It is poignantly so with many. The liability of fear is constant, and this fact is perhaps the explanation for many a suicide. I asked one who sought in a despondent hour to snuff out the candle of life, and was prevented from so doing: ''Why did you wish to end your life?'' And the pathetic answer was given: ''I was afraid to go on with life.'' People are afraid, for one thing, because they are so dependent. They are utterly dependent upon God and greatly dependent upon one another. Sometimes the proud expression is heard: ''I am independent.'' Let such a one tell us of whom he is independent, and how and where and when? We are all bound together in the bundle of life. ''For none of us liveth to himself, and no man dieth to himself.''

Again, we are afraid because we are continually in the presence of great mysteries, such as the mystery of sin, of sorrow, of God, of one's own personality, and of the strange and ofttimes trying providences that come to us in the earthly life.

Still again, the responsibilities of life are such that serious men and women must often tremble. Piercing questions arise to probe our hearts to the depths. Often do we ask: ''Will I make good in the stern battle of life?'' ''Will I disappoint the expectations of my loved ones and friends?'' Even Moses trembled before his mighty responsibilities, thus voicing his fear: "O my Lord, I am not eloquent, neither heretofore, nor since thou hast spoken unto thy servant: but I am slow of speech, and of a slow tongue." And even Solomon shrank before his vast responsibility, saying: "And now, O Lord my God, thou hast made thy servant king instead of David my father; and I am but a little child: I know not how to go out or come in." Often come the testing hours in life, when we cry out with Paul: "Who is sufficient for these things?" Many times are we provoked to ask that very question, as we are called upon to make important decisions and meet the critically testing experiences of life. Verily, we are many times made to tremble before the immeasurably responsible facts of life. Jesus graciously comes to us, saying: "Do not be afraid of life." "I will never leave thee, nor forsake thee."

2. Again, he bids us be unafraid of death. He reminds us, "I was dead, and behold, I am alive for evermore." The shuddering fear of death is a very real fact in many a life. Some are in bondage all their earthly lifetime, through fear of death. Maeterlinck confesses in his autobiography: "I am a frightened child in the presence of death." It is not to be wondered at that the thought of death casts its oppressive shadows about us, because death is an experience utterly strange to every one of us. "It is a bourne whence no traveler returns." "The black camel kneels at every gate." "With equal pace, impartial fate knocks at the palace and the cottage gate." It is not surprising that numbers of people have a strange fascination for prying into the secrets of death. This gruesome curiosity sometimes leads its possessor into strange quests and still stranger claims. What shall be said of these uncanny efforts to pry into the secrets of the dead? Such efforts are both profitless and presumptuous. Jesus has told us all that we need to know about death. He knows all about the grave, for He has explored its every chamber, and He has met this Waterloo of death and won. He is not now in the grave. He is alive. He is the Living One who is now bringing to bear the resources of His wisdom, mercy, power, and love upon our needy world, and His will is bound to prevail. We are told that "Ideas rule the world." Very well, compare the ideas proclaimed by Jesus, with all others, and at once we see how preeminent His ideas are. The hands on His clock never turn backward. "For he must reign, till he hath put all enemies under his feet." Some day, thank God! war will be under His feet forever. And so will be all forms of intemperance, and selfishness, and sin. And so will be death itself, because it is divinely decreed that "The last enemy that shall be destroyed is death." "O death, where is thy sting? O grave, where is thy victory? . . . But thanks be to God which giveth us the victory through our Lord Jesus Christ."

And still further—Jesus is with His people when they come to die. The evidences of this fact are countless and glorious. Often and joyfully did John Wesley declare: "Our people die well." Many of us, even in our limited and very humble sphere, can give the same glad testimony. "Our people die well." Indeed, when we see how well they can die, how unafraid and triumphant they are when they face the last enemy, we are fortified afresh for our work of testifying to the sufficiency of Christ's help in every possible human experience.

Not long ago, I saw a timid mother die. Hers was a very humble home, the husband was a carpenter, the children were very modestly clothed, and the limitations imposed by a meager income for the home were markedly in evidence. With a calmness, fearlessness, and joyfulness indescribable, that modest woman faced the final chapter of the earthly journey. She gave her sublime Christian testimony to her sorrowing husband and children; she confidently bound them to the heart of God in a prayer that can never be forgotten by those that heard it. Then she passed into the valley of the shadows, smilingly whispering the victorious words: "Yea, though I walk through the valley of the shadow of death, I will fear no evil: for thou art with me; thy rod and thy staff they comfort me." The next day, I saw a strong husband and father pass to the great beyond. He requested that the pastor pray that the whole household might unreservedly accept God's will. When the prayer was concluded, the strong man who was rapidly hurrying down to death sublimely said to the poignantly sorrowing wife and sons: "This is God's way; He doeth all things well; I accept His will without a question; tell me, O my dear wife and children, will you not likewise accept His will in this hour, and through all the unfolding future?" And with one voice, they said: "We will." And then, the strong man was gone, and the peace and calm of heaven filled all that house. A third day came, and I was called to witness the passing of an unusually timid girl in the Sunday school. The modest child of little more than a dozen years of age anxiously said to her mother: "Everything is getting dark, Mamma, come close to me, I'm afraid." And the gentle mother said to the little daughter: "Jesus is with us in the dark, my child, as well as in the light, and He will surely take care of all who put their trust in Him." And the child's face was immediately lighted up with a joyful smile, as she said: "I am trusting Him, and I'll just keep on trusting Him, and He will stay close to me, for He said He would, and He always does what He says He will do." And a little later, even in life's closing moments, her voice could be heard singing: "There'll be no dark valley when Jesus comes to gather His children home." Such illustrations of triumph in the hour of death could be indefinitely multiplied. The pastors of your churches are privileged to witness such triumphs, week by week, and they are able, therefore, to stand in their pulpits and victoriously shout with Paul, "But thanks be to God, which giveth us the victory through our Lord Jesus Christ."

3. Not only does Jesus bid us be unafraid of life and of death, but He also bids us to be unafraid of eternity. The word He speaks here in His great promise is: "I have the keys of hell and of death." That little word "keys" carries with it a large meaning. It means guidance, it means authority, it means control. Just as Jesus cares for His people in life and in death, even so will He care for them in eternity. "I go to prepare a place for you. And if I go and prepare a place for you, I will come again, and receive you unto myself; that where I am, there ye may be also."

Belief in God and in immortality go together. The age-old question: "If a man die, shall he live again?" is a question that will not be hushed. It is no wonder that such a question has been eagerly asked by myriads, in the recent years. The Great War laid millions of young men under sod and sea and has sent other millions to stagger on with broken health, even down to the grave. Suffering hearts all around the encircling globe have asked and are continually asking if death is an eternal sleep and if the grave ends all. To such questions we must give our most positive answer. The grave does not end all. The doctrine of immortality is not a dead creed, an empty speculation, an intellectual curiosity, an interesting question. The doctrine of immortality is a fact, a force, a great moral dynamic, which lifts life to high levels and drives it to great ends. Yes, we are to live again, beyond the sunset and the night, to live on consciously, personally, and forever.

The nature of man demands immortality. The instinct of immortality is the prophecy of its fulfilment. Where in all nature can you find instinct falsified? The wings of the bird mean that it was made to fly. The fins of the fish mean that it was made to swim. The deathless yearnings of the heart imperiously cry out for immortality. On the modest monument that marks the last resting place in France of President Roosevelt's son, who fell in the Great War, is inscribed this death-defying sentence: "He has outsoared the shadows of our night." The human heart refuses to be hushed in its cry for immortality.

The character of God presages immortality. When Job thought of men, he said: "If a man die, shall he live again?" When he thought of God, he said: "I know that my redeemer liveth." Then Job went on to voice the deathless cry of the heart for immortality. God is infinitely interested in us, He cares for us, He provides for us. If He cares for the birds, as He does, surely He cares also for us. He bids us to put fear away, reminding us: "But even the very hairs of your head are all numbered. Fear ye not, therefore: ye are of more value than many sparrows." Abraham was "the friend of God." Death has not dissolved that friendship. "Enoch walked with God: and he was not; for God took him." A little girl, who heard a preacher's sermon on this sentence, gave this report of the sermon to a little neighbor girl who did not hear the sermon: "The preacher said that Enoch took a long walk with God, and they walked, and they walked, and they walked; and at last, God told Enoch that he need not go back to live at his house any more, but he could just go on home with God, to live with Him, in His house, forever." Surely, the little girl's interpretation is what our hearts demand, and it is what we steadfastly and joyfully believe to be the plan of God for His friends.

But the crowning argument for immortality is the experience of Jesus. He has incontestably proved it. He came to earth, and really lived, and died, and was buried, and rose again, just as He said He would do. Long years ago, the men of the Old World wondered if there was some other land beyond the waters, to the far West. One day, a bolder spirit than others had been set sail toward the West. And by and by Columbus set his feet upon the shores of a new land. Even so, Jesus was the divine Columbus who has explored all the chambers of the grave, and has come back therefrom, the victorious Conqueror of death. He comforts His friends with the gracious words: "I am the resurrection, and the life: he that believeth in me, though he were dead, yet shall he live. And whosoever liveth and believeth in me shall never die." In the incomparable chapter of guidance and comfort, the fourteenth chapter of John, Jesus would anchor us, once for all, with His divinely assuring words: "Because I live, ye shall live also."

Low in the grave He lay—Jesus, my Saviour!
    Waiting the coming day—Jesus, my Lord!
Up from the grave He arose,
    With a mighty triumph o'er His foes;
He arose a Victor from the dark domain,
    And He lives forever with His saints to reign:
He arose! He arose! Hallelujah! Christ arose!

With our faith in that victorious Saviour, we may sing with Whittier in his exquisite poem, "Snowbound":

Alas for him who never sees
    The stars shine through his cypress-trees!
Who, hopeless, lays his dead away,
    Nor looks to see the breaking day
Across the mournful marbles play!
    Who hath not learned, in hours of faith,
The truth to flesh and sense unknown,
    That Life is ever lord of Death,
And Love can never lose its own!

Are you trusting in Christ as your personal Saviour, and do you gladly bow to Him as your rightful Master? If your hearts answer "Yes," go your many scattered ways, I pray you, without hesitation or fear. Your personal relations to Christ will determine your relations to the three vast matters: life, death, and eternity, concerning which he would have us put all our fears away, now and forevermore. He is our Pilot, our Righteousness, our Savior, our Advocate, our promised and infallible Guide, even unto death and throughout the vast beyond, forever. Well do we often sing: "He leadeth me." As we sing it now, who wishes openly to confess Him and follow Him?

G. Campbell Morgan
(1863—1945)

George Campbell Morgan is rated by many as the greatest Bible expositor of modern times. Born in 1863 into a Christian home in Tetbury, England, Morgan preached his first sermon before he was thirteen. He was a schoolteacher and a lay preacher until his ordination as a Congregationalist minister in 1889.

As Morgan pastored for several years in England, his reputation as a Bible expositor spread to the United States. Accepting D.L. Moody's invitation to teach at the Northfield Bible Conference, Morgan left for America in 1901 and stayed for several years. His ministry was to teach the converts from Moody's evangelistic campaigns.

He returned to England in 1904 to pastor Westminster Congregational Chapel in London. Under his leadership it became one of the largest and most influential churches in the country. Morgan resigned the position in 1919 to do itinerant work in England and America. For fourteen years he was in wide demand as a preacher and conference teacher, crossing the Atlantic Ocean more than fifty times in his lifetime. He returned to London in 1933 to again pastor Westminster Chapel, where he remained until retirement in 1943. Morgan died two years later.

Famous for his sound Bible interpretation and expository ability, Morgan was a man of intense and passionate Bible study. He was largely self-educated and held no formal degrees from college or seminary. However, the scores of religious books and commentaries he wrote bear witness to his profound knowledge of the Scriptures. The father of four sons who all became preachers, G. Campbell Morgan was recognized as the prince of expositors in the English-speaking world.

21

The Perfect Ideal of Life
By G. Campbell Morgan

Then said Jesus unto them, When ye have lifted up the Son of man, then shall ye know that I am he, and that I do nothing of myself; but as the Father hath taught me, I speak these things. And he that sent me is with me: the Father hath not left me alone; for I do always those things that please him. As he spake these words, many believed on him (John 8:28-30).

The Master, you will see, in this verse lays before us three things. First of all, He gives us the perfect ideal of human life in a short phrase, and that comes at the end, "the things that please him." Those are the things that create perfect human life, living in the realm of which man realizes perfectly all the possibilities of his wondrous being—"the things that please him." So I say, in this phrase, the Master reveals to us the perfect ideal of our lives. Then, in the second place, the Master lays claim—one of the most stupendous claims that He ever made—that He utterly, absolutely, realizes that ideal. He says, "I do always the things that please him." And then, thirdly, we have the revelation of the secret by which He has been able to realize the ideal, to make the abstract concrete, to bring down the fair vision of divine purpose to the level of actual human life and experience, and the secret is declared in the opening words: "He that sent me is with me; my Father hath not left me alone."

The perfect ideal for my life, then, is that I live always in the realm of the things that please God; and the secret by which I may do so is here unfolded—by living in perpetual, unbroken communion with God: communion with which I do not permit anything to interfere. Then it shall be possible for me to pass into this high realm of actual realization.

It is important that we should remind ourselves in a few sentences that the Lord has indeed stated the highest possible ideal for human life in these words: "The things that please him." Oh, the godlessness of men! The godlessness that is to be found on every hand! The godlessness of the men and women that are called by the name of God! How tragic, how sad, how awful it is! Because godlessness is always not merely an act of rebellion against God, but a falling short in our own lives of their highest and most glorious possibilities.

Here is my life. Now, the highest realm for me is the realm where all my thoughts, and all my deeds, and all my methods, and everything in my life please God. That is the highest realm, because God only knows what I am; only perfectly understands the possibilities of my nature, and all the great reaches of my being. You remember those lines that Tennyson sang—very beautifully, I always think:

Flower in the crannied wall,
    I pluck you out of the crannies;—
    Hold you here, root and all, in my hand,
    Little Flower—but if I could understand
What you art, root and all, and all in all,
    I should know what God and man is.

Beautiful confession! Absolutely true. I hold that flower in my hand, and I look at it, flower and leaves and stem and root. I can botanize it, and then I tear it to pieces—that is what the botanist mostly does—and you put some part of it there, and some part of it there, and some part of it there. There is the root, there the stem, and there are the leaves, and there is everything; but where is the flower? Gone. How did it go? When did it go? Why, when you ruthlessly tore it to bits. But how did you destroy it? You interfered with the principle that made it what it was— you interfered with the principle of life. What is life? No man can tell you. "If I could but know what you are, little flower, root and all, and all in all," I would know what life is, what God is, what man is. I cannot.

Now, if you lift that little parable of the flower into the highest realm of animal life, and speak of yourself—we don't know ourselves; down in my nature there are reaches that I have not fathomed yet. They are coming up every day. What a blessed thing it is to have the Master at hand, to hand them over to Him as they come up, and say, "Lord, here is another piece of Thy territory; govern it; I don't know anything about it." But there is the business. I don't know myself, but God knows me, understands all the complex relationships of my life, knows how matter affects mind, and physical and mental and spiritual are blended in one in the high ideal of humanity. Oh, remember, man is the crowning and most glorious work of God of which we know anything yet. And God only knows man.

But here is a Man that stands amid His enemies, and He looks out upon His enemies, and He says, "I do the things that please him"—not

"I teach them," not "I dream them," not "I have seen them in a fair vision," but "I do them." There never was a bigger claim from the lips of the Master than that: "I do always the things that please him."

You would not thank me to insult your Christian experience, upon whatever level you live it, by attempting to define that statement of Christ. History has vindicated it. We believe it with all our hearts—that He always did the things that pleased God. But I have got onto a level that I can touch now. The great ideal has come from the air to the earth. The fair vision has become concrete in a Man. Now, I want to see that Man; and if I see that Man I shall see in Him a revelation of what God's purpose is for men, and I shall see, therefore, a revelation of what the highest possibility of life is. Now this is a tempting theme. It is a temptation to begin to contrast Him with popular ideals of life. I want to see Him; I want, if I can, to catch the notes of the music that make up the perfect harmony which was the dropping of a song out of God's heaven upon man's earth, that man might catch the key-note of it and make music in his own life. What are the things in this Man's life? He says: "I have realized the ideal—I do." There are four things that I want to say about Him, four notes in the music of His life.

First, spirituality. That is one of the words that needs redeeming from abuse. He was the embodiment of the spiritual ideal in life. He was spiritual in the high, true, full, broad, blessed sense of that word.

It may be well for a moment to note what spirituality did not mean in the life of Jesus Christ. It did not mean asceticism. During all the years of His ministry, during all the years of His teaching, you never find a single instance in which Jesus Christ made a whip of cords to scourge Himself. And all that business of scourging oneself—an attempt to elevate the spirit by the ruin of the actual flesh—is absolutely opposed to His view of life. Jesus Christ did not deny Himself. The fact of His life was this—that He touched everything familiarly. He went into all the relationship of life. He went to the widow. He took up the children and held them in His arms, and looked into their eyes till heaven was poured in as He looked. He didn't go and get behind walls somewhere. He didn't get away and say: "Now, if I am going to get pure I shall do it by shutting men out." You remember what the Pharisees said of Him once. They said: "This man receiveth sinners." You know how they said it. They meant to say: "We did hope that we should make something out of this new man, but we are quite disappointed. He receives sinners."

And what did they mean? They meant what you have so often said: "You can't touch pitch without being defiled." But this Man sat down with the publican and He didn't take on any defilement from the publican. On the other hand, He gave the publican His purity in the life of Jesus Christ. Things worked the other way. He was the great negative of God to the very law of evil that you have—evil contaminates good. If you will put on a plate one apple that is getting bad among twelve others that are pure, the bad one will influence the others. Christ came to drive back every force of disease and every force of evil by this strong purity of His own person, and He said: "I will go among the bad and make them good." That is what He was doing the whole way through. So His spirituality was not asceticism. And if you are going to be so spiritual that you see no beauty in the flowers and hear no music in the song of the birds; if the life which you pass into when you consent to the crucifixion of self does not open to you the very gates of God, and make the singing of the birds and the blossoming of the flowers infinitely more beautiful, you have never seen Jesus yet.

What was His spirituality? The spirituality of Jesus Christ was a concrete realization of a great truth which He laid down in His own beatitudes. What was that? "Blessed are the pure in heart: for they shall see God." Now, the trouble is we have been lifting all the good things of God and putting them in heaven. And I don't wonder that you sing:

My willing soul would stay
    In such a frame as this,
And sit and sing itself away
    To everlasting bliss.

No wonder you want to sing yourself away to everlasting bliss, because everything that is worth having you have put up there. But Jesus said: "Blest are the pure in heart: for they shall see God." If you are pure you will see Him everywhere—in the flower that blooms, in the march of history, in the sorrows of men, above the darkness of the darkest cloud; and you will know that God is in the field when He is most invisible.

Second, subjection. The next note in the music of His life is His absolute subjection to God. You can very often tell the great philosophies which are governing human lives by the little catchwords that slip off men's tongues: "Well, I thank God I am my own master." That is your trouble, man. It is because you are your own master that you are in danger of hell. A man says: "Can't I do as I like with my own?" You have got no "own" to do what you like with. It is because men have forgotten the covenant of God, the kingship of God, that we have all the wreckage and ruin that blights this poor earth of ours. Here is the Man who never forgets it.

Did you notice those wonderful words: "I do nothing of myself; but as my Father taught me, I speak." He neither did nor spoke anything of Himself. It was a wonderful life. He stood forevermore between the next moment and heaven. And the Father's voice said, "Do this," and He said "Amen, I came to do thy will," and did it. And the Father's voice said, "Speak these words to men," and He, "Amen," and He spoke.

You say: "That is just what I do not want to do." I know that. We want to be independent; have our own way. "The things that please God"—this Man was subject to the divine will. You know the two words—if you can learn to say them, not like a parrot, not glibly, but out of your heart—the two words that will help you: "Hallelujah" and "Amen." You can say them in Welsh or any language you like; they are always the same. When the next dispensation of God's dealings faces you look at it and say: "Hallelujah! Praise God! Amen!"

Third, sympathy. Now, you have this Man turned toward other men. We have seen something of Him as He faced God: Spirituality, a sense of God; subjection, a perpetual amen to the divine volition. Now, He faces the crowd. Sympathy! Why? Because He is right with God, He is right with men; because He feels God near, and knows Him, and responds to the divine will; therefore, when He faces men He is right toward men. The settlement of every social problem you have in this country and in my own land, the settlement of the whole business, will be found in the return of man to God. When man gets back to God he gets back to men. What is behind it? Sympathy is the power of putting my spirit outside my personality, into the circumstances of another man, and feeling as that man feels.

I take one picture as an illustration of this. I see the Master approaching the city of Nain, and around Him His disciples. He is coming up. And I see outside the city of Nain, coming toward the gate a man carried by others, dead, and walking by that bier a mother. Now, all I want you to look at is that woman's face, and, looking into her face, see all the anguish of those circumstances. She is a widow, and that is her boy, her only boy, and he is dead. Man cannot talk about this. You have got to be in the house to know what that means. But look at her face— there it is. All the sorrow is on her face. You can see it.

Now turn from her quickly and look into the face of Christ. Why, I look into His face—there is her face. He is feeling all she is feeling; He is down in her sorrow with her; He has got underneath the burden, and He is feeling all the agony that that woman feels because her boy is dead. He is moved with compassion whenever human sorrow crosses His vision and human need approaches Him. And now I see Him moving toward the bier. I see Him as He touches it. And He takes the boy back and gives him to his mother. Do you see in yon mountain a cloud, so somber and sad, and suddenly the sun comes from behind the cloud, and all the mountainside laughs with gladness? That is that woman's face. The agony is gone. The tear that remains there is gilded with a smile, and joy is on her face. Look at Him. There it is. He is in her joy now. He is having as good a time as the woman. He has carried her grief and her sorrow. He has given her joy. And it is His joy that He has given to her. He is with her in her joy.

Wonderful sympathy! He went about gathering human sorrow in His own heart, scattering His joy, and having fellowship in agony and in deliverance, in tears and in their wiping away. Great, sympathetic soul! Why? Because He always lived with God, and, living with God, the divine love moved Him with compassion. Ah, believe me, our sorrows are more felt in heaven than on earth. And we had that glimpse of the eternal love in this Man, who did the things that pleased God, and manifested such wondrous sympathy.

Fourth, strength. The last note is that of strength. You talk about the weakness of Jesus, the frailty of Jesus. I tell you, there never was any one so strong as He. And if you will take the pains of reading His life with that in mind you will find it was one tremendous march of triumph against all opposing forces. About His dying—how did He die? "At last, at last," says the man in his study that does not know anything about Jesus; "at last His enemies became too much for Him, and they killed Him." Nothing of the sort. That is a very superficial reading. What is the truth? Hear it from His own lips: "No man taketh it [my life] from me, but I lay it down of myself. I have power to lay it down and I have power to take it again." What do you think of that? How does that touch you as a revelation of magnificence in strength? And then, look at Him, when He comes back from the tomb, having fulfilled that which was either an empty boast or a great fact—thank God, we believe it was a great fact! Now He stands upon the mountain, with this handful of men around Him, His disciples, and He is going away from them. "All authority," He says, "is given unto me. I am King not merely by an of-fice conferred, but by a triumph won. I am King, for I have faced the enemies of the race—sin and sorrow and ignorance and death—and my foot is upon the neck of every one. All authority is given to me."

Oh, the strength of this Man! Where did He get it? "My Father hath not left me alone. I have lived with God. I have walked with God. I always knew Him near. I always responded to His will. And my heart went out in sympathy to others, and I mastered the enemies of those with whom I sympathized. And I come to the end and I say, All authority is given to me." Oh, my brother, that is the pattern for you and for me! Ah, that is life! That is the ideal! Oh, how can I fulfil it? I am not going to talk about that. Let me only give you this sentence to finish with. "Christ in you, the hope of glory." If Christ be in me by the power of the Spirit, He will keep me conscious of God's nearness to me. If Christ be in me by the consciousness of the Spirit reigning and governing, He will take my will from day to day, blend it with His, and take away all that makes it hard to say, "God's will be done."

Gypsy Smith
(1860—1947)

Rodney Smith was born in a tent in 1860 near Leytonstone, England. His nomadic family peddled baskets and tinware, and they were never in one place long enough for the children to have formal education. Smith was fifteen years old when his mother died and his father accepted Christ, but Rodney was not saved until two years later. He then began to learn to read and write and to show an interest in the ministry.

Smith joined William Booth's Salvation Army in 1877 and was soon preaching to crowds of over 1,000 people. It was probably during this time that he was nicknamed "Gypsy." Several years later he became an itinerant evangelist and conducted many successful campaigns. Out of the Edinburgh meeting, Smith formed the Gypsy Gospel Wagon Mission in 1892, and he traveled the world ministering to his own people. In 1897 he became a special missionary of the National Free Church Council.

Although he had no formal education, Gypsy Smith was praised for his use of the English language. With a heart of tenderness and compassion for lost men, he preached a gospel of love that resulted in the conversion of thousands. He conducted evangelistic campaigns in Scotland and America for over seventy years. In Paris he saw 150 up-and-outers come to Christ. Twice he traveled around the world as an evangelist and it is said that he never held a meeting in which there were no conversions. His love for all kinds of people, his deep faith and commitment, and genuine humility combined to make him one of the most effective evangelists in the history of the church. Gypsy Smith died of a heart attack at sea en route to America at the age of eighty-seven.

As Jesus Passed By
By Gypsy Smith

And as Jesus passed forth from thence, he saw a man, named Matthew, sitting at the receipt of custom: and he saith unto him, Follow me. And he arose, and followed him (Matt. 9:9).

This is Matthew's modest way of telling all generations how he was converted. Matthew could have made a great deal more of that epoch-making moment in his life. Sometimes I think when he wrote just as much as my text he would not write any more that day. Can you not see between the lines what a story is there untold? He does not even tell you that he lived in a big house. He does not tell you that he made a big feast. He does not tell you that he invited all his old friends to come and meet with Jesus at the feast. He leaves others to tell you that little bit of the story. He simply says there was a feast. Very modest is Matthew. He says Jesus saw a man, and said to that man, "Follow Me," and the man followed; that is all. Some of us at certain moments of our lives cannot trust ourselves to tell all the story. We keep something back; we cannot trust ourselves to put the story into words. There are pages in every life that will never be written. There are stories untold to mortal ear over which the angels rejoice. There are moments when only the sky and the sun, the moon and the stars, the birds and the flowers, and the heaven eternal can hear all we have to say of His wonderful grace and mercy. We can only tell a bit of it, just a little bit of it. I want you to think of this wonderful moment—and it was a wonderful moment, a moment when Gospels were born, a moment in which history began to breathe, a moment when in his soul there was placed the germ-joy that will make heaven pulsate with hallelujahs. It was a wonderful moment in his life when he saw Jesus standing there calling him by name, speaking to him as a man would to his friend, appealing to him.

Why should Jesus go to this man? Because this man needed Jesus. I believe deep down in this man's heart he was longing for Christ. I am not so sure that he had not heard John the Baptist preach. I am not so sure that he was not already a convicted sinner. I am not so sure that he had not heard John say, "Behold the Lamb of God!" There were moments in his life when he longed to get a look at that dear face, to hear the music of that voice, and catch some inspiration from His life-giving message, and to feel the touch that healed. And I can imagine that even that day he could not see his books for his tears. He was at his business, you remember; he sat at the place of toll, everything in front of him, and while he was thinking of the inward longings, while the soul-hunger was gnawing, while the man within the man was talking to him and setting in motion thoughts and feelings that were eternal, I can imagine him saying, "Oh, shall I ever see Him?" And maybe he laid his head on his hands in his grief, and at that moment Jesus said, "Matthew, Matthew, follow Me." You know Matthew was ready to do it. He did it instantly, without asking a question, without any hesitation. He acted as though he had made his plans as to what he would do if he had the chance. He left all. He does not tell you that; he leaves the others to add that bit to the story—and his all was the possibility of becoming very rich. He left it all: he left his books, he left his business, he left his office, he left his position, he left his friends, he left **all** to follow Jesus. Matthew had counted the cost and knew what he would do if the chance came. Jesus knew it too. He knew where Matthew sat, just as He knew where Nathanael prayed under the fig-tree. He knows where you are, Matthew at the place of toll, or Nathanael under the fig-tree, or Zacchaeus in the tree. He knows, He sees. There is no look heavenward, there is no desire heavenward, there is no aspiration after goodness, there is not an honest struggle for a nobler life in your heart, in your home, anywhere, everywhere, but what God sees and God knows. And, listen to me, there never is a good desire, there never is a noble thought, there never will be an aspiration for a holier life, but what is God-given and God-inspired. He knows. And He knows where you sit, my brother. Here is a man handicapped, a jewel in an unlikely place; here is a man that nobody wanted, ostracized by his very profession, separated from decent folk by his calling, unpopular and hated. There he was; he never had had a chance. The church did not want him when Jesus Christ took the trouble to save him. The church of his day did not want him, and I am afraid there are some churches in England who would not thank you to fill them with the harlots, the publicans, the gamblers, the drunkards, and the sinners. And yet they are the sort that heaven opens its doors to. Don't forget that. They are the people for whom Christ died—not the righteous, but sinners. And there are people who would sit in committee and dictate to the Son of God as to who He is to save. They did it in Matthew's day. There are people who would sit in judgment on the Christ of God. They would question the authority of Omnipotence to save the sinner. "This Man eateth with sinners." It shows how much they knew of this Man and His mission to the world. What does this story mean? It means this: that for every man there is a chance. The Christ I have to preach gives a chance to the worst, to the most unlikely, to the most degraded, to the most hated, to the most sinful, to the most despised, to the people who were born into the world with the devil in their blood, the blood of the gambler in their veins, the blood of the harlot in their veins. And when I think of it all and look at some people, the wonder to me is that they are not worse than they are. God have pity on the little boys and girls in the world who are made drunk before they are a year old! God have pity on the child-life of today! For such Jesus came.

And He chooses to find out about these people, the people that nobody wants, and He says, "I want you; I am after you." It is a new way of treating sinners. Did you ever think of it? A new way of treating sinners, wrongdoers. Prison for wrongdoers, the law courts for wrong-goers; the whole fabric of society is built up to keep off wrongdoers, to keep away wrongdoers, to keep out wrongdoers, to shut up and shut off wrongdoers, and Jesus Christ comes and opens His arms to them, and says, "Come to Me; I will receive you." That is the Christ for me! To set the prisoner free, to break the chains of them that are bound, to open the prison doors and say, "March out; I will make you free by My mighty power." It means a chance for every man. And Jesus sees far more in these people that are far from Him than we have seen yet. If you and I had the eyes of Christ we should see in the filthiest wretch that walks the street something worth saving. If you and I only had the vision of Calvary we should never weary, we should never tire, we should never lose heart, and we should never lose hope. We should believe that for the worst there is a throne, a song, an anthem. May God help us to believe our gospel!

Why did Jesus go to Matthew? Because Jesus knew that Matthew needed Him. Nobody could do for Matthew what Jesus could. Don't forget that. Matthew had never had a chance. Nobody but Jesus could give him one. He was in a bad setting; his whole life was a tangle; his whole life was knots. Nobody wanted him. And you know people like that. There are some connected with you that you would rather not see. You tremble when you see them and when their name is mentioned. There are some names you do not talk about to others; you try to forget; you won't talk about them. There is a skeleton in every cupboard. The most of us here have somebody connected with us that we do not like to mention; we try to forget; and yet, God knows, the agony of it eats the life out of us. They are the people who need Him.

It is no good to say to some people, "Believe, believe." They need somebody's fingers to unravel the knots, to untie and straighten things out, and who is to do it? Those whose whole life has been cursed from their very birth, they are handicapped in their very blood, and who is to deliver them? Can anybody do it? Is there no God who can do it? Listen—the fingers that weaved the rainbow into a scarf and wrapped it around the shoulders of the dying storm, the fingers that painted the lily-bell and threw out the planets, the fingers that were dipped in the mighty sea of eternity and shook out on this old planet, making the ocean to drop and the rivers to stream—the same fingers can take hold on these tangled lives and can make them whole again, for He came to make the crooked straight and the rough places plain. Blessed be God, Jesus can do for Matthew what nobody else can, and He can do for you, my brother, what your friends cannot do. He can take the desire for drink out of you; He can cure the love of gambling that is eating the soul out of you; He can put out the fires of lust that are burning in your being and consuming you by inches. He can take the devil of lying out of you, the devil of cheating out of you, of fraud out of you, of hypocrisy out of you. Jesus can do what nobody else can; the preacher cannot, the Church cannot; but the Lord Jesus, who loves you, is mighty to save.

Let me go another step. There was something that Matthew could do for Jesus that nobody else could—and I say that reverently. Jesus needed Matthew. Ay, and He needs you. They looked at Him and said, "He is a sinner." "Yes," said Jesus, "and he will write My first Gospel." Only give him a chance; you do not know what there is hidden in the drunkard. There may be a preacher, there may be an evangelist, there may be a Gospel. You do not know. Give them a chance; give them all a chance. "A sinner." They were fond of using these words. "He is a sinner." They used them about the man in the tree. "Yes," said Jesus, "he is a sinner, and he is a son of Abraham." And it was Jesus who spoke on both occasions. You would not have gone for a scribe for the Son of God to a publican. No! But Jesus has a wonderful way of showing what He can do with unlikely material. A little child cried just now. Its little voice in coming days may startle the nation. The waving of its little hand may marshal the hosts of God. Who can tell? That little boy at your side may become a Spurgeon, a Maclaren, a Whitefield, a Wesley. Who can tell the possibilities of a child? That little girl may be a Mrs. Fletcher, a Florence Nightingale, a Catherine Booth. Who can tell? And God wants them all. There are Gospels hidden away, untold yet, but they will shine out and flash in letters, golden capitals, and make the world glad with a great gladness.

You saw the sinner; Jesus saw the man. He saw the sinner too, and He knew what the sinner would be when grace had had a chance. The world sees the face and the clothes and the house, the street you live on, where you work, and reckons you up by how much your salary is. Jesus does not reckon that way. See that sailor—drunken, filthy, vile of lip and impure in soul—a drunken sailor. Nobody wanted him; nobody cared for him. God looked at him and saved him; and his name was John Newton, the poet, the preacher, but God could see the theologian, the preacher, in the drunken sailor. See that man, a swearing tinker; so swearing, he says of himself, that when he began to swear his neighbors shuddered. Nobody wanted that tinker. But God looked at him and saved him; and his name was John Bunyan, the immortal dreamer. You would not have looked for the *Pilgrim's Progress* in that swearing tinker. God looked at that man, a publican—and you know what a publican is—helping his brother to sell beer in Gloucester. God looked at him and saved him; and his name was George Whitefield, the mighty preacher. Look at that man selling boots and shoes in a shoe store in Chicago. God looked at him and saved him, and when He took the trouble to save him and that young fellow offered himself to a Congregational church as a church member, they saw so little in him that they put him back on trial for twelve months; and his name was Moody. And Moody has put one hand on America and another hand on Britain, and they moved towards the Cross. See that man, the plaything of the village, full ·of devilry, mischief, roguery, fond of pleasure and sin. Nobody cared for him except his mates, and God saved him; and his name was Peter Mackenzie, a sunbeam in the lives of thousands. Look at this picture—a gypsy tent; there is a father and five little motherless children, without a Bible, without school. Nobody wanted them—who does want a gypsy? Nobody—outsider, ostracized, despised, and rejected. But God looked on that poor father and those five motherless little things and saw them in their ignorance and heathenism, hungry for God. And He looked again, and He said, ''There are six preachers in that tent.'' And He put those arms that were nailed to the tree round the father and the children and saved them all; and I am one of them. It takes love to see. Love saw more in Matthew than anybody. And love sees more in you, my brother, than anybody else; and if no one wants you, He does; and if no one loves you, He does. If no one cares, He cares; and if you think there is not a friend in the world, you have more friends than you think, and they are closer to you than you dream. God is here, and He says, ''Come to Me, follow Me, and I will save you; I will give you a chance for this world and the next. Only follow Me.''

Matthew never did a wiser or nobler thing than when he took Christ home. Everybody there had a chance of blessing that day. Think of what it would mean for your home if you, my brother, took Christ home with you. Your wife and children would have a chance they have never had before. If both of you—husband and wife—bow at His dear feet together, what joy there will be in heaven and on earth! It would mean your home for Jesus. You will give Christ a chance with every child in your home by taking Him there. Matthew took Jesus home with him; and He will go home with you if you will ask Him, and He will go with you this night. God help you!

I can believe there are scores and hundreds who mean to follow Jesus. Who will leave all to follow Jesus? Who will sacrifice everything for Jesus' sake? Who will take their stand for Jesus, and who will go home and say to their friends, "I have come to tell you what great things the Lord hath done for me"? Jesus calls to you. Will you follow?

G.B. Vick
(1901—1975)

George Beauchamp Vick was born in 1901 in Russellville, Kentucky, in a pastor's home. After conversion at age nine, he moved with his family to Louisville. His interest in mathematics assisted him in obtaining a job with a railroad company after high school graduation.

His work took him to Fort Worth, Texas, in 1928, where he became a member of the First Baptist Church, then pastored by J. Frank Norris. Vick became actively involved in the church and later served on its staff for eight years.

In 1936 Vick moved to Detroit, Michigan, to continue working with Norris in Temple Baptist Church, and he remained there until his homegoing in 1975. Under his leadership, the Sunday school of Temple Baptist Church experienced unprecedented growth, and he became co-pastor in 1947. In 1950 Vick was influential in organizing the Baptist Bible Fellowship, with 119 other pastors. They began Baptist Bible College and chose him as its first president, a position he held until his death. That college in Springfield, Missouri, reportedly grew to an enrollment of over 2,000 under his leadership. Vick himself became known as ''Mr. Baptist Bible Fellowship.'' He also became pastor of Temple Baptist Church during this time and saw its membership increase to 15,000.

G.B. Vick is remembered as one of the great Fundamentalist leaders and spokesmen of his day. He was recognized as an authority on Sunday school growth and church administration. He was a great motivator of young people; over 350 persons entered full-time Christian service under his ministry. Vick was also primarily responsible for the world missions outreach of the Baptist Bible Fellowship International, which today has some 600 missionaries serving in sixty-four countries of the world. Vick's own church contributed large sums of money to world missions, totaling almost a quarter of a million dollars in 1974. One of the great leaders in Baptist history, G.B. Vick was respected by fundamental Christians everywhere for his dynamic stand for the faith.

Heaven
By G.B. Vick

In my Father's house are many mansions: if it were not so, I would have told you. I go to prepare a place for you. And if I go and prepare a place for you, I will come again, and receive you unto myself; that where I am, there ye may be also (John 14:2,3).

The most stupendous thought that can occupy the mind of man is heaven and how to go there. God has not left us to grope our uncertain way through a dark, starless night, with no light for our pathway and no guide for our faltering footsteps. We can shout with the sweet singer of Israel, "Thy word is a lamp unto my feet, and a light unto my path."

Yes, the Bible has much to say concerning heaven and life after death. In fact, the Word of God was written to show us how to go to heaven. How true, then, are the inspired words, "If in this life only we have hope in Christ, we are of all men most miserable" (most to be pitied).

In spite of that, most men are living in the opening words of that sentence—"In this life only." They plan for *this life only*. They work for *this life only*. They prepare for *this life only*. Oh, how true are the words of our Lord, "For what is a man profited, if he shall gain the whole world, and lose his own soul? or what shall a man give in exchange for his soul?" Therefore, my friend, you are making a fool bargain if you have prepared for "this life only."

The only certain thing about this life is death. "The boast of heraldry, the pomp of power, all that beauty, all that wealth ere gave awaits alike the inevitable hour, the paths of glory lead but to the grave."

Sometimes when we have to stand beside the open grave over the earthly remains of one who is the dearest and the nearest of all earthly companions to us, we cover that mound with a blanket of flowers and water those flowers with our tears. Sometimes in our loneliness our hearts re-echo the words of the Lord Jesus as He hung upon the cross, "My God, my God, why?"

Does Jesus care when I've said good-by
To the dearest on earth to me,
And my sad heart aches till it nearly breaks—
Is it aught to Him? Does He see?
Oh yes, He cares; I know He cares,
His heart is touched with my grief;
When the days are weary, the long nights dreary,
I know my Saviour cares.

Yes, my friends, we do have a Saviour who cares. "For we have not an high priest which cannot be touched with the feeling of our infirmities; but was in all points tempted like as we are, yet without sin." The Lord Jesus Christ, when He was here, was called the "Man of sorrows, and acquainted with grief." He has drained to the bitterest dregs the cup of every human sorrow, suffering, and woe. Therefore, He is able to help us when all human help is in vain.

Yes, there is a heaven. The Bible says so and all laws of logic demand it. Have you ever stopped to think that there is no instinct in animals, nor intuition given to man by the Creator that does not respond to a fact?

Who taught the newborn kitten, even before its eyes are open, to seek nourishment at its mother's breast? God the Creator placed that instinct in the kitten and that instinct responds to a fact. It is a fact that nourishment has there been provided.

Who taught the birds to fly south in the autumn, then to return north in the spring? The Creator has given them an instinct—a response to a fact. Cold weather is coming and they cannot endure the rigors of the northern winters, therefore must seek a warmer clime.

So God has also given man certain intuitions and desires and everyone responds to a fact. God has given me eyes to see light; He has created light for the eyes. God has given me ears to hear sound; He has created sound for the ears. God has created me with a hunger; He has provided food to satisfy that hunger. He has created me with a thirst; that thirst responds to a fact for He has created water to satisfy my thirst.

But deeper than any instinct in animal or intuition or desire given to man, there is a deeper longing in my soul, stronger than hunger for food or desire for water; there is a longing in my soul for something better than this old world can offer—for a better life, a fairer land. This longing too responds to a fact, for God has created that better land.

There's a land that is fairer than day,
And by faith we can see it afar;
For the Father waits over the way,
To prepare us a dwelling-place there.

The Lord Jesus Christ, the Son of God, has told us about that fair land. Listen to the immortal words of our Lord as recorded in John the 14th chapter, verses 1 to 6:

Let not your heart be troubled: ye believe in God, believe also in me. In my Father's house are many mansions: if it were not so, I would have told you. I go to prepare a place for you. And if I go and prepare a place for you, I will come again, and receive you unto myself; that where I am, there ye may be also. And whither I go ye know, and the way ye know. Thomas saith unto him, Lord, we know not whither thou goest; and how can we know the way? Jesus saith unto him, I am the way, the truth, and the life: no man cometh unto the Father but by me.

My friends, let's give urgent heed to these blessed words which fell from the lips of the Son of God. Listen to the opening verse:

"Let not your heart be troubled."

Only the Son of God has the right, the power, the authority to speak such words as those to a troubled world. Only He has power to speak such words as those to hearts that are bowed in sin and in sorrow and bereavement.

And naturally the disciples, when they heard that the Master they loved so dearly was now so soon to go away, were heartbroken. They felt as sheep scattered without a shepherd. It was on that occasion that the Lord spoke these words of love and of comfort and sustaining grace to them. But He also spoke those words for us and for those of all coming time who would face similar experiences of sorrow and trouble. "Let not your heart be troubled."

And then the next few verses give us a number of reasons why, even in the midst of sorrow and heartbreak and good-byes, the child of God can still have an untroubled heart. And the first reason He advances is, "Ye believe in God, believe also in me." In other words, He was showing us that the only basis for an untroubled heart is an individual, personal, vital, living faith in the Lord Jesus Christ as the all-sufficient Saviour.

In verse 2 the Lord Jesus gives us another reason why the child of God may have an untroubled heart even in the midst of sorrow and bereavement. He says, "In my Father's house are many mansions: if it were not so, I would have told you."

My friend, I can never read or quote that verse of Scripture without reminding myself afresh that the word "house" there means "home." "In my Father's home are many mansions: if it were not so, I would have told you." Somehow the word home seems to make it a little sweeter to us, a little more personal, and a little more real. "In my Father's home are many mansions." When I hear the word home I believe there are several reasons why the Lord Jesus in His sublime omniscience selected that word to best convey to us something of the beauty, of the wonders, of the glories of the eternal abiding place of His children.

When I say home, your mind goes back across the years, perhaps across hundreds of miles of intervening space to that spot which will forever be hallowed in your memories among all the places of earth. That place where you grew up as a boy or a girl, playing around the yard with brothers and sisters and neighbor children, sitting around the hearthside upon a winter's evening with Mother, Dad, and others in the family. You know there are several things about that old home place which are not true about any other spot on earth as far as you are concerned.

First, home is a place where love reigns supreme. I am talking about the old-fashioned Christian home, not one of these modern homes which is just a sort of glorified roominghouse where the members of the family meet each other in the halls occasionally on the way from one busy social engagement to another. Not a place where there is confusion, bickering, fussing, and fighting, where the father and mother live like mad cats and where the children are anxious to get just as far away as possible, as soon as possible. Not that sort of a home. I am talking about the old-fashioned Christian home where the father can come home at the end of a busy day and there he can sit as the uncrowned king, honored, respected, and obeyed. Where he can shut the world out with its mad business competition and strife. Where the mother is respected and honored and revered as the uncrowned queen. In such a home love reigns supreme, and perhaps that is the nearest approach to heaven that earth knows anything about.

And so heaven itself is a place where love reigns supreme, where peace shall flow like a river.

Second, home is a place of ample provision and room whenever the children arrive. Perhaps my experience has been duplicated by nearly everyone here. I have sometimes been away from my old home place yonder in Louisville, Kentucky, for years at a time. Because of the stress of my work, I have been unable to turn my steps homeward.

But after those years of absence, how wonderful it was to turn back homeward for an old-fashioned family reunion! I suppose I have arrived there most every hour of the day or night. Sometimes as twilight shades would gather I have driven up in front of the old home place. There I would see Mother sitting in her accustomed familiar place on the porch, and I would go in. After greeting the members of the family, we would go into the dining room and I'd sit down again at the same old place there at the table. The intervening years would seem to slip away into nothingness. I would seem just like a boy again.

Then I have arrived at the old home place in the wee small hours of the morning—two, three, four o'clock in the morning after driving many weary miles. Yet no matter at what unearthly hour I did arrive, I would walk up on the porch, ring the doorbell, and I could never imagine Mother coming to the door, opening it just a little crack and then saying, "Son, I am sorry, but all the beds are occupied; the house is full. Your brothers, your sister, and their families have already arrived and there is no more room. You'll have to take your family and go to the hotel or somewhere else." No, my friends, I cannot imagine such a welcome or lack of welcome as that. Nor can you from your mother or from your home.

So home is a place where there is always room, no matter when the children arrive. And so it is with the heavenly home above. I care not how soon or how late I shall gather there for God's great family reunion. I am not concerned about how many of God's children shall have preceded me, for there is ample provision for His own. For the Lord Jesus said, "In my Father's home are many mansions: if it were not so, I would have told you;" and He continues by saying, "I go to prepare a place for you."

But somebody says, "But where is heaven?" I cannot describe to you the geographic location of that fair land. I cannot tell you the longitude or latitude of that place, nor am I greatly concerned about that. After all, that is not what makes any place dear to our hearts. That is not what endeared your old family home in your memories. Heaven is sweet to us because of those who are there. And though I cannot tell you the longitude and latitude of that city, yet, I think, after all, I can tell you just a little of where heaven is. Heaven, to the believer, to the child of God, is but one step beyond that narrow veil which separates this world from the next, time from eternity.

Heaven to the believer is just one step beyond the end of this little life's pilgrimage. Not only so, but I think I can tell you something else about where heaven is. Heaven is a place where Jesus is, for He says, "I go to prepare a place for you. And if I go and prepare a place for you, I will come again, and receive you unto myself; that where I am, there ye may be also." Yes, my friends, it is where Jesus is, and that is enough for me. I love the words of the old song, "Where Jesus is 'tis Heaven to me."

Not only so, but heaven is a place where all of our loved ones who have died with their faith fixed unfalteringly in Jesus Christ as the all-sufficient Savior have preceded us and where they await us. Heaven, therefore, is a place of grand and glorious and unending reunion.

Have you ever stopped to think that the very word "good-bye" is erased from the vocabulary of heaven? Therefore—today to any lonely heart who mourns the homegoing of some loved one whom you have loved long since and have lost awhile, may I say that if you and I could do the unthinkable, the impossible; if today we could call back our loved ones from yonder shore, it would be the height of selfishness for us to do so after they for this little while have tasted the joys which await the people of God on the other side. After they have experienced some of the unspeakable joys of the many mansions it would be the height of selfishness for us to want them back here to endure and to undergo the sorrows and the heartbreaks which are the common portion of all mankind here upon an old earth marred by sin.

Who of us would not gladly exchange Detroit, Michigan, or any other city of earth for that city which hath foundations, whose builder and maker is God? Who of us wouldn't gladly exchange an old city like this, with its sin and temptation, its filth, its bickerings, its imperfections, its tears for that city built by God's own hand where nothing that destroys or mars or blemishes can enter? That, my friends, is the sure portion of the child of God.

Who of us wouldn't gladly exchange an old world like this that is torn by wars and rumors of wars for that beautiful place of ineffable joy where peace shall flow like a river?

Who of us wouldn't gladly exchange bodies like these, subject to heat and to cold, to hunger and to thirst, to pain and disease, temptations, sin, weariness, death itself, for bodies over which none of these things—heat and cold and hunger and thirst, pain and weariness, and sin and temptation and disease and death—shall have any power? That I say is the sure portion of the people of God.

Who of us wouldn't exchange bodies like these, where the eye grows dim with the shedding of many salty tears, where the shoulders become stooped with the bearing of the burdens of years, where the footsteps become faltering, where the face is lined with the pen of time and etched upon our countenance is the story of every sorrow which besets us? Thank God, we will one day exchange these old bodies for bodies which are fashioned anew like unto the glorified body of our resurrected Lord!

Who of us wouldn't gladly exchange the companionships of earth, companionships with people like you and me, so imperfect, so quick-tempered, so apt to speak the hasty, thoughtless word that would wound even those we love best, for the companionship and the fellowship with God's heroes of the faith, for patriarchs, prophets, priests, and kings, for those children of God who have borne the burdens of life, who have fought its battles and have won the incorruptible crown? That, my friends, is the sure portion of the children of God.

No wonder the apostle Paul says, "I find a longing in my soul to depart and be with Christ which is far better." No wonder that the same inspired apostle says, "To die is gain."

Now notice in verse 4 the Lord Jesus continues by saying, "And whither I go ye know, and the way ye know." Then Thomas, one of the Twelve, interrupted the Lord with a question.

I have always been glad for that interruption and that question. It was a perfectly natural question and the Lord Jesus Christ did not rebuke Thomas for that interruption. He answered that question for him and for us. I say it was a perfectly natural question, for Thomas said unto Him, "Lord, we know not whither thou goest; and how can we know the way?" In substance Thomas was asking a question which I believe has been re-echoed in the heart of every normal, thinking person from that day until now. Thomas was actually saying, "Lord, can a man be sure? Can we be certain of the way from earth to heaven? Can we know beyond all shadow of a doubt?"

My friends, Jesus answered that question for him and for us. The answer was so clear and unmistakable that no man need misunderstand.

What is your conception of the way to heaven? I hear some man say, "Why, I believe the way to heaven is to live a good life, to live upon a high moral plane, to be a good father, a good husband, a good citizen in the community, to live by the Golden Rule, to do unto others as I would have them do unto me."

My friends, these are wonderful virtues which should characterize the life of every child of God, but that is *not* the way from earth to heaven. And if today you are dependent upon your own good works, your own moral life, your own good citizenship, or your own moral rectitude, you are building your hopes upon a false foundation. That is NOT the way to heaven.

Some other man would say, "I believe the way to heaven is to unite with the church, to be baptized, to submit oneself to the ordinances of the church, to be regular in attendance, and faithful to the church's requirements."

Well, friends, these things, too, should be prominent characteristics of every Christian life; but that is not the way from earth to heaven, for neither the Temple Baptist Church of Detroit with which I am affiliated, nor any church to which you may belong, has the power to forgive a single sin or to cleanse a single stain from your guilty, hell-deserving soul.

That is NOT the way to heaven.

What is it? Listen, as Jesus replied to Thomas's question, "How can we know the way?" Jesus answered and said unto him, "I am the way, the truth, and the life; no man cometh unto the Father, but by me." In other words, the Lord Jesus was telling us that all we need from a spiritual standpoint in time and in eternity, in this life and in the next, as far as salvation is concerned, is found in Him. "Neither is there salvation in any other: for there is none other name under heaven given among men, whereby we must be saved.''

Jesus said, ''I am the way''—without the way there is no going. Jesus said, ''I am the truth''—without the truth there is no knowing. Jesus said, ''I am the life''—without the life there is no living. All that we need is found in Christ.

I care not whatever else you may have—a good reputation, a good moral character, many lovable characteristics—if you do not have the Son of God as your Savior, you do not have eternal life.

My friends, that is what the Lord Jesus Christ was talking about when He said, ''For what is a man profited, if he shall gain the whole world, and lose his own soul? or what shall a man give in exchange for his soul?''

When all the great plants of our cities,
    Have turned out their last finished work;
When our merchants have made the last bargain,
    And dismissed the last tired clerk;
When our banks have raked in the last dollar,
    And have paid out the last dividend;
When the Judge of the Earth says,
    ''Closed for the Night!''
And asks for a balance—WHAT THEN?

When the choir has sung its last anthem,
    And the preacher has said his last prayer;
When the people have heard their last sermon,
    And the sound has died out on the air;
When the Bible lies closed on the pulpit,
    And the pews are all empty of men;
When each one stands facing his record,
    And the Great Book is opened—WHAT THEN?

When the actors have played their last drama,
    And the mimic has made his last fun;
When the movies have flashed the last picture,
    And the billboard displayed its last run;
When the crowds seeking pleasure have vanished,
    And have gone into darkness again;
And the world that rejected its Saviour
    Is asked for a reason—WHAT THEN?

When the bugle's last call sinks in silence,
    And the long marching columns stand still;

When the captain has giv'n his last order,
    And they've captured the last fort and hill;
When the flag has been hauled from the masthead,
    And the wounded afield have checked in;
When the Trumpet of Ages is sounded
    And we stand up before Him—WHAT THEN?

Several years ago an old engineer on the Baltimore and Ohio
Railroad was retiring from active service. He was a great Christian and
his testimony ran something like this:

I suppose it is perfectly natural that my mind should go back
forty years or so ago when, just out of school, I got my first job on
the old B & O. I was the child of my parents' old age; therefore
just as soon as I reached young manhood and was able to get a
job, my father who was old had to retire from active work and the
sole support of the family fell on me.

All my life I had wanted to be a railroad man, but in those
early days before many of the modern safety devices had been
perfected, my mother seemed to live in a haunted dread and fear
that one of these days I would be involved in a terrible railroad
accident and would thus lose my life. Every morning when I
would go out on the run, Mother, having prepared my lunch
with her own hands, would put the lunch basket in my hands and
place an arm about my shoulders and I would kiss her good-bye
and she would say, "O God, please watch over our boy today
and bring him back home safe tonight." And I would go out on
my run, climbing up on my engine with those words ringing in
my ears, "O God, please watch over my boy today and bring
him back safe tonight."

Then in the late afternoon as I was coming in from my run
when the old engine would round that last curve on the outskirts
of our little town, I would look up on the hillside to a little vine-
covered cottage, then I'd reach up and give one long blast of the
old whistle; winter or summer a little white-haired mother would
always come over to the window and lean out and wave her handkerchief. The neighbors would tell me that she would always say,
"Thank God, my boy is safe home at last."

In the fullness of time Mother passed on and I had to get a
hired woman to come and cook and keep house for my dad in his
old age. While the hired woman would always fix my lunch, yet
Dad took up where Mother left off and he would not allow
anyone else to put that lunch basket in my hand. Every morning
when I would go out on the run, he placed a trembling hand on

my shoulder and he too would say, "O God, please watch over and protect my boy. Bring him back home safe tonight."

Then just as of yore, when I would come in from my run in the late afternoon and the old engine rounded that last curve, I would reach up again and give a long blast of the whistle and winter or summer, no matter how cold the weather, that old white-headed dad would totter over to the window, lean out and wave his handkerchief. The neighbors told me that he, too, would always say, "Thank God my boy is safe home at last."

Then in the fullness of time, my dad went on Home and my life has been so lonely since then, living in boarding houses.

Now, boys, my hair, too, is white with the frosts of many winters, and it won't be long, according to the laws of nature, before I'll make my last long run.

When that time comes, I have always been so accustomed to riding up at the front end of the train that I am going to ask my Great Engineer to let me ride in the cab with Him on my final run on the old Gospel Train.

When the engine rounds the last curve and my eyes fall for the first time upon the gleaming lights and battlements of the City of God, just as we are about to glide into the Grand Central Station of the Skies, I want to reach up and give one long blast of the whistle. As I climb down from the cab on that last run and I walk into the station, I know that on either side of the Beautiful Gate there will be an old white-haired mother and an old white-haired dad, and the very moment the Gates of Pearl click upon my heels and my feet press for the first time the gold-paved streets of the City of God, I know that old white-haired mother and white-haired dad will throw their arms around me, the first thing they'll say will be, "Thank God, my boy is safe at last."

R.G. Lee
(1886—1978)

Born in a log cabin in 1886 near Fort Mill, South Carolina, Robert Green Lee had a humble sharecropper's beginning. Young Robert was convicted by a Sunday morning sermon when he was twelve. He struggled over his decision as he plowed corn the next day and finally stopped at the end of a row and committed his life to Christ.

As a teenager, he worked for a year on the construction of the Panama Canal to earn money for college. An avid sports enthusiast, he was a track star at Furman University, where he graduated in 1913. He received his doctor's degree from the Chicago Law School in 1919.

Lee pastored for two years in Edgefield, South Carolina, before going to the First Baptist Church of New Orleans, Louisiana, in 1921. Four years later he returned to South Carolina to pastor the Citadel Square Baptist Church in Charleston.

Lee became pastor of Bellevue Baptist Church in Memphis, Tennessee, in 1927. He is best remembered for this great ministry, which lasted for over thirty-two years. Under his leadership the church grew from a membership of 1,400 to over 9,400, and became one of the greatest churches in America. While in Memphis he served as president of the Southern Baptist Convention for three terms. After resigning the church in 1960, Lee traveled around the world preaching for several years, covering over 100,000 miles annually as he neared his eightieth birthday. He died in 1978 at the age of ninety-one.

R.G. Lee was a pulpiteer of the highest caliber. Spending long hours in his study, he shared his deep knowledge of the Scriptures in gifted speech flavored with choice phrases and sentences long to be remembered. His anointed eloquence exalted Christ and never failed to carry the reader heavenward. Dr. Lee's most famous sermon, "Pay Day—Some Day," was preached hundreds of times all across America and in many foreign countries; an estimated 10,000 people were saved under the preaching of this one sermon.

Pay Day—Some Day
By R.G. Lee

Arise, go down to meet Ahab king of Israel, which is in Samaria: behold, he is in the vineyard of Naboth, whither he is gone down to possess it. And thou shalt speak unto him, saying, Thus saith the Lord, Hast thou killed, and also taken possession? And thou shalt speak unto him, saying, Thus saith the Lord, In the place where dogs licked the blood of Naboth shall dogs lick thy blood, even thine. And of Jezebel also spake the Lord, saying, The dogs shall eat Jezebel by the wall of Jezreel (1 Kings 21:18,19,23).

I introduce to you Naboth. Naboth was a devout Israelite who lived in the foothill village of Jezreel. Naboth was a good man. He abhorred that which is evil and clave to that which is good. In spite of the persecution of the prophets he did not shrink from making it known that he was a worshiper of Jehovah. He was an example of one who had not bowed the knee nor given a kiss to Baal.

Naboth would not change his heavenly principles for loose experiences. He would not dilute the stringency of his personal righteousness for questionable compromises. Now Naboth had a vineyard surrounding his house. This little vineyard, fragrant with blossoms in the days of the budding branch and freighted with fruit in the days of the vintage, was a cherished ancestral possession. This vineyard was near the summer palace of Ahab—situated about twenty miles from Samaria—a palace unique in its splendor as the first palace inlaid with ivory.

I introduce to you Ahab—the vile, egotistical, covetous toad who squatted upon the throne of Israel—the worst of Israel's evil kings. King Ahab had command of a nation's wealth and a nation's army, but he had no command of his lusts and appetites. Ahab wore rich robes, but he had a sinning and wicked and troubled heart beneath them. Ahab ate the finest food the world could supply—and this food was served to him in dishes splendid by servants obedient to his every beck and nod—but he had a starved soul. Ahab lived in palaces sumptuous within and without, yet he tormented himself for one bit of land more.

Ahab was a king, with a throne and a crown and a scepter, yet he lived all of his life under the thumb of a wicked woman—a tool in her hands. Ahab has pilloried himself in the contempt of all right-thinking, right-living, God-fearing men as a mean and selfish rascal who was the curse of his country. The Bible introduces him to us in words more appropriate than these when it says: "But there was none like unto Ahab, which did sell himself to work wickedness in the sight of the Lord, whom Jezebel his wife stirred up. And he did very abominably in following idols, according to all things as did the Amorites, whom the Lord cast out before the children of Israel" (1 Kings 21:25,26).

"And Ahab made a grove; and Ahab did more to provoke the Lord God of Israel to anger than all the kings of Israel that were before him" (1 Kings 16:33).

I introduce to you Jezebel, daughter of Ethbaal, King of Tyre (1 Kings 16:31), and wife of Ahab, the King of Israel—a king's daughter and a king's wife, the evil genius at once of her dynasty and of her country. Infinitely more daring and reckless was she in her wickedness than was her wicked husband. Masterful, indomitable, implacable, the instigator and supporter of religious persecution, called "the authentic author of priestly inquisitions," a devout worshiper of Baal, she hated anybody and everybody who spoke against or refused to worship her false and helpless god. As blunt in her wickedness and as brazen in her lewdness was she as Cleopatra, fair sorceress of the Nile. She had all the subtle and successful scheming of Lady Macbeth, all the adulterous desire and treachery of Potiphar's wife (Gen. 39:7-20), all the boldness of Mary Queen of Scots, all the cruelty and whimsical imperiousness of Katherine of Russia, all the devilish infamy of a Madame Pompadour, and, doubtless, all the fascination of personality of a Josephine of France.

Most of that which is bad in all evil women found expression through this painted viper of Israel. She had that rich endowment of nature which a good woman ought always to dedicate to the service of her day and generation. But—alas!—this idolatrous daughter of an idolatrous king of an idolatrous people engaging with her maidens in worship unto Ashtoreth—the personification of the most forbidding obscenity, uncleanness, and sensuality—became the evil genius who wrought wreck, brought blight, and devised death. She was the beautiful and malicious adder coiled upon the throne of the nation.

I introduce to you Elijah the Tishbite, the prophet of God at a time when by tens of thousands the people had forsaken God's covenants, thrown down God's altars, slain God's prophets with the sword (1 Kings 19:10). The young prophet, knowing much of the glorious past of the now apostate nation, must have been filled with horror when he learned of the rank heathenism, fierce cruelties, and reeking licentiousness of Ahab's idolatrous capital—at a time when Jezebel "set herself, with Ahab's tacit consent, to extirpate the religion of Jehovah from the land of Israel." Holy anger burned within him like an unquenchable Vesuvius or the flames of Martinique.

Elijah! Heir to the infinite riches of God he! Elijah! Attended by the hosts of heaven he! Little human companionship he had! But he was not lonely—because God was with him, and he was sometimes attended by the hosts of heaven. He wore a rough sheepskin cloak, but there was a peaceful, confident heart beneath it. He ate bird's food and widow's fare, but was a physical and spiritual athlete. He had no lease of office or authority, yet everyone obeyed him. He grieved only when God's cause seemed tottering. He passed from earth without dying—into celestial glory. Everywhere where courage is admired and manhood honored and service appreciated he is honored as one of earth's heroes and one of heaven's saints. He was "a seer, and saw clearly; a hero, and dared valiantly; a great heart, and felt deeply."

And now with these four persons introduced we want to turn to God's Word and see the tragedy of pay day some day! We will see the corn they put into the hopper and then behold the grist that came out the spout.

The first scene in this tragedy of "pay day—some day" is—

I. The Real Estate Request

"And it came to pass after these things, that Naboth the Jezreelite had a vineyard, which was in Jezreel, hard by the palace of Ahab king of Samaria. And Ahab spoke unto Naboth, saying, Give me thy vineyard, that I may have it for a garden of herbs, because it is near unto my house: and I will give thee for it a better vineyard than it; or, if it seem good to thee, I will give thee the worth of it in money" (1 Kings 21:1,2).

Thus far Ahab was quite within his rights. No intention had he of cheating Naboth out of his vineyard or of killing him to get it. Honestly did he offer to give him its worth in money. Honestly did he offer him a better vineyard for it.

Ahab had not, however, counted upon the reluctance of all Jews to part with their inheritance of land. By peculiar tenure every Israelite held his land, and to all land-holding transactions there was another party, even God, "who made the heavens and the earth." Throughout Judah and Israel, Jehovah was the real owner of the soil; and every tribe received its territory and every family its inheritance by lot from Him, with the added condition that the land should not be sold forever. "The land shall not be sold for ever: for the land is mine; for ye are strangers and sojourners with me" (Lev. 25:23). "So shall not the inheritance of the children of Israel remove from tribe to tribe: for every one of the children of Israel shall keep himself to the inheritance of the tribe of his fathers.... But every one of the tribes of the children of Israel shall keep himself to his own inheritance" (Num. 36:7-9).

Thus we see that the permanent sale of the paternal inheritance was forbidden by law. Ahab forgot—if he had ever really known it—that for Naboth to sell for money or to swap for a better vineyard his little vineyard would seem to that good man like a denial of his allegiance to the true religion to sell it when jubilee restoration was neglected in such idolatrous times.

Fearing God most and man least, and obeying the One whom he feared the most and loved the most, he said: "The Lord forbid it me, that I should give the inheritance of my fathers unto thee" (1 Kings 21:3).

True to the religious teachings of his father with real-hearted loyalty to the convenant God of Israel, he believed he held the land in fee simple from God. His father and grandfather, and doubtless grandfather's father, had owned the land before him. All the memories of childhood were tangled in its grapevines. His father's hand, folded now in the dust of death, had used the pruning blade among the branches, and because of this every branch and vine were dear. His mother's hands, now doubtless wrapped in a duststained shroud, had gathered purple clusters from those bunchladen boughs, and for this reason he loved every spot in his vineyard and every branch on his vines. The ties of sentiment, of religion, and of family pride bound and endeared him to the place. So his refusal to sell was quick, firm, final, and courteous.

So with "the courage of a bird that dares the wild sea," he took his stand against the king's proposal.

And that brings us to the second scene in this tragedy. It is—

II. The Pouting Potentate

Naboth's quick, firm, courteous, final refusal took all the spokes from the wheels of Ahab's desire and changed it into a foiled and foaming whirlpool of sullen sulks.

"And Ahab came into his house heavy and displeased because of the word which Naboth the Jezreelite had spoken to him: for he had said, I will not give thee the inheritance of my fathers. And he laid him down upon his bed, and turned away his face, and would eat no bread" (1 Kings 21:4).

What a ridiculous picture! A king acting like a spoiled and sullen child—impotent in disappointment and ugly in petty rage! A king, whose victories over the Syrians have rung through many lands—a conqueror, a slave to himself—whining like a sick hound! A king, rejecting all converse with others, pouting like a spoiled and petulant child that has been denied one trinket in the midst of one thousand playthings! A king, in a chamber "ceiled with cedar, and painted with vermilion" (Jer. 22:14), prostituting genius to theatrical trumpery.

What an ancient picture we have of great powers dedicated to mean, ugly, petty things. Think of it! In the middle of the day, the commander-in-chief of an army seized by Sergeant Sensitive. General Ahab made prisoner by Private Pouts! The leader of an army laid low by Corporal Mopishness! A monarch moaning and blubbering and growlingly refusing to eat because a man, a good man, because of the commandments of God and because of religious principles, would not sell or swap a little vineyard which was his by inheritance from his forefathers.

What an ancient picture of great powers and talents prostituted to base and purposeless ends and withheld from the service of God! What an ancient spectacle! And how modern and up-to-date, in this respect, was Ahab, king of Israel. What a likeness to him in conduct today are many talented men and women. I know men and women—you know men and women—with diamond and ruby abilities who are worth no more to God through the churches than a punctured Japanese nickel in a Chinese bazaar!

So many there are who, like Ahab, withhold their talents from God—using them in the service of the Devil. People there are, not a few, who have pipe-organ abilities and make no more music for the cause of Christ than a wheezy saxophone in an idiot's hands. People there are, many of them, who have incandescent-light powers who make no more light for God than a smoky barn lantern, with smoke-blackened globe, on a stormy night. People there are—I know them and you know them—with locomotive powers doing pushcart work for God. People there are—and how sad 'tis true—who have steam-shovel abilities who are doing teaspoon work for God. Yes!

Now look at this overfed bull bellowing for a little spot of grass outside his own vast pasture lands—and, if you are withholding talents and powers from the service of God, receive the rebuke of the tragic and ludicrous picture.

And now, consider the third scene in this tragedy of "pay day—some day." It is—

III—The Wicked Wife

When Ahab would "eat no bread," the servants went and told

Jezebel. What she said to them, we do not know. Something of what she said to Ahab we do know. Puzzled and provoked at the news that her husband would not eat—that he had gone to bed when it was not bed-time—Jezebel went to investigate. She found him in bed with his face turned to the wall, his lips swollen with mulish moping, his eyes burning with cheap anger-fire, his heart stubborn in wicked rebellion. He was groaningly mournful and peevishly petulant—having, up to the moment when she stood by his bedside, refused to eat or cheer up in the least.

At first, in a voice of solicitousness, she sought the reason of his choler. In "sweet" and anxious concern she said: "Why is thy spirit so sad, that thou eatest no bread?" (1 Kings 21:5). And then, as the man-ner of women is unto this day, she doubtless put her hand on his forehead to see if he had temperature. He had temperature all right. Like the tongue of the wicked, he was set on fire of hell. Then he told her, every word full of petulance and mopish peevishness as he spoke: "Because I spake unto Naboth the Jezreelite, and said unto him, Give me thy vineyard for money; or else, if it please thee, I will give thee another vineyard for it: and he answered I will not give thee my vineyard!" (1 Kings 21:6).

With her tongue, sharp like a razor, she prods Ahab as an ox driver prods with sharp goad the ox which does not want to press his neck into the yoke, or as one whips with a rawhide a stubborn mule. With profuse and harsh laughter this old gray and gaudy guinea of Satan derided this king of hers for a cowardly buffoon and sordid jester.

What hornet-like sting in her sarcasm! What wolf-mouth fierceness in her every reproach! What tiger-fang cruelty in her expressed displeasure! What fury in the shrieking of her rebuke! What bitter bit-terness in the teasing taunts she hurled at him for his scrupulous timidity! Her bosom with anger was heaving! Her eyes were flashing with rage under the surge of hot anger that swept over her.

"Are you not the king of this country?" she chides bitingly, her tongue sharp like a butcher's blade. "Can you not command and have it done?" she scolds as a common village hag who has more noise than wisdom in her words. "Can you not seize and keep?" she cries with reproach. "I thought you told me you were king in these parts! And here you are crying like a baby and will not eat anything because you do not have courage to take a bit of land. You! Ha! Ha! Ha! Ha! You the king of Israel, and allow yourself to be disobeyed and defied by a common clodhopper from the country. You are more courteous and considerate of him than you are of your queen! Shame on you! But you leave it to me! I will get the vineyard for you, and all that I require is that you ask no questions. Leave it to me, Ahab!"

"And Jezebel his wife said unto him, Dost thou now govern the

kingdom of Israel? arise, and eat bread, and let thine heart be merry: I
will give thee the vineyard of Naboth the Jezreelite!'' (1 Kings 21:7).

Ahab knew Jezebel well enough to know assuredly that she would do
her best, or her devil's worst, to do what she said she would do. So slowly, as a turtle crawls out of the cold mud when the hot sunshine hits it, he
came out of his sulks, somewhat as a snake arouses and uncoils from
winter sleep. He doubtless asked her, with a show of reluctant eagerness,
how she was going to get Naboth's vineyard. She, if she acted as human
nature naturally expresses itself, tickled him under the chin with her lily
white and bejeweled fingers, or kissed him peckingly on the cheeks with
her lips screwed in a tight knot, and said something akin to these words:
''That's my secret just now; just leave it to me!''

She was the polluted reservoir from which the streams of his own
iniquity found mighty increase. She was the poisonous pocket from
which his cruel fangs fed. She was the sulphurous pit wherein the fires of
his own iniquity found fuel for intenser burning. She was the Devil's
grindstone which furnished sharpening for his weapons of wickedness.

I suppose Ahab considered himself the master of his wife. But it was
her mastery over him that stirred him up to more and mightier
wickedness than his own heart was capable of conceiving, than his own
mind was capable of planning, than his own will was capable of
executing.

What a tragedy when any woman thinks more of paint than purity,
of vulgarity than virtue, of pearls than principles, of adornment than
righteous adoration, of hose and hats than holiness, of dress than duty, of
mirrors than manners! What a tragedy when any woman sacrifices
decency on the altar of degradation—visualizing the slimy, the tawdry,
the tinseled!

Know ye not yet, ye women, that the degeneracy of womanhood
helps the decay of manhood? Know ye not that when woman is lame
morally man limps morally?—that when woman slips morally man
slumps morally?—when woman fags in spiritual ideals man sags in
spiritual ideals? Study history as much as you please and read the Bible
as often as you will, and you will see that the moral and spiritual life of no
nation, no community, no city, no village, no countryside, no home, no
school, no church ever rises any higher or flows any stronger than the
spiritual life of the women.

Who was it who caused Samson to have his eyes punched out and to
be a prisoner of the Philistines, after he had been judge in Israel for twenty years? Delilah—a woman! Who was it caused David to stake his
crown for a caress? Bathsheba—a woman. Who was it danced Herod into hell? Herodias—a woman! Who was it who was like a heavy chain
around the neck of Governor Felix for life or death, for time and eterni-

ty? Drusilla—a woman! Who was it, by lying and diabolical strategem, sent the spotless Joseph to jail because he refused her dirty, improper proposal? Potiphar's wife.

So also it was a woman, a passionate and ambitious idolatress, even Jezebel, who mastered Ahab. Take the stirring crimes of any age, and at the bottom more or less consciously concerned, the world, almost invariably, finds a woman. Only God Almighty knows the full story of the foul plots hatched by women. This was true, as we shall presently see, with the two under discussion now. But let me say, incidentally, if women have mastered men for evil, they have also mastered them for good—and we gladly make declaration that some of the fairest and most fragrant flowers that grow in the garden of God and some of the sweetest and most luscious fruit that ripens in God's spiritual orchards are there because of woman's faith, woman's love, woman's prayer, woman's virtue, woman's tears, woman's devotion to Christ.

But we must not depart further from the objective of this message to discuss that. Let us come to the next terrible scene in this tragedy of sin.

The next scene is—

IV—A Message Meaning Murder

Jezebel wrote letters to the elders of Jezreel. And in these letters she made definite and subtle declaration that some terrible sin had been committed in their city for which it was needful that a fast should be proclaimed in order to avert the wrath of heaven.

"So she wrote letters in Ahab's name, and sealed them with his seal, and sent the letters unto the elders and to the nobles that were in his city, dwelling with Naboth. And she wrote in the letters, saying, Proclaim a fast, and set Naboth on high among the people: and set two men, sons of Belial, before him, to bear witness against him, saying, Thou didst blaspheme God and the king. And then carry him out, and stone him, that he may die" (1 Kings 21:8-10).

This letter, with cynical disregard of decency, was a hideous mockery in the name of religion. Once get the recusant citizen accused of blasphemy, and, by a divine law, the property of the blasphemer and rebel went to the crown. "Justice! How many traitors to sacred truth have dragged the innocent to destruction!"

Surely black ink never wrote a fouler plot or death scheme on white paper since writing was known among men. Every syllable of every word of every line of every sentence was full of hate toward him who had done only good continually. Every letter of every syllable was but the thread which, united with other threads, made the hangman's noose for him who had not changed his righteous principles for the whim of a king. The whole letter was a diabolical death-warrant.

Moreover, Jezebel's deeds showed that when she went down to market, as it were, she would have in her basket a nice vineyard for her husband when she returned. She said to herself: "This man Naboth has refused my honorable lord on religious grounds, and by all the gods of Baal, I will get him yet on these very same grounds." She understood perfectly the passion of a devout Jew for a public fast; and she knew that nothing would keep the Jews away. Every Jew and every member of his household would be there.

"Proclaim a fast." Fasting has ever been a sign of humiliation before God, of humbling one's self in the dust before the "high and lofty One that inhabiteth eternity." The idea in calling for a fast was clearly to declare that the community was under the anger of God on account of a grave crime committed by one of its members, which crime is to be exposed and punished. Then, too, the fast involved a cessation of work, a holiday, so that the citizens would have time to attend the public gathering.

"Set Naboth on high!" "On high" meant before the bar of justice, not in the seat of honor. "On high" meant that Naboth was put where every eye could watch him closely and keenly observe his bearing under the accusation. "And set two men, base fellows, before him."

And let them "bear witness against him!" In other words, put him out of the way by judicial murder, not by private assassination. "And then carry him out, and stone him, that he may die!" A criminal was not to be executed within a city, as that would defile it! Thus Christ was crucified outside the walls of Jerusalem! We see that Jezebel took it for granted that Naboth would be condemned.

And so one day, while Naboth worked in his vineyard, the letters came down to Jezreel. And one evening, while Naboth talked at the cottage door with his sons or neighbors, the message meaning murder was known to the elders of the city. And that night, while he slept with the wife of his bosom, the hounds of death let loose from the kennels of hell by the jewel-adorned fingers of a king's daughter and a king's wife were close on his heels. The message meaning murder was known to many but not to him, until they came and told him that a fast had been proclaimed—proclaimed because God had been offended at some crime and that His wrath must be appeased and the threatening anger turned away, and he himself, all unconscious of any offense toward God or the king, set in the place of the accused, even "on high among the people," to be tried as a conspicuous criminal.

Consider now—

V—The Fatal Fast

And what concern they must have created in the household of

Naboth, when they knew that Naboth was to be "set on high," even in the "seat of the accused," even before the bar of "justice," because of a ferocious message calling religion in to attest a lie. And what excitement there was in the city when, with fawning readiness to carry out her vile commands, the elders and nobles "fastened the minds" of the people upon the fast—proclaimed as if some great calamity were overhanging the city for their sins like a black cloud portending a storm, and proclaimed as if something must be done at once to avert the doom. Curious throngs hurried to the fast to see him who had been accused of the crime which made necessary the appeasing of the threatening wrath of an angered God.

And they did! "And there came in two men, children of Belial, and sat before him" (1 Kings 21:13). Satan's hawks ready to bring death to God's harmless sparrow! Satan's eagles ready to bury their cruel talons in God's innocent dove. Satan's bloody wolves ready to kill God's lamb! Satan's boars ready with keen tusks to rip God's stag to shreds! Reckless and depraved professional perjurers they were! "And the men of Belial witnessed against him, even against Naboth, in the presence of the people, saying, Naboth did blaspheme God and the king" (1 Kings 21:13).

Then strong hands jerked Naboth out of the seat of the accused. Doubtless muttering curses the while, they dragged him out from among the throngs of people, while children screamed and cried, while women shrieked in terror, while men moved in confusion and murmured in consternation. They dragged him roughly to a place outside the walls of the city and with stones they beat his body to the ground. Naboth fell to the ground as lily by hailstones beaten to earth, as stately cedar uprooted by furious storm. His head by stones is crushed, as eggs crushed by heel of giant. His legs are splintered! His arms are broken! His ribs are crushed. Bones stick out from the mass of human flesh as fingers of ivory from pots of red paint. Brains, emptied from his skull, are scattered about. Blood spatters like crimson rain. Naboth's eyes roll in sockets of blood. His tongue between broken jaws becomes still. His mauled body becomes—at last—still. His last gasp is a sigh. Naboth is dead—dead for cursing God and the king as many were led to believe!

And we learn from 2 Kings 9:26, that by the savage law of those days his innocent sons were involved in his overthrow. They, too, that they might not claim the inheritance, were slain. And Naboth's property, left without heirs, reverted to the crown.

No doubt Naboth's righteous austerity had made him extremely unpopular in many ways in "progressive Jezreel." And since Jezebel carried out her purpose in a perfectly legal and orderly way and in a "wonderfully" democratic manner, we see a fine picture of autocracy working by democratic methods. And when these "loyally patriotic citizens" of Jezreel had left the bodies of Naboth and his sons to be devoured by the wild dogs which prowled after night-fall in and around the city, they sent and told Queen Jezebel that her bloody orders had been bloodily and completely obeyed! "Then they sent to Jezebel, saying, Naboth is stoned, and is dead" (1 Kings 21:14).

I do not know where Jezebel was when she received the news of Naboth's death. Maybe she was out on the lawn watching the fountains splash. Maybe she was in the sun parlor, or somewhere listening to the musicians thrum on their instruments. But, if I judge this painted human viper by her nature, I say she received the tragic news with devilish delight, with jubilant merriment.

What was it to her that yonder, over twenty miles away, sat a little woman who the night before had her husband but who now washes her crushed and ghastly face with her tears? What did it matter to her that in Jezreel only yesterday her sons ran to her at her call but today are mangled in death? What did it matter to her that outside the city walls the dogs licked the blood of a godly husband? What mattered it to her that Jehovah God had been defied, His commandments broken, His altars splattered with pagan mud, His holy Name profaned? What mattered it to her that the worship of God had been dishonored?

What did she care if a wife, tragically widowed by murder, walked life's way in loneliness? What did she care that there was lamentation and grief and great mourning,   Rachel weeping for her children because they were not? What did she care if justice had been outraged just so she had gotten the little plot of land close by their place within which was evil girt with diadem? Nothing! Did pang grip her heart because innocent blood had been shed? Just as well ask if the ravenous lion mourns over the lamb it devours.

Trippingly, as a gay dancer, she hurried in to where Ahab sat. With profuse caresses and words glib with joy she told him the "good" news. She had about her the triumphant manner of one who has accomplished successfully what others had not dared attempt. Her "tryout" in getting the vineyard was a decided "triumph." She had "pulled the stunt." She had been "brave" and "wise"—and because of this her husband now could arise and hie him down to the vineyard and call it his own.

"And it came to pass, when Jezebel heard that Naboth was stoned, and was dead, that Jezebel said to Ahab, Arise, take possession of the vineyard of Naboth the Jezreelite, which he refused to give thee for money: for Naboth is not alive, but dead" (1 Kings 21:15).

And it was the plot hatched in her own mind and it was her hand, her lily-white hand, her queen's hand, that wrote the letters that made this tragic statement true.

And the next scene in this tragedy of "pay day—some day" is—

VI. The Visit to the Vineyard

How Jezebel must have paraded with pride before Ahab when she went with tidings that the vineyard which he wanted to buy was now his for nothing! How keen must have been the sarcasm of her attitude when she made it known by word and manner that she had succeeded where he failed—and at less cost! How gloatingly victorious were the remarks which she made which kept him warmly reminded that she had kept her "sacred" promise! What a lovely fabric, stained and dyed red with Naboth's blood, she spread before him for his "comfort" from the loom of her evil machinations!

"And it came to pass, when Ahab heard that Naboth was dead, that Ahab rose up to go down to the vineyard of Naboth the Jezreelite, to take possession of it" (1 Kings 21:16). Ahab rose up to go down—from Samaria to Jezreel. He gave orders to his royal wardrobe keeper to get out his king's clothes, because he had a little "business" trip to make to look over some property that had come to him by the shrewdness of his wife in the real estate market!

Jehu and Bidkar, the royal charioteers, make ready the great horses such as kings had in those days. Jehu was the speed-breaking driver of his day, known as the one who drove furiously. The gilded chariot is drawn forth. The fiery horses are harnessed and to the king's chariot hitched. The outriders, in gorgeous garments dressed, saddle their horses and make ready to accompany the king in something of military state. Then, amid the clatter of prancing hoofs and the loud breathing of the chariot horses—eager-eyed, alert, strong-muscled, bellows-lunged, stouthearted, and agile of feet—Jehu drives the horses to the chariot hitched up to the palace steps.

Out from the palace doors, Jezebel walking, almost strutting, proudly and gaily at his side, comes Ahab. Down the steps he goes while Jezebel, perhaps, waves a bejeweled hand to him or speaks a "sweet" good-bye. Bidkar opens the chariot door. Ahab steps in. Then, with the crack of his whip or a sharp command by word of mouth, Jehu sends the great horses on their way—away from the palace steps, away from the palace grounds, away through the gates, away, accompanied by the outriders, away down the road to Jezreel!

Where is God? Where is God? Is He blind that He cannot see? Is He deaf that He cannot hear? Is He dumb that He cannot speak? Is He paralyzed that He cannot move? *Where is God?* Well, wait a minute, and we shall see.

Over there in the palace Jezebel said to Ahab, her husband: "Arise! Get thee down and take possession of the vineyard of Naboth." And over yonder in the wilderness way, out yonder where the tall cedars waved like green plumes against a silver shield, against the moon blossoming in its fulness like a great jonquil in the garden of the patient stars, out yonder where the only music of the night was the weird call of whippoorwill and the cough of coyote and the howl of wolf, out yonder God had an eagle-eyed, hairy, stouthearted prophet, a great physical and spiritual athlete, Elijah. "And the word of the Lord came to Elijah." and God said to Elijah: "Arise, go down."

Over here, in the palace, Jezebel said to Ahab: "Arise, get thee down!" And out there, near Carmel, God said to Elijah: "Arise!" I am so glad that I live in a universe where, when the Devil has his Ahab to whom he can say, "Arise," God has His Elijah to whom He can say, "Arise!"

"And the word of the Lord came to Elijah the Tishbite, saying, Arise, go down to meet Ahab king of Israel, which is in Samaria: behold, he is in the vineyard of Naboth, whither he is gone down to possess it. And thou shalt speak unto him, saying, Thus saith the Lord. Hast thou killed, and also taken possession? And thou shalt speak unto him, saying, Thus saith the Lord, In the place where the dogs licked the blood of Naboth shall dogs lick thy blood, even thine" (1 Kings 21:17-19).

As Ahab goes down to Jezreel, the voice of Jehu, as he restrains the fiery horses, or the lash of his whip as he urges them on, attracts the attention of the grazing cattle on adjacent pasture land. The sound of clanking hoofs of cantering horses resounds in every glen by the roadway. The gilded chariot catches the light of the sun and reflects it brightly, but he who rides therein is unmindful of the bloodstains on the ground where Naboth died.

And that brings us to the other scene in this tragedy of "pay day—some day." It is—

VII. The Alarming Appearance

The journey of twenty-odd miles from Samaria to Jezreel is over. Jehu brings the horses to a stop outside the gate to the vineyard. The horses stretch their necks trying to get slack on the reins. They have stood well the furious pace at which they have been driven. Around the rim of their harness is the foam of their sweat. On their flanks are, perhaps, the marks of Jehu's whip. They breathe as though their great lungs were a tireless bellows. The outriders line up in something of military formation. The hands of ready servants open the gate to the vineyard. Bidkar opens the chariot door. And Ahab steps out into Naboth's vineyard. There, no doubt, he sees, in the soft soil, Naboth's footprints. Close by doubtless, the smaller footprints of his wife he sees.

Naboth is dead, and the coveted vineyard is now Ahab's through the "gentle scheming" of the queen of his house. Perhaps Ahab, as he walks into the vineyard, sees Naboth's pruning hook among the vines. Or he notices the fine trellis work which Naboth's hands had fastened together for the growing vines. Perhaps, in a corner of the vineyard, is a seat where Naboth and his sons rested after the day's toil, or a well where sparkling waters refreshed the thirsty or furnished water for the vines in time of drouth.

And while Ahab strolls among the vines that Naboth tended, what is it that appears? Snarling wild beasts? No. Black clouds full of threatening storm? No, not that. Flaming lightning which dazzles him? No. War chariots of his ancient enemies rumbling along the road? No. An oncoming flood sweeping things before it? No; not a flood. A tornado goring the earth? No. A huge serpent threatening to encircle him and crush his bones in its deadly coils? No; not a serpent. What then? What alarmed Ahab so? Let us follow him and see.

As he converses with himself, suddenly a shadow falls across his path. Quick as a flash Ahab whirls on his heels, and there before him stands Elijah, prophet of the living God. Elijah's cheeks are swarthy; his eye is keen and piercing; like coals of fire, his eyes burn with righteous indignation in their sockets; his bosom heaves; his head is held high. His only weapon is a staff; his only robe a sheepskin, and a leather girdle about his loins.

Like an apparition from the other world, like Banquo's ghost at Macbeth's feast, Elijah, with suddenness terrifying, stands before Ahab. Ahab had not seen Elijah for five years. Ahab thought Elijah had been cowed and silenced by Jezebel, but now the prophet confronts him with his death-warrant from the Lord God Almighty.

To Ahab there is an eternity of agony in the few moments they stand thus, face to face, eye to eye, soul to soul! His voice is hoarse, like the cry of a hunted animal. He trembles like a hunted stag before the mouths of fierce hounds. Suddenly his face goes white. His lips quiver. He had gone to take possession of a vineyard, coveted for a garden of herbs; and there he is face to face with righteousness, face to face with honor, face to face with judgment. The vineyard, with the sun shining upon it now, is as black as if it were part of the midnight which has gathered in judgment.

"And Ahab said to Elijah, Hast thou found me, O mine enemy?" (1 Kings 21:20). And Elijah, without a tremor in his voice, his eyes burning their way into Ahab's guilty soul, answered: "I have found thee: because thou hast sold thyself to work evil in the sight of the Lord." Then, with every word a thunderbolt, and every sentence a withering denunciation, Elijah continued: "God told me to ask you this: Hast thou killed, and also taken possession? . . . Thus saith the Lord, In the place where dogs licked the blood of Naboth shall dogs lick thy blood, even thine. . . . Behold, I will bring evil upon thee, and will take away thy posterity. . . . And will make thine house like the house of Jeroboam the son of Nebat, and like the house of Baasha the son of Ahijah, for the provocation wherewith thou hast provoked me to anger, and made Israel to sin!''

And then, plying other words mercilessly like a terrible scourge to the cringing Ahab, Elijah said: "And of Jezebel also spake the Lord, saying, The dogs shall eat Jezebel by the wall of Jezreel. Him that dieth of Ahab in the city the dogs shall eat; and him that dieth in the field shall the fowls of the air eat."

And, with these words, making Ahab to cower as one cowers and recoils from a hissing adder, filling Ahab's vineyard to be haunted with ghosts and the clusters thereof to be full of blood, Elijah went his way—as was his custom so suddenly to appear and so quickly to disappear. Ahab had sold himself for nought, as did Achan for a burial robe, and a useless ingot, as did Judas for thirty pieces of silver which so burned his palms and so burned his conscience and so burned his soul until he found relief in the noose at the rope's end.

And when Ahab got back in the chariot to go back to Jezebel—the vile toad who squatted upon the throne to be again with the beautiful adder coiled upon the throne—the hoofs of the horses pounding the road pounded into his guilty soul Elijah's words: "Some day—the dogs will lick thy blood! Some day the dogs will eat Jezebel—by the ramparts of Jezreel." God had spoken! Would it come to pass?

And that brings us to the last scene in this tragedy of "pay day— some day." It is—

VIII. Pay Day—Some Day

Does pay day come? As to Ahab and Jezebel, pay day comes as certainly as night follows day, because sin carries in itself the seed of its own fatal penalty. Dr. Meyer says: "According to God's constitution of the world, the wrong-doer will be abundantly punished." The fathers sow the wind and the children reap the whirlwind. One generation labors to scatter tares, and the next generation reaps tares and retribution immeasureable.

To the individual who goes not the direction God points, a terrible pay day comes. To the nation which forgets God, pay day will come in the awful realization of the truth that the "nations that forget God shall be turned into hell." When nations trample on the principles of the Almighty, the result is that the world is beaten with many stripes. We have seen nations slide into Gehenna—and the smoke of their torment has gone up before our eyes day and night.

The certainty of pay day—some day for all who regard not God or man is set forth in the words of an unknown poet:

You'll pay. The knowledge of your acts will weigh

Heavier on your mind each day.

The more you climb, the more you gain,

The more you'll feel the nagging strain.

Success will cower at the threat

of retribution. Fear will fret

Your peace and bleed you for the debt;

Conscience collects from every crook

More than the worth of what he took.

You only thought you got away

But in the night you'll pay and pay.

All these statements are but verification of Bible truth:

"Whoso diggeth a pit shall fall therein: and he that rolleth a stone, it will return upon him" (Prov. 26:27).

"Therefore shall they eat of the fruit of their own way, and be filled with their own devices. For the turning away of the simple shall slay them, and the prosperity of fools shall destroy them" (Prov. 1:31,32).

"Even as I have seen, they that plow iniquity, and sow wickedness, reap the same" (Job 4:8).

"The gods are just—and of our vices made instruments to scourge us."

When I was pastor of the First Baptist Church of New Orleans, all that I preached and taught was sent out over the radio. In my "fan mail" I received letters from a young man who called himself "Chief of the Kangaroo Court." Many nasty, critical things he said. Sometimes he wrote a nice line—and a nice line was in all the vulgar things he wrote like a gardenia in a garbage can.

One day I received a telephone call from a nurse in the Charity Hospital of New Orleans. It was about this fellow who so often dipped his pen in slop, who seldom thrust his pen into nectar. She said: "Pastor, there is a young man down here whose name we do not know, who will not tell us his name. All he will tell us is that he is chief of the Kangaroo Court. He is going to die. He says that you are the only preacher he has ever heard—and he has never seen you. He wants to see you. Will you come down?" "Yes," I replied. And I quit what I was doing and hurried down to the hospital.

The young nurse met me at the entrance to the charity ward and took me in. Inside were several beds against the wall on one side and against the wall on the other side. And in a place by itself was another bed. To this bed, on which lay a young man about eighteen or nineteen years old, slender, hollow-eyed, nervous, the nurse led me. "This is the chief of the Kangaroo Court," she said simply.

I looked upon the young man, "Hello," I said kindly.

"Howdy do?" he answered, in a voice that was half a snarl.

"What can I do for you?" I asked, trying to make him see my willingness to help him.

"Not a thing! Nothin' 'tall" he said grouchily, "unless you throw my body to the buzzards when I am dead—if the buzzards will have it!"

A rather painful silence, in which I looked kindly at him and he wildly at me, ensued.

Then he spoke again. "I sent for you, sir, because I want you to tell these young fellows here something for me. I sent for you because I know you go up and down the land and talk to many young people. And I want you to tell 'em and tell 'em every chance you get, that the Devil pays only in counterfeit money."

This was in desperate earnestness, in his eyes and in his voice. I held his hand as he died. I saw his eyes glaze. I heard the last gurgle in his throat. I saw his chest heave like a bellows and then become quiet.

When he died, the little nurse called me to her, excitedly. "Come here!" she called.

"What do you want, child?" I asked.

"I want to wash your hands! It's dangerous to *touch* him."

Pay day had come!

But what about Ahab? Did pay day come for him? Yes. Consider how. Three years went by. Ahab is still king. And I dare say that during those three years Jezebel had reminded him that they were eating herbs out of Naboth's vineyard. I can hear her say something like this as they sat at the king's table: "Ahab, help yourself to these herbs. I thought Elijah said the dogs were going to lick your blood. I guess his dogs lost their noses and lost the trail."

But I think that during those three years, Ahab never heard a dog bark that he did not jump.

One day Jehoshaphat, king of Judah, visited Ahab. The Bible tells us what took place—what was said, what was done.

"And the king of Israel said unto his servants. Know ye that Ramoth in Gilead is ours, and we be still, and take it not out of the hand of the king of Syria? And he said unto Jehoshaphat, Wilt thou go with me to battle to Ramoth-gilead? And Jehoshaphat said to the king of Israel, I am as thou art, my people as thy people, my horses as thy horses" (1 Kings 22:3,4).

"So the king of Israel and Jehoshaphat the king of Judah went up to Ramoth-gilead" (1 Kings 22:29).

Ahab, after Jehoshaphat had promised to go with him, in his heart was afraid, and had sad forebodings, dreadful premonitions, horrible fears. Remembering the withering words of Elijah three years before, he disguised himself—put armor on his body and covered this armor with ordinary citizen's clothes.

"And the king of Israel said unto Jehoshaphat, I will disguise myself, and enter into the battle; but put thou on thy robes. And the king of Israel disguised himself, and went into the battle" (1 Kings 22:30).

The Syrian general had given orders to slay only the king of Israel—Ahab.

"But the king of Syria commanded his thirty and two captains that had rule over his chariots, saying, Fight neither with small nor great, save only with the king of Israel" (1 Kings 22:31).

Jehoshaphat was not injured, although he wore his royal clothes.

"And it came to pass, when the captains of the chariots saw Jehoshaphat, that they said, Surely it is the king of Israel. And they turned aside to fight against him: and Jehoshaphat cried out. And it came to pass, when the captains of the chariots perceived that it was not the king of Israel, that they turned back from pursuing him" (1 Kings 22:32,33).

While war steeds neighed and war chariots rumbled and shields clashed on shields and arrows whizzed and spears were thrown and swords were wielded, a death-carrying arrow, shot by an aimless and nameless archer, found the crack in Ahab's armor.

"And a certain man drew a bow at a venture, and smote the king of Israel between the joints of the harness: wherefore he said unto the driver of his chariot, Turn thee thine hand, and carry me out of the host; for I am wounded. And the battle increased that day: and the king was stayed up in his chariot against the Syrians, and died at even: and the blood ran out of the wound into the midst of the chariot.... And one washed the chariot in the pool of Samaria; and the dogs licked up his blood; and they washed his armour; *according unto the word of the Lord which He spake"* (1 Kings 22:34,35,38).

But what about Jezebel? Did her pay day come? Yes—after twenty years. After Ahab's death, after the dogs licked the blood, she virtually ruled the kingdom. But I think that she went into the temple of Baal on occasions and prayed her god Baal to protect her from Elijah's hounds.

Elijah had been taken home to heaven without the touch of the deathdew upon his brow. Elisha had succeeded him.

"And Elisha the prophet called one of the children of the prophets, and said unto him, Gird up thy loins, and take this box of oil in thine hand, and go to Ramoth-gilead: and when thou comest thither, look out there Jehu the son of Jehoshaphat the son of Nimshi, and go in, and make him arise up from among his brethren, and carry him to an inner chamber; then take the box of oil, and pour it on his head, and say, Thus saith the Lord, I have anointed thee king over Israel. Then open the door, and flee, and tarry not. So the young man, even the young man the prophet, went to Ramoth-gilead. And when he came, behold, the captains of the host were sitting; and he said, I have an errand to thee, O captain. And Jehu said, Unto which of all us? And he said, To thee, O captain. And he arose, and went into the house; and he poured the oil on his head, and said unto him, Thus saith the Lord God of Israel, I have anointed thee king over the people of the Lord, even over Israel. And thou shalt smite the house of Ahab thy master, that I may avenge the blood of my servants the prophets, and the blood of all the servants of the Lord, at the hand of Jezebel. . . . And I will make the house of Ahab like the house of Jeroboam the son of Nebat, and like the house of Baasha the son of Ahijah: And the dogs shall eat Jezebel in the portion of Jezreel, and there shall be none to bury her. And he opened the door, and fled" (2 Kings 9:1-7,9,10).

"Then Jehu came forth to the servants of his lord: and one said unto him, Is all well? wherefore came this mad fellow to thee? And he said unto them, Ye know the man, and his communication. And they said, It is false; tell us now. And he said, Thus and thus spake he to me, saying, Thus saith the Lord, I have anointed thee king over Israel. Then they hasted, and took every man his garment, and put it under him on the top of the stairs, and blew with trumpets, saying, Jehu is king" (2 Kings 9:11-13).

Mounting his chariot, commanding and taking with him a company of his most reliable soldiers, furiously did he drive nearly sixty miles to Jezreel.

"And when Jehu was come to Jezreel, Jezebel heard of it." Pause! Who is Jehu? He is the one who, twenty years before the events of this chapter from which we quote, rode down with Ahab to take Naboth's vineyard, the one who throughout those twenty years never forgot those withering words of terrible denunciation which Elijah spoke. And who is Jezebel? Oh! The very same one who wrote the letters and had Naboth put to death. And what is Jezreel? The place where Naboth had his vineyard and where Naboth died, his life pounded out by stones in the hands of ruffians. "And when Jehu was come to Jezreel, Jezebel heard of it; and she painted her face, and tired her head, and looked out at a window. And as Jehu entered in at the gate, she said, Had Zimri peace, who slew his master?"

Pause again just here. "Had Zimri peace, who slew his master?" No; "there is no peace, saith my God, to the wicked." And he lifted up his face to the window, and said, "Who is on my side? who? And there looked out to him two or three eunuchs. And he said, Throw her down" (2 Kings 9:30-33).

These men put their strong men's fingers into her soft feminine flesh and picked her up, tired head and all, painted face and all, bejeweled fingers and all, silken skirts and all—and threw her down. Her body hit the street and burst open. Some of her blood splattered on the legs of Jehu's horses, dishonoring them. Some of her blood splattered on the walls of the city, disgracing them.

And Jehu drove his horses and chariot over her. There she lies, twisting in death agony in the street. Her body is crushed by the chariot wheels. On her white bosom are the black crescent-shapes of horses' hoofs. She is hissing like an adder in the fire.

"And when he was come in, he did eat and drink, and said, Go, see now this cursed woman, and bury her: for she is a king's daughter. And they went to bury her: but they found no more of her than the skull, and the feet, and the palms of her hands" (2 Kings 9:34,35).

God Almighty saw to it that the hungry dogs despised the brains that conceived the plot that took Naboth's life. God Almighty saw to it that the mangy lean dogs of the back alleys despised the hands that wrote the plot that took Naboth's life. God Almighty saw to it that the lousy dogs which ate carrion despised the feet that walked in Baal's courts and then in Naboth's vineyard.

These soldiers of Jehu went back to Jehu and said: "We went to bury her, O king," but the dogs had eaten her.

And Jehu replied: "This is the word of the Lord, which he spake by his servant Elijah the Tishbite, saying, In the portion of Jezreel shall dogs eat the flesh of Jezebel."

"And the carcass of Jezebel shall be as dung upon the face of the field in the portion of Jezreel; so that they shall not say, This is Jezebel" (2 Kings 9:37).

Thus perished a female demon, the most infamous queen that ever wore a royal diadem.

Pay day—some day! God said it—and it was done! Yes, and from this we learn the power and certainty of God in carrying out His own retributive providence, that men might know that His justice slumbereth not. Even though the mill of God grinds slowly, it grinds to powder; "and though His judgments have leaden heels, they have iron hands."

And when I see Ahab fall in his chariot and when I see the dogs eating Jezebel by the walls of Jezreel, I say, as the Scripture saith: "O that thou hadst hearkened to my commandments; then had thy peace been as a river, and thy righteousness as the waves of the sea!" And as I remember that the gains of ungodliness are weighted with the curse of God, I ask you: "Wherefore do ye spend money for that which is not bread? and your labour for that which satisfieth not?"

And the only way I know for any man or woman on earth to escape the sinner's pay day on earth and the sinner's hell beyond—making sure of the Christian's pay day on earth and the Christian's heaven beyond the Christian's pay day—is through Christ Jesus, who took the sinner's place upon the cross, becoming for all sinners all that God must judge, that sinners through faith in Christ Jesus might become all that God cannot judge.

John R. Rice
(1895—1980)

Called by many "the twentieth century's mightiest pen," John R. Rice is credited as having done more to promote the cause of soulwinning and revival than any other man in this century. He was born in 1895 in Gainesville, Texas, and had a godly mother who exerted a great influence on him, even though she died when he was only five years old. Four years later he was converted.

Upon graduation from high school, Rice entered Decatur Baptist College and graduated in 1918. After attending Baylor University, he enrolled in Southwestern Baptist Theological Seminary in 1921; he conducted evangelistic meetings in the meantime. In 1932 he moved with his family from Fort Worth to Dallas where he organized Galilean Baptist Church, which he pastored for eight years. He began the *Sword of the Lord*, a weekly newspaper containing sermons and articles on soulwinning and revival in 1934, moving the operation to Wheaton, Illinois, in 1940 and then on to Murfreesboro, Tennessee, in 1963.

John R. Rice came on the evangelistic scene when mass evangelism and citywide campaigns had almost disappeared, but his tent revivals and open-air services received tremendous response. Rice conducted hundreds of conferences that motivated thousands of preachers across the country to greater soulwinning efforts. At the time of his death on December 29, 1980, the *Sword of the Lord* had grown to a circulation of over 300,000, serving effectively as a faithful promoter of the fundamentals of the faith.

Maintaining a prolific writing ministry throughout his active life, Rice authored over 200 books and pamphlets that have been circulated in thirty-nine languages in over 60 million copies. His "Voice of Revival" radio broadcast is still being aired with his taped messages.

Only eternity will reveal the full impact of the ministry of John R. Rice, a valiant defender of the faith. Tens of thousands of souls have been converted through his preaching and publications. The following sermon has been one of the most effective tools toward that end. "What Must I Do to Be Saved?" has been printed in millions of copies in approximately forty languages. It continues to be used of God in leading people to Christ in this generation.

What Must I Do to Be Saved?

By John R. Rice

Sirs, what must I do to be saved? And they said, Believe on the Lord Jesus Christ, and thou shalt be saved, and thy house (Acts 16:30,31).

Paul and Silas, jailed in the city of Philippi, one night sang and prayed until God, with a mighty earthquake, opened all the doors and loosened their bonds. The poor jailer, frightened and convicted of his sins, came to these two preachers and asked this question. Read it in Acts 16:29-31: "Then he called for a light, and sprang in, and came trembling, and fell down before Paul and Silas, and brought them out, and said, Sirs, what must I do to be saved? And they said, Believe on the Lord Jesus Christ, and thou shalt be saved, and thy house."

"What must I do to be saved?" "Believe on the Lord Jesus Christ, and thou shalt be saved!" This is God's plan of salvation—the only plan He has for every man, woman, and child who was ever born into the world.

What Must I Do?

There is something each of us must do if we desire salvation. There was hope for this jailer because he saw himself a lost sinner and came trembling to inquire, "What must I do?" Reader, all of us are sinners. The Word of God from beginning to end emphasizes that fact. In Isaiah 53:6, we read, "All we like sheep have gone astray; we have turned every one to his own way; and the Lord hath laid on him the iniquity of us all."

All of us have gone astray! The Lord is not content for sinners to be left believing themselves good. In Romans 3:9-12, we read: "What then? are we better than they? No, in no wise: for we have before proved

258

both Jews and Gentiles, that they are all under sin; As it is written, There is none righteous, no, not one: there is none that understandeth, there is none that seeketh after God. They are all gone out of the way, they are together become unprofitable; there is none that doeth good, no, not one."

In verses 22 and 23, it is stated again that "there is no difference: for all have sinned, and come short of the glory of God." That is the reason Jesus said to Nicodemus, "Marvel not that I said unto thee, Ye must be born again" (John 3:7). Then reading verse 18 of that same chapter we learn that Jesus also taught that anyone who did not believe on Him as the Son of God was already condemned.

Certainly these Scriptures must make it clear to all who believe the Word of God that every individual is a lost sinner until he or she believes in Christ and accepts His atoning sacrifice.

Only God can make a wrong heart right. If we genuinely want to be saved, we each must admit, "I am a sinner. I am lost, and I need to be saved." No one ever was saved without coming for salvation as a sinner.

Oh, I beg you, see it today! We are poor, lost sinners, hell-bound sinners! Our hearts are as black as coal. We have hardened our hearts, resisted the call of God, and rejected Christ. However good we may be in man's sight, we are terrible sinners, and unless we turn to Christ we must spend eternity in hell. We need salvation more than we need anything else in the world.

Once we have settled that matter in our hearts, we are ready to learn God's answer to our question, "What must I do to be saved?"

Believe on the Lord Jesus Christ

Here is God's simple way to be saved. We are sinners; our hearts are wrong; we cannot save ourselves; we are already condemned. Then what we must do to be saved is to simply trust the Lord Jesus with the matter. When we do trust Him, then we have God's promise, "Thou shalt be saved" (Acts 16:31).

I do not mean that we are just to believe that there is a God or that there is a Savior. Devils believe that and tremble (cf. James 2:19).

We can believe that a certain physician is a good doctor without calling him to be our doctor when we are sick. We can believe that a certain man is a good lawyer without taking him as our lawyer to defend our cases. We are not just to believe the truth about Jesus; we are to believe on Him, that is, to depend upon Him, to risk Him, to trust Him; and when we do, we are saved.

Not Saved by Good Works

Of course, none of us deserves salvation. There is nothing we can do that will make us worthy of it. We cannot be saved by keeping the Ten Commandments, for the Scriptures clearly show that no person has kept them. In Romans 3:20, we read, "Therefore by the deeds of the law there shall no flesh be justified in his sight: for by the law is the knowledge of sin."

The same point is emphasized in Galatians 3:11, "But that no man is justified by the law in the sight of God, it is evident: for, The just shall live by faith."

"Not by works of righteousness which we have done, but according to his mercy he saved us, by the washing of regeneration, and renewing of the Holy Ghost" (Titus 3:5).

"For by grace are ye saved through faith; and that not of yourselves: it is the gift of God: not of works, lest any man should boast" (Eph. 2:8,9).

We had as well admit that no man deserves saving and no man can save himself. Salvation must be free or the sinner could never get it. In fact, it takes blood to pay for sin.

"Without Shedding of Blood Is No Remission" (Heb. 9:22)

"For when we were yet without strength, in due time Christ died for the ungodly" (Rom. 5:6).

"All we like sheep have gone astray; we have turned every one to his own way; and the Lord hath laid on him the iniquity of us all" (Isa. 53:6).

Peter wrote that all of us are bought by the blood of Christ:

"Forasmuch as ye know that ye were not redeemed with corruptible things, as silver and gold, from your vain conversation received by tradition from your fathers; but with the precious blood of Christ, as of a lamb without blemish and without spot" (1 Peter 1:18,19).

Every lamb, bullock, heifer, goat, turtledove, and pigeon offered on the altar in Old Testament times pictured this: man, a guilty sinner, must have some innocent one shed his blood to pay for man's sins. Jesus died for our sins; and salvation is bought for every man in the world, if he will have it, as the free gift of God.

"For the wages of sin is death; but the gift of God is eternal life through Jesus Christ our Lord" (Rom. 6:23).

We must realize and remember that church membership will not save us. Baptism does not save, nor does it keep anybody saved. It is only an act of duty for those who have already accepted Christ as their Savior. A moral life or lodge membership or good citizenship will not bring salvation, for it is "not by works of righteousness which we have done, but according to his mercy he saved us" (Titus 3:5). We must not depend for salvation on what we do, but on what Jesus did and what He promises to do for us.

What About Repentance?

Doesn't the Bible say that we must repent? Yes, we read that "God...commandeth all men everywhere to repent" (Acts 17:30), and again, "Except ye repent, ye shall all likewise perish" (Luke 13:3,5).

This was the preaching of John the Baptist, of Jesus, of Peter, and of Paul. Certainly repentance is God's plan of salvation.

The trouble here, however, is that men have misunderstood what repentance means; and an idea has grown up that repentance involves a period of weeping and mourning over sin. This understanding originated with the Douay Version of the Bible which, instead of telling one to "repent" says "do penance." Thus, in revival meetings the place of inquiry where people should be taught the plan of salvation from the Bible became "the mourner's bench" and thousands of people have been taught that God would not hear their prayers or forgive their sins until they went through a process of sorrow and mourning over their failures.

Do not misunderstand me. God is anxious for us to have penitent, broken hearts because of sins. We have gone away from God. We have trampled underfoot the blood of Jesus Christ and wasted years of our lives that might have been lived to His glory. As sinners, we have served our father, the Devil.

There is plenty for us to weep about, and I am not surprised if we feel deep shame and sorrow that we have so mistreated the God who made us and the Savior who died for us. I am not surprised if we cannot keep back the tears. Nevertheless, what I want you to know is that tears and sorrow alone cannot save us.

Certainly we should be sorry and ashamed because of our sins. "Godly sorrow worketh repentance" (2 Cor. 7:10). The right kind of sorrow leads to immediate repentance, but mourning is not itself repentance.

To repent literally means to have a change of mind or spirit toward God and toward sin. It means to earnestly turn from sins and to trust in Jesus Christ for salvation.

We can see, then, how the man who believes in Christ repents and the man who repents believes in Christ. The jailer repented when he turned from sin to believe in the Lord Jesus Christ.

Instant Salvation!

The jailer did not go through a period of mourning. He was told to believe on the Lord Jesus Christ; he did just that and was saved, and his whole family was saved the same way—immediately, the same hour of the night. (cf. Acts 16:30-34).

Throughout the New Testament you read that people were saved all at once, without any process and without any period of mourning. Zacchaeus, up a tree, trusted Jesus and made haste and came down, and received Him joyfully (cf. Luke 19:6-9). Jesus said, "This day is salvation come to this house."

When Peter told Cornelius and his assembled household that they could be saved by believing, immediately, "while Peter yet spake these words," the Holy Spirit came on them and they were happily saved (cf. Acts 10:44-48).

The thief on the cross, although he was a wicked sinner, experienced immediate salvation when he inquired of Jesus (cf. Luke 23:42,43).

From John 1:35-49, we learn that one by one Andrew, Simon Peter, Philip, and Nathanael were immediately converted by faith in Christ.

The Bible contains no record of any person who was ever told to wait, or mourn, or weep over his sins, before trusting Jesus and being saved. One who believes in Christ has repented. Repentance and faith are alike in that neither requires a long period of time nor a process of mourning and sorrow. We can experience instantaneous salvation when we turn with believing hearts to Jesus.

Salvation is instantaneous. All that keeps you from being saved today is the wickedness of your heart that holds on to sin and will not turn to Jesus to trust in Him for salvation.

I beg you to turn, in shame and sorrow, from your sins this minute, and trust in Christ and be saved!

Can One Be Saved Without Prayer?

The Bible records the prayers of many sinners. For example, remember the thief on the cross and the publican in the temple. In fact, we read in Romans 10:13, "For whosoever shall call upon the name of the Lord shall be saved."

Many people believe that a sinner cannot be saved without a period of prayer, without consciously calling on God. However, nowhere does the Bible say a sinner must pray in order to be saved. In fact, the verses following Romans 10:13 point out that calling on God is an evidence of faith in the heart; and it is faith that is necessary for salvation.

The Lord encourages the sinner to pray, and the Lord hears and answers the sinner's prayer when it is based on trust in Jesus Christ for salvation. He heard the prayers of the thief on the cross, of the publican in the temple, and of blind Bartimaeus.

However, in Romans 10:14, we read, "How then shall they call on him in whom they have not believed?"

Certainly each individual who is to be saved must believe. Prayer is evidence of faith. No matter how long one prays, if he does not trust in Christ, he can never be saved. If he trusts in Christ without conscious prayer, then he is saved already. There is just one plan of salvation: the only step a sinner must take to be saved is to believe on the Lord Jesus Christ!

Somehow we preachers have left the impression that God is hard-hearted and that He requires of penitent sinners many tears, loud cries, and long periods of sorrow before He will hear and save them. We have left the impression that God does not care whether people are saved or not, and that they must find a way to touch His heart before He will forgive. This is slanderous to a good and holy God who "so loved the world, that he gave his only begotten Son, that whosoever believeth in him should not perish, but have everlasting life" (John 3:16).

Man's sins are already paid for; God's wrath is already turned away from any sinner who wants salvation, and He is anxious to freely offer this gift to all His children. Thank God, we do not have to beg God to forgive our sins! He will do it the minute we trust Him.

This way of being saved by faith seems so easy, and it is. Some of us may say, "But I thought one must have a change of heart." So we must. But that is God's part. Jesus was talking to Nicodemus when He said, "Ye must be born again" (John 3:7), and in the same chapter we read that He told Nicodemus how to obtain the new birth. "For God so loved the world, that he gave his only begotten Son, that whosoever believeth in him should not perish, but have everlasting life" (John 3:16).

How Should I Feel?

The change in our sinful heart is God's part, to which He will attend. Your part is to believe in Him. Whatever else is necessary in our eternal salvation the Lord takes care of when we trust in Him.

Some people have an idea that the change of heart is a matter of feeling, and so they hesitate to claim Christ as Savior until they have experienced some change in attitude or outlook. Do not let the Devil deceive you here.

I believe in heartfelt religion, and thank God for the joy He gives day by day. However, nowhere in the Bible can we find information on how one must feel before he is saved or after he is saved.

Feeling varies with the person saved. Some cry when they are saved, some laugh, and a few shout aloud the praises of God. But no one is more saved than another. What we want is salvation, and we should be satisfied to feel any way that will please the Lord, as long as He forgives our sins.

We must also be aware that we cannot feel right until we get right. Rejoicing does not come before we trust the Lord. One does not feel the result of medicine before he takes it. The children of Israel, bitten by fiery serpents and at the point of death in the wilderness, were not and did not feel healed until they looked to the brass serpent on the pole (cf. Num. 21:6-9).

People are not saved by feeling; they are saved by trusting in Christ. The prodigal son, away from home in the hogpen, decided to arise and go to his father but he did not feel good. Clothed in rags, he was without shoes, without the ring of sonship, without any evidence of his father's forgiveness, and was perishing of hunger. Yet he arose and came to his father, not by feeling, but by faith in his father. Thank God, his father received him, just as God receives every sinner who will come.

When the prodigal boy sat down at his father's table, with shoes of the gospel of peace, clothed in the garments of the righteousness of Christ, with the ring of sonship on his finger, eating the fatted calf at the right hand of the father, happy in his love, then you may be sure he had plenty of feeling.

Feeling comes after salvation. After we are saved, we receive peace and joy by following the Lord in baptism, reading His Word, winning souls, and otherwise pleasing Him. We need to go to the Lord day by day for the joy of a Christian life, but salvation is settled once and for all when we simply depend upon Christ as our Savior.

What About Public Confession?

Every person who is saved ought to publicly confess Christ. Matthew 10:32 and Romans 10:9 teach that God will claim as His child any who will claim Christ as Savior; but we confess with our mouths what we have already trusted in our hearts.

Concerning that very matter, in Romans 10:10, we read, "For with the heart man believeth unto righteousness; and with the mouth confession is made unto salvation."

To claim Christ as our Savior proves that we trust Him. So it is with all the other promises in the Bible concerning how one is saved. In John 6:37, we read, "Him that cometh to me I will in no wise cast out"; and in John 1:12, salvation is promised to "as many as receive" Jesus. However, we could not come to Christ without trusting Him, and John 1:12 shows that receiving Jesus is the same as believing on His name.

We must not make salvation a difficult matter. There is one simple step between us and Jesus. When we trust Him, everything is settled. We have repented and have come to Christ. When we have received Him, we have done everything necessary in order to be saved. Take the answer in Acts 16:31 at face value: "Believe on the Lord Jesus Christ, and thou shalt be saved."

In dozens of Scriptures throughout the Bible, salvation is promised to those who believe. Read carefully the following passages and see that again and again God has promised all any poor sinner will ever need when he believes on the Lord Jesus Christ:

"But as many as received him, to them gave he power to become the sons of God, even to them that believe on his name" (John 1:12).

"And as Moses lifted up the serpent in the wilderness, even so must the Son of man be lifted up: that whosoever believeth in him should not perish, but have eternal life. For God so loved the world, that he gave his only begotten Son, that whosoever believeth in him should not perish, but have everlasting life" (John 3:14-16).

"He that believeth on him is not condemned: but he that believeth not is condemned already, because he hath not believed in the name of the only begotten Son of God" (John 3:18).

"He that believeth on the Son hath everlasting life: and he that believeth not the Son shall not see life; but the wrath of God abideth on him" (John 3:36).

"Verily, verily, I say unto you, He that heareth my word, and believeth on him that sent me, hath everlasting life, and shall not come into condemnation; but is passed from death unto life" (John 5:24).

"And this is the will of him that sent me, that every one which seeth the Son, and believeth on him, may have everlasting life: and I will raise him up at the last day" (John 6:40).

"Verily, verily, I say unto you, He that believeth on me hath everlasting life" (John 6:47).

"To him give all the prophets witness, that through his name whosoever believeth in him shall receive remission of sins" (Acts 10:43).

"And by him all that believe are justified from all things, from which ye could not be justified by the law of Moses" (Acts 13:39).

Read again the Scripture we began with:

"What must I do to be saved? And they said, Believe on the Lord Jesus Christ, and thou shalt be saved" (Acts 16:30,31).

Trust Jesus, the Great Physician

If any of us were sick and about to die, and there were some good doctor whom we could trust, would we not risk him to take our cases, give us the necessary treatments, and with God's help, get us well? Then just like that, we should trust in Christ, depend on Him for our salvation, and turn our cases over to Him today.

With the same kind of faith we exercise to call in a doctor and risk him for our bodies' sake, we can call in the Lord Jesus Christ and risk Him to forgive our sins and save our poor lost souls. He said, "They that are whole need not a physician; but they that are sick" (Luke 5:31). He is the Great Physician and will heal our souls instantly if we will trust Him. As we would trust a doctor, submit to his treatments, and depend on him for results, so we should trust Jesus today regarding our souls.

Jesus Is Our Lawyer

If we had committed a crime and were thrown in jail, probably the first thing we would do would be to send for a lawyer in whom we had confidence; and we would trust him with the entire matter of our defense. In God's sight we are criminals, condemned already with the wrath of God upon us day after day.

However, God has provided someone to take the part of the poor sinners, criminals before the bar of His justice, and Jesus is that lawyer. "If any man sin, we have an advocate [or lawyer] with the Father, Jesus Christ the righteous: and he is the propitiation for our sins: and not for ours only, but also for the sins of the whole world" (1 John 2:1,2).

Jesus will not only be our lawyer to defend our cases; He has already paid the penalty and we may safely trust Him to have us immediately pardoned and justified! Therefore, why not simply risk Jesus as we would risk a good lawyer? Jesus is far superior to any lawyer; of course, we do not have to pay Him a fee, and He never fails.

A Wedding

A young man and woman stand side by side before the preacher. In their marriage vows they profess their intentions to love, cherish, and honor each other and to be faithful to this commitment until death separates them. Then the preacher pronounces them husband and wife, and they are married in the sight of God and man.

What a simple picture of salvation! Jesus is the Bridegroom and we who trust Him are to be His bride. Already Jesus has loved us and has long urged us to accept His love. Jesus invites us to believe in Him right now and be saved and so become a part of his bride. If you have not made this commitment, will you right now, with the same simple faith of that young woman who takes a husband, accept Jesus as your Savior and say to Him, "I do"?

Make It Sure—Claim Him Today!

The way is plain and you can be saved this moment.

Surely it has become plain that without Jesus we are lost sinners without excuse for our condition. Will you hold on to your sin and go to hell for your stubbornness? Nothing in the world could show your wickedness like postponing this matter. You can be saved right now. I beg you to turn your whole heart from sin to trust in Christ. Choose for heaven against hell; choose for Christ against Satan. Do not let Satan deceive you any longer. Your delay may result in a hardened heart, a wasted life, and a soul tortured in hell; and if you are not saved, when God has made the way so plain and has paid the price for your sins, then you have no one to blame but yourself. Will you trust Jesus Christ today and be saved?

"Boast not thyself of tomorrow; for thou knowest not what a day may bring forth" (Prov. 27:1).

"Behold, now is the accepted time; behold, now is the day of salvation" (2 Cor. 6:2).

"Today if ye will hear his voice, harden not your hearts" (Heb. 3:7,8).

God has given you this heartbeat, this breath, this moment in order to trust Christ, but there is no promise of another. I beg you do it right now, and then publicly profess Him as your Savior. Then you will have the assurance that Jesus promised, "Whosoever therefore shall confess me before men, him will I confess also before my Father which is in heaven" (Matt. 10:32).

BIBLIOGRAPHY

Carey, William. *An Enquiry Into the Obligation of Christians to Use Means for the Conversion of the Heathen.* London: Carey Kingsgate Press, (1792), 1962.

Chapman, J. Wilbur. *And Judas Iscariot.* New York: Hodder & Stoughton, 1906.

Cranfill, J.B. *Sermons and Life Sketch of B.H. Carroll.* Philadelphia: American Baptist Publication Society, 1893.

Fant, Clyde E., Jr. and Pinson, William M., Jr. eds. *Twenty Centuries of Great Preaching.* Waco, Texas: Word Books, 1971.

Hickman, Edward, ed. *The Works of Jonathan Edwards,* Vol. 2. Carlisle, Pennsylvania: The Banner of Truth Trust, (1884), 1974.

Jones, Sam. *Sam Jones' Gospel Sermons.* Chicago: Rhodes & McClure Publishing Company, 1897.

Kleiser, Grenville, ed. *The World's Greatest Sermons.* Introduction by Lewis O. Brastow. New York: Funk & Wagnall's, 1908.

Lee, R.G. "Pay Day—Some Day." *The Sword of the Lord,* June 3, 1960.

McCartney, Clarence Edward, ed. *Great Sermons of the World.* Grand Rapids: Baker Book House, 1958.

McCheyne, Robert Murray. *A Basket of Fragments.* Fearn, Ross-Shire, Scotland: Christian Focus Publications, 1975.

McFarlan, D. *The Revivals of the Eighteenth Century.* Edinburgh, Scotland: Johnston & Hunter, 1947. Reprinted, Wheaton, Illinois: Richard Owen Roberts Publishers, 1980.

Meyer, F.B. Introduction by Robert G. Lee. *Great Pulpit Masters* series, no. 6. New York: Fleming H. Revell, 1950.

Moody, D.L. *Twelve Select Sermons.* Chicago: Fleming H. Revell, 1884.

Rice, John R., ed. *The Rice Reference Bible.* Nashville, Tennessee: Thomas Nelson Publishers, 1981.

Scott, Robert and Stiles, William C. eds. *Modern Sermons by World Scholars.* Introduction by Newell Dwight Hillis. New York: Funk & Wagnall's, 1909.

Smith, Gypsy. *As Jesus Passed By*. Chicago: Fleming H. Revell, 1905.

Spurgeon, C.H. *The Metropolitan Tabernacle Pulpit*. London: The Banner of Truth Trust, 1971. Reprinted, Pasadena, Texas: Pilgrim Publications, 1973.

Stonehouse, Ned B., ed. *God Transcendant & Other Selected Sermons*. Grand Rapids: William B. Eerdmans Publishing Company, 1949.

Sunday, Billy. *The Best of Billy Sunday*. Murfreesboro, Tennessee: The Sword of the Lord Publishers, 1965.

Talmage, T. DeWitt. *Sermons By the Reverend T. DeWitt Talmage*. Wakefield: William Nicholson & Sons, n.d.

Torrey, R.A. Introduction by William Culbertson. *Great Pulpit Master* series, no. 3. New York: Fleming H. Revell, 1950.

Truett, George W. *Follow Thou Me*. New York: Harper Brothers Publishers, 1932.

Vick, G. Beauchamp. "Heaven." *The Sword of the Lord,* January 2, 1981.

Wiersbe, Warren. *Treasury of the World's Great Sermons*. Grand Rapids: Kregel Publications, 1977.